SELECT PRAISE FOR THE FIRST EDITION

"Batchelor successfully shows how this dreamer and risk-taker perfectly captured the cultural zeitgeist and assisted in creating 'fairy tales for grown-ups.'"
—*Publishers Weekly*

"A fun ride through an extraordinary life for new fans and longtime comic book readers alike."—*New York Daily News*

"This is a solidly researched and written biography of Lee. . . . [Lee] is a hugely entertaining story, and the author tells it well."—*Booklist*

"Where Batchelor succeeds most is fleshing out the settings and context along the narrative spine of Lee's life. . . . Batchelor delves into not only how Lee worked as an editor—the creative freedom he gave many artists worked to his advantage, too—but also how he built himself into a celebrity brand synonymous with the Marvel name."—*The Washington Post*

"Bob Batchelor's bio of Stan Lee is not only thorough and accurate, it's also extremely well written. If you enjoy reading Stan's stories, you'll enjoy the story of Stan just as much."—**Steve Englehart, novelist and comic book writer (*The Avengers, Captain America*)**

"An insightful and candid look at one of the twentieth century's greatest myth-makers."—**Mark Waid, writer (*Daredevil, The Fantastic Four, Kingdom Come*)**

"Bob Batchelor's book takes us on a journey into the life and imagination of Stan Lee, whose collaborations with Jack Kirby and Steve Ditko laid the foundation of the Marvel Universe and unleashed a creative explosion that continues to impact—and transform—all of popular culture."—**J. M. DeMatteis, writer (*The Amazing Spider-Man, Silver Surfer*)**

"Definitive!"—**Lindsay Graham, podcast host (*Business Movers, Wondery*)**

"Impressively informed and informative, exceptionally well written, organized and presented, Stan Lee is an extraordinary biography that is a 'must read' for the legions of Stan Lee fans."—**Midwest Book Review**

Stan Lee

Stan Lee

A Life

Centennial Edition

Bob Batchelor

ROWMAN & LITTLEFIELD
Lanham • Boulder • New York • London

Published by Rowman & Littlefield
An imprint of The Rowman & Littlefield Publishing Group, Inc.
4501 Forbes Boulevard, Suite 200, Lanham, Maryland 20706
www.rowman.com

86-90 Paul Street, London EC2A 4NE

Distributed by NATIONAL BOOK NETWORK

British Library Cataloguing in Publication Information Available

Library of Congress Cataloging-in-Publication Data
Name: Batchelor, Bob, author.
Title: Stan Lee : a life / Bob Batchelor.
Description: Centennial edition. | Lanham : Rowman & Littlefield, [2022] | Includes
    index. | Summary: "Creative icon, visionary, and dreamer, Stan Lee co-created many
    of pop culture's most significant characters, including Spider-Man, Black Panther, and
    the Avengers. Stan Lee: A Life is the definitive biography of the Marvel legend by
    noted cultural historian Bob Batchelor, celebrating the centennial of Lee's birth"—
    Provided by publisher.
Identifiers: LCCN 2022007180 (print) | LCCN 2022007181 (ebook) | ISBN
    9781538162033 (cloth) | ISBN 9781538162040 (epub)
Subjects: LCSH: Lee, Stan, 1922–2018. | Cartoonists—United States—Biography.
Classification: LCC PN6727.L39 Z54 2022 (print) | LCC PN6727.L39 (ebook) | DDC
    741.5/973092 [B]—dc23/eng/20220222
LC record available at https://lccn.loc.gov/2022007180
LC ebook record available at https://lccn.loc.gov/2022007181

To the loving memory of
Josette Percival Valois (1940–2021)

Contents

Foreword

$\mathcal{W}$alking through downtown San Diego on a warm summer evening, I saw countless children dressed as goblins, aliens, wizards, and robots. Across the street were space-fighters, zombies, and vampires—legions of creatures. But the odd thing—holding their hands were their parents.

The fathers and mothers of these supernatural specimens were dressed just the same. There were flags, banners, and toys being handed out. Lines of teenagers were waiting in the hot sun to get a $200 ticket to enter. Buses were wrapped in an infinite array of color, text, and good ol' sci-fi wholesomeness. Yes, I was at Comic-Con. My own son was even dressed as a Transformer—Optimus Prime. I watched him become overwhelmed with the immersion. He stood there drowning in complete sensory overload. This was seriously the FIRST time I'd ever seen a celebration of *imagination* of this magnitude—where a parent could be a kid—*with their kid.*

When I was young, I cut my teeth playing with Legos. I built my sci-fi chops by filling my backyard with spaceships, secret spaceports, and flying astronauts. I envisioned a multidimensional environment. My space-faring soldiers explored every object. Over time, we started to imagine that they were heroes or had special powers. I remember that moment specifically because Batman and Spider-Man cartoons were seeping into my head.

Later, in creating Blink-182, Angels & Airwaves, and the entertainment company To the Stars★, I realized that I could create a whole new multimedia world across music, books, video, and film—a kind of transmedia art project that would project my hopes, dreams, and aspirations for the world the way I saw it with superheroes as a kid. For example, my character Poet Anderson is an antihero (like Spider-Man!) who grapples with dreams and nightmares as a Dream Walker, a guardian of the Dreamscape charged with protecting sleeping innocents from the nightmares that threaten both worlds. Poet led to an award-winning short film, a chart-topping album, an acclaimed comic book series, a graphic novel, and a YA science-fiction novel. Who says you can't bring dreams to life?

When I look back now, I realize that Stan Lee and his contemporaries had started playing with ideas and contracts that would honestly lead me to wonder what started this flow of consciousness in the first place. I thought about the clones from outer space in *Star Wars* with a rebel band of heroes that have special Jedi powers. Or the clones that come from the ground in *Lord of the Rings*, while advanced elves and wizards with extraordinary (natural) powers fight them off. And, again, the Avengers—who battle insects from another dimension that, like the other replicas, are missing that empathy component that seems exclusive to our human souls.

With the current UFO phenomenon, there is a ton of evidence suggesting that ETs are interdimensional, don't share our consciousness, and may have insectile or cloning origins. So does consciousness beam a signal to humanity directly into our minds that we need to hear, like a radio receiver? Do people like Stan Lee bring it out in a way that gets us to think and ponder? This is complicated stuff! Maybe our great sci-fi writers and creators are having a grand time preparing us for what's next. Perhaps they have no clue of the enormity and weight behind their (seemingly common) ideas.

After I went to Comic-Con and experienced the Marvel, *Star Wars*, and Disney overload, I wanted to follow in their footsteps—constructing amazing new narratives that would change the world. At To the Stars★, we're utilizing our deep connections to bring to light an amazing story (and possibly) . . . *the story of the millennium*. I often wondered the best way to tell an important story like this, especially one that most people might not be ready for. I wanted to give people a newfound appreciation of the profound yet unresolved mysteries involving science and the universe through entertainment directly informed by science.

Each time I thought about it, I remembered what Stan did to prepare the way for all of us. He made the supernatural world blend seamlessly into our physical world. Stan's vision is similar to what I expect will be the next great scientific leap for humanity—a collision of physics and metaphysics. The result will be a unified theory of everything, only possible with the discovery of *consciousness*. And Stan gave us a glimpse of *what could be*. For me, someone who sits in a chair next to former high-ranking CIA, DOD, and military officials, Stan may be right about a few things . . . although possibly minus the supersuits.

No one could have imagined how important these comic stories would be to so many people or the gravitational impact that those first superhero films would have when they hit our culture. Just like the Spider-Man animated TV series that was so important to me, the Marvel universe has become a game changer. Countless people across all age groups now have a north star. Stan paved a path for artists like me to be creative *and* make a living from our creative energy. What a wonderful idea: legions of young people creating and imagining a better world, but one that might actually be a bit more on the nose than anyone would suspect . . . but minus the supersuits. Or not?

—Tom Delonge, Blink-182 and To the Stars★

How the Marvel Universe
Conquered the Globe

*H*ow did Marvel storytelling conquer the globe?

Since the early 1960s, there has been only one answer: Stan Lee. His unique voice and narrative define the Marvel universe.

It's a creation that may just go on into infinity. According to Marvel executive Victoria Alonso, "There's about 6,000 characters in the Marvel library. . . . If this goes right, we will be telling these stories for many, many, many, many generations to come." From this viewpoint, Marvel's future success centers on the "many different characters that you can actually voice." Alonso's instincts are pure—having many thousands of characters will enable the company to open up worlds and ideas that haven't even been considered yet. However, what makes these characters fit into the Marvel universe—the consistent thread—is the style (and attitude) that Stan created.[1]

Lee's voice from the dawn of the superhero age became Marvel's house style. Other comic book writers mimicked his style, and later so did scribes across other mediums. In subsequent generations, his voice has become American mythology. Need proof? Surf over to Disney+ and listen to Robert Downey Jr. play Iron Man or check out a YouTube clip of Tom Holland as Spider-Man. What you hear in their banter is instantly recognizable.

While there are generations of great science-fiction films and action movies, the difference between the Marvel cinematic universe (MCU) and the others is voice. The contrasts are startling. For example, if you examine the Star Wars films, you'll find many iconic lines or catchphrases, but there isn't a consistent voice or recognizable cadence. Just juxtapose Peter Parker's wit when he's in costume versus Darth Vader—the latter's most memorable feature is the sound of his breathing apparatus. The emphasis for Vader is visual impact, not what or how the character speaks. As a filmmaker, George Lucas isn't focused on dialogue. In *Star Wars*, he wanted to create an interconnected universe where the visual power propelled the story. Plus, Lucas started from a different wellspring, not decades of tales that someone like Lee dialogued or were created by others who mimicked his house style. The Star Wars hero tropes are drawn from literature and film, but there is not a distinct, unifying dialogue. At least since the earliest animation efforts, countless writers, directors, and actors have attempted to imitate or mimic Stan's dialogue from the comic books because that cadence is the voice of Marvel.

Many directors and producers can make a film packed with action-filled fight scenes, stunning visuals, and out-of-this-world computer-generated imagery, but what these others can't replicate is that verbal expression. The Marvel feeling is so ingrained in the heads of fandom that it feels subconscious. It's driven by Lee's voice. No matter who directs an MCU film or plays a superhero or supervillain, the internal consistency prevails: Thor's humor and stilted formality, Iron Man's snark, Spider-Man's relentless patter and earnestness. This is Stan's enduring legacy.

Here's a quick history lesson: in the early 1960s, after those first several superhero comic books became hits (Fantastic Four, Spider-Man, Avengers), Marvel grew into, then fused with, the emerging cultural zeitgeist. The comics were suddenly as cool as the latest rock band or film star (thus appearing in hip publications like *Rolling Stone* and *Esquire*). In other words, Marvel joined the movement as it formed, then worked its way to the forefront of changing the culture through Lee's guidance, though it would be hard to imagine that he thought of what was happening in these terms. Riding that cultural wave, Stan stumbled into—then later carefully crafted—a role as the face of comic books. Eager to hit the road, he barnstormed college campuses swollen to the breaking point with baby boomers who wanted to take over the world and had the numbers to bend culture to their wills. Stan turned out to be engaging—nearly mesmerizing—in his belief in the power of comic books, propelling Marvel into the psyche of college-aged readers as if he were some kind of pied piper.

Within the comics themselves, Stan utilized tools to blow up the fourth wall, thus speaking directly (and frequently!) to readers. Tens of thousands of young people joined Marvel fan clubs, demonstrating the appeal of Lee's message that something special was going on inside comics that belonged solely to *them*, not the voices of authority in their lives. Soon, journalists started poking around, wondering what "today's youth" found so interesting about comic books. Suddenly, Stan's *the* guy to tell adults what's happening. Lee's effervescence and wit shimmered as he provided attention-grabbing sound bites and interview fodder. Here was someone who had insight into these crazy young people!

What happened over the course of a decade or so couldn't possibly be duplicated, so formulaic in retrospect that it seems impossible that it happened.

Unlike Bob Dylan or Jann Wenner, for example, Stan didn't plan this revolution. He didn't say to himself that he would cocreate a character that would become part of American folklore. It wasn't planned, yet it seems totally intentional. Baby boomers grew up with Stan's voice in their heads. Interestingly, Lee spoke for Marvel's superheroes to eager audiences talking about the characters, while at the same time creating the dialogue in the actual comics. So he was the person talking about the characters he himself was voicing. In addition, he wasn't just in the media; Stan was talking directly to readers within the pages. He was Spider-Man's voice, while also talking about the comics, the company, his colleagues, and the world to a captivated audience.

By the time Gen Xers started reading comics, Marvel's style was wholly entrenched. As each generation ages out of traditional comic book reading age, Lee's voice becomes commensurate with nostalgia—a part of our lives we look back to with fondness and equate with better times. Immersed in a heavily capitalistic, entertainment-driven culture, embedded stories are ones that get retold, and Marvel superheroes become a balm for a cultural explosion driven by cable television, global box office calculations, and the web. In what seems like the blink of an eye, the Marvel voice became *the* voice of modern storytelling.

Yet the term *voice* is difficult to comprehend. Jerome Charyn, one of the most important writers in American literary history, describes it instead as "music." Charyn's concept, although focused on books, can be applied to Lee's comic book writing: "Writing . . . is about the music, it's about the voice. This is what predominates. The music is all, the music is total, it's absolute." Stan's dialogue provided Marvel with a kind of music that readers could hear and that matched their internal rhythms, resulting in an experience that transformed them. "It's music alive with extreme sympathy," Charyn explained. "There is no space between you and the text."[2] As a result, readers could feel the Marvel style, while simultaneously Lee's patter paralleled the cultural explosion booming across society. We hear this in the Beatles' *Sgt. Pepper's Lonely Hearts Club Band*, Stanley Kubrick's *Dr. Strangelove* and *2001: A Space Odyssey*, and J. D. Salinger's short stories.

For this revolution to unfold, the spark needed an accelerant, like Bob Dylan, the Beatles, James Brown, or *Star Wars*. In terms of sheer numbers, one could argue that, based on Stan's voice and attitude, Marvel has a wider reach around the world than any other entertainment vehicle or single entertainer. The past success of Marvel film and television properties and the billions of dollars bet on its continued popularity ensure that Marvel will remain at the heart of global popular culture.

★   ★   ★

There is a *secret* to all this MCU success, isn't there? It can't have been an accident.

Let's not rest our argument for Marvel storytelling's conquest of the globe on opinion or anecdote. Researchers have attempted to pin down the reasoning behind why the MCU has been so dominant and pervasive. An academic study in *Harvard Business Review* by Spencer Harrison, Arne Carlsen, and Miha Škerlavaj gets at the primary rationale: "The secret seems to be finding the right balance between creating innovative films and retaining enough continuity to make them all recognizably part of a coherent family."[3]

Next, the team looked at individual aspects of the MCU. They studied scripts, film crews, directors, and critical reaction, leading to several additional points emerging: the movies "showcase differing emotional tones" and are "visually different," and the most critically acclaimed films "are the very ones that are viewed as violating the superhero genre."[4] In other words, *Iron Man* is funny, but *Thor* is often sad (though frequently hilarious). *Guardians of the Galaxy* is a space opera zipping across galaxies, while *Spider-Man* is set in Queens and Manhattan. *Black Panther* is filled with social commentary, as is *Captain Marvel*. Again, the through point is voice.

Mold the entire MCU into a ball, but don't expect the contraption to roll straight—purposely. Moviegoers recognize (and have been taught) that each film will be different in tone, look, and outcome. They know the origin stories (and, with Spider-Man, have seen them several times on film). Yet fans also know that each new film or television series is going to seem fresh and new—an *experience*, not just a piece of entertainment. The MCU is giving people something created for the masses, but the stories are so infused within the culture that we each take something *personal* from the films. For me, it may be the Avengers coming to life—literally a dream come true—while you may find inspiration in T'Challa and Wakanda's progressivism. Whether it's the MCU's commentary about life in contemporary America or the nostalgia of the good ol' days reading comics as a kid, something is being triggered for people all over the world.

For contemporary audiences, that experience is also inclusive, another point Alonso identified: "You cannot have a global audience and not somehow start to represent it." The success of *Black Panther*, for example, went against unofficial Hollywood rules that a film wouldn't open if it had "a completely Black cast." According to Alonso, 51 percent of the Marvel audience is female and 28 percent Hispanic: "If we don't represent the people that watch what we make, eventually they'll go elsewhere because somebody else will figure it out." Disney isn't alone in this strategic thinking, but the results confirm the point.[5]

And let's not forget how important the consistent use of Easter eggs has been, not only within the films but as the credits roll. The anticipation alone gets the fan community revved up for future installments (as did Stan's cameo appearances, which most fans still yearn for, even years after his passing).

An even more elemental facet of Marvel's success is its commitment to a shared set of core values via storytelling. According to best-selling author and comics writer Brad Meltzer, Stan "gave an entire generation creeds to live by . . . vital cornerstones of their belief systems." The power of his stories was in how people assimilated them. "Stan Lee gave them real-world applications for all those values. And unlike politicians, corporations, advertising, or anything else, those lessons were *good*. For the sake of good."[6] The idea is not that Marvel entertainment must live up to these principles at every moment, but overall the ideals Stan punctuated established a tone and framework that could support a universe.

The superheroes that Lee and his cocreators brought to life in Marvel comic books remain at the heart of contemporary storytelling. Lee created a narrative foundation that has fueled pop culture across all media for nearly six decades. By establishing the voice of Marvel superheroes and shepherding the comic books to life as the creative head of Marvel, Lee cemented his place in American history. According to veteran industry analyst Paul Dergarabedian, the results have been breathtaking: "The profound impact of Stan Lee's creations and the influence that his singular vision has had on our culture and the world of cinema is almost immeasurable and virtually unparalleled by any other modern day artist."[7]

From my perspective, this viewpoint does not diminish the role Jack Kirby or Steve Ditko played in cocreating the superheroes or the thousands of additional hands it took to create the comic books, animated series, TV shows, or films over parts of the last ten decades. Kirby and Ditko were phenomenal talents, but in contrast to Lee, they focused on one part of the production process. Obviously, the look of the superheroes and the plots they developed were instrumental in the final product. Then, like now, the artists and writers needed one another. Creative products are built on teams acting in concert.

Yet there must be a boss. Stan directed, managed, or supervised it all. Lee was Jack and Steve's supervisor and could change their work at any time. This concept adds a level of managerial and creative acumen to Stan's Marvel story that is not usually discussed in evaluations of his role in modern mythmaking. The view will rankle some readers who would counter that Lee needed Kirby and Ditko more than they needed him. The argument is counterfactual because the fusion of their collective talents could not have occurred if the fusion hadn't taken place. This thinking is great for pop culture debates: "What if Mick and Keith hadn't seen each other on the train platform?" or "What if

Joe Maneely didn't die tragically?" I'm more interested in what happened *after* the spark that created the Marvel universe. Roy Thomas, Stan's protégé and comic book historian, explained: "To Stan, it wasn't all that important whose idea a particular story was; what mattered was that it sold comic books, and Stan had every reason to believe that both his editorial guidance and his command of the dialogue contributed materially to that popularity."[8]

Every successful idea, person, organization, or entity is built by many, but again, what was the accelerant?

★   ★   ★

Your favorite superhero . . . your favorite comic book. If you "got" Marvel—if you loved Marvel—then you heard or saw something that you shared with your friends but that you could also cherish alone. All the while, you felt that someone (or some*thing*) was behind all this, creating these treasured objects. You could find him on the front cover and in the letters page—talking to *you*! "Smilin' Stan."

Who was this guy? Maybe you were too young to understand, but what you could *feel* was that he was talking to you—in a voice that your parents didn't understand. This is yours, not theirs. Former Marvel editor and Lee biographer Danny Fingeroth described his fascination with that link between Stan and Marvel readers: "In the stories, he and his—and *your*—bullpen pals delivered exciting adventures filled with (angst-fueled) moments of insight. . . . He was *better* than a friend or a relative. He was *Stan Lee*."[9]

In the 1960s and 1970s, no matter the tiny hamlet, thriving city, or rural enclave, if a kid got their hands on a Marvel comic book, they understood they had a friend in New York City named Stan Lee. Each month (seemingly like magic), Lee and the Mighty Marvel Bullpen put these colorful gifts into our hands (in my youth, under the ever-present "Stan Lee Presents" banner), which enabled us to travel the galaxies along with Thor, Iron Man, the Avengers, and the X-Men.

How did the Marvel universe come to dominate global popular culture? Largely based on Stan supplying a voice to a mythology. Certainly, the creation of the Marvel universe was a team effort, like all forms of entertainment; nothing is created in a vacuum. There are unheralded people in the process and those who deserve as much credit as Lee for their roles. Yet it was the unmistakable "music" that Lee conceived that launched a cultural revolution.

Crisscrossing the nation while speaking at college campuses, sitting for interviews, and conversing with readers in the "Stan's Soapbox" pages in the back of comic books, Lee paved the way for intense fandom. His work gave readers a way to engage with Marvel and rejoice in the joyful act of being a fan. Geek/nerd culture began with "Smiley" and his Merry Marauding Bull-pen nodding and winking at fans each issue. Lee's commitment to building a fan base took fandom beyond sales figures and consumerism to authentically creating communities. The Marvel cinematic universe has spun this idea into global proportions. It is the fans of the MCU across film and television that have reinforced and spread Stan's voice across the world.

★   ★   ★

Imagine the scene—at the height of the Great Depression, a desperately poor teenager who just graduated from high school enters a nondescript office building. He has a hunch about this interview. His Uncle Robbie works there, but the kid has no clue what takes place inside its towering concrete walls. *Will this be it?*

The teen emerges a little later with a full-time job—$8 a week. Even someone with Stan Lee's imagination could not have conjured up in that moment what would unfold in his marvelous life or its consequences on modern storytelling.

Yet he did give us a hint of what was in store, mischievously scribbling, "Stan Lee is God" on a high school ceiling where he was certain that all his friends would see the message.

This is his story—Excelsior!

• *2* •

Origin Story

*W*indow shoppers cautiously ventured out onto Times Square on Thursday, December 28, 1922, flipping up their collars against the icy wind. A wintry mix of rain and snow pelted New York City. The dark gray clouds matched the city's mood as pedestrians bundled up against the dismal weather. A sudden gust could nearly knock a woman off the sidewalk or send a man scurrying out into the street to retrieve his errant hat. The stubborn storm dumped rain and snow up and down the East Coast.

In a tiny Manhattan apartment on Ninety-Eighth Street and West End Avenue, Jack and Celia Lieber barely noticed the dreary weather. They were about to welcome their first child. They named the little tyke Stanley Martin.

The newborn entered the world at a chaotic time in American history. The nation was still recovering from the upheaval of World War I and the Spanish Flu epidemic that had killed millions globally. Leaders from around the world yearned to secure a peaceful future. At home, the American economy had slipped and sputtered after war production dropped, but manufacturing picked up in 1922 as consumer goods companies produced everything from sleek automobiles to new clothing styles and electric kitchen gadgets.

Newfound wealth fueled the "Roaring Twenties," an era filled with jazz, dance crazes, illegal alcohol, and glamour. Yet those on the lower end of the economic spectrum faced a more difficult journey. The 1929 Wall Street crash swept the Lieber family to near destitution. Despite their woes, Celia and Jack raised the boy to believe in his own bright future. Stanley emerged an optimist, bedeviling the clouds that filled the sky that day and the dark era of the Great Depression.

This is how superheroes are born.

★   ★   ★

Young Stanley's parents were among the millions of immigrants to enter America in the early twentieth century. Born in Romania in 1886, his father docked in the New York City Harbor in 1905. Hyman, who later went by Jacob (or the Americanized "Jack"), was just nineteen years old. He traveled with fourteen-year-old Abraham (possibly a relative or maybe even his brother). The teens joined the wave of Jewish immigrants fleeing Eastern Europe. After decades of anti-Jewish pogroms (anti-Semitic terror campaigns) across Europe and Russia that left countless thousands of Jewish people murdered, immigration to the United States skyrocketed from 5,000 in 1880 to 258,000 in 1907. In total, some 2.7 million people of Jewish descent from all over Europe migrated to America between 1875 and 1924.

Jacob left behind life in gritty Romania, a country at that time sandwiched between Austria-Hungary, Serbia, Bulgaria, and Russia, during the reign of monarch Carol I (ruling from 1881 until his death in 1914). The voyage to America would have cost Hyman and Abraham about 179 rubles each (roughly $90), an enormous sum back then. There was no guarantee that immigrants would be let into the US, even if they were fleeing oppression, especially if they were from the poor or working class. The boys would have to prove to Ellis Island immigration inspectors that they had the means to subsist (about 50 rubles).[1]

The brutality against Jewish Romanians meant that most immigrants would never return home, particularly since they were from a nation that did not permit them to have religious freedom or the right to pursue meaningful work. The monarchy forbade Jews from becoming lawyers, outlawed rabbinical seminaries, and made entrance into medicine nearly impossible. Several laws passed in the 1890s outlawed Jewish education, and anti-Semitism was openly taught in Romanian high schools. All people of Jewish heritage were considered "aliens" or "foreigners," regardless of how long their ancestors had lived in Romania. Being considered a minority meant permanent subservience and discrimination. The psychological terror had significant consequences.

The semisecret pogroms led to countless anti-Jewish riots and widespread looting. Neither the police nor the army stopped the rampage, and in many instances the authorities joined in on the pillage. "The economic depression that became dire in Romania towards the close of the nineteenth century was accompanied by an increased level of violence," explained historian Dana Mihailescu.[2] Yet, since there were relatively few Romanians in the US, the American media rarely reported on the violence. Like so many times in world history, nations that could have attempted to stop the anti-Semitic terror campaigns turned a blind eye to the atrocities.

Life in America offered the potential for a better life, but it was not easy for the millions of Europeans flooding into the country. Most were unskilled laborers, so work in early twentieth-century factories proved dangerous, re-sulting in high rates of workplace injuries and deaths. Romanian immigrants gained religious freedom and were shielded from the wanton violence they faced back home, but they also faced hardships that altered their traditional family values.

Teenaged Jacob scraped out a meager existence in New York. Like other single immigrant men, he lived in boardinghouses or with Romanian families that rented rooms, frequently in heavily Romanian neighborhoods. Since Jewish immigrants also faced anti-Semitism, living with their countrymen pro-vided some insulation and protection. Relatively few of the new immigrants could speak or read English, adding to the kinship and solidarity when they faced the English-speaking world. Remembering a Romanian Jewish restau-rant on the Lower East Side, Maurice Samuel recalled people gathered "to eat karnatzlech, beigalech, mammaligge, and kachkeval, to drink . . . and to play six-six and tablanette," all while speaking in Romanian Yiddish. The men in these taverns filled the air with nostalgic tales about their homeland, but the stories were also tinged with regret since they recalled the evils and violence of the pogroms.[3]

Jacob and Abraham entered the clothing industry at a time when the gar-ment district clamored for workers. Although most immigrants were unskilled, many Jewish immigrants were skilled craftsmen (about 65 percent); however, no evidence exists that would help us determine if Jacob and Abraham had previous experience. One historian explained: "Upon arrival in the United States, the immigrants became tailors, even if they had not been tailors before, because this trade was in demand in Manhattan."[4] On-the-job training was the norm in garment industry.

Many first-generation immigrants did not discuss their ancestry in detail or how they had journeyed to America. While they retained specific cultural attributes, such as food and music, the outward goal was to become "Ameri-can." As a result, many families simply did not pass down their stories. Dis-cussions centered on the future, not past hardships.[5] A clearer picture of the Lieber family emerges if examined within the larger wave of émigrés. Their struggles and the aftereffects were similar to other Jewish families attempting to blend in.

In 1910, both Jacob and Abraham were boarders with Gershen Mosh-kowitz, a fifty-two-year old Russian, and his Romanian wife, Meintz, along with their two children, on Avenue A in Manhattan. Census takers reported that the young men attended school and could read and write English but supplied no additional details. They almost certainly spoke Romanian Yiddish at home and in the neighborhood.[6]

Ten years later, in 1920, thirty-four-year-old Jacob was still living as a boarder—with the family of David and Beckie Schwartz and their three young children—in an apartment on 114th Street in Manhattan. The Schwartzes immigrated to America from Romania in 1914. Unlike Jacob, they could not speak, read, or write in English. Both Jacob and David worked in the garment industry. The 114th Street apartment building and surrounding neighborhood was predominantly Jewish immigrants from Russia and Romania, so Yiddish was more commonplace.

We know little about Jacob's romance with Celia Solomon. In 1920, Lieber was living with the Schwartz family, but by the end of 1922, he married Celia. Stanley arrived just before the New Year.

The Solomons had a more typical immigrant experience, arriving in the US in 1901. Immigrating as a family would have been a costly endeavor but important in keeping them together. Various documents list Celia's father (Sanfir or Zanfer) and mother (Sophia or Sophie) with different first names. Sanfir (born in 1865) and Sophia (1866) had eight children. In 1903, Robbie, their youngest child, was the first born in the United States.

In 1910, the family lived in an apartment building on Fourth Street in a Romanian neighborhood. Celia worked as a salesperson in a five-and-dime store. She and older brother Louis (trimming store salesman) did not attend school, unlike her four younger siblings (Frieda, Isidor, Minnie, and Robbie). In many immigrant families, older children provided needed financial support, thus enabling younger siblings to go to school. The Solomons settled into life in the US, aspiring to a higher standard of living, benefiting from free education, and embracing American culture. While Sanfir and Sophia spoke Yiddish, their children were fluent in English. Later, they moved to West 152nd Street.

Celia's life between 1910 and 1922 is a mystery, as are the early years of her marriage to Jacob. They later moved from West Ninety-Eighth and West End Avenue to Washington Heights, around the time Stanley's sibling, Larry, was born (October 26, 1931). The move signaled a downsizing in the family's fortunes. Like so many others, the Great Depression cut the heart out of the Lieber family, halting their progress toward the American Dream.

★   ★   ★

A bone-chilling wind whipped down Twenty-Ninth Street in Manhattan as some two thousand men braced against the frigid air. Breadlines snaked up Fifth Avenue. When food ran out, a quarter of them would be turned away hungry. Many families would starve that night. The sight of destitute men at wit's end unnerved New Yorkers. They were humiliated by accepting charity, doing so reluctantly, even to survive. Most had no choice. Soup lines created a riveting picture of national despair—a defeated country in financial collapse.

The economic breakdown left the nation angry and despondent. Money had been at the core of American culture in the 1920s. Investment bankers reigned as society's new celebrities—the type of men described by Nick Carraway in F. Scott Fitzgerald's *The Great Gatsby* (1925). The overheated economy put the kindling in place; greed provided the spark.

The economic calamity devastated the Liebers. "My earliest recollections were of my parents talking about what they would do if they didn't have the rent money," Stanley remembered. "Luckily we were never evicted."[7] The struggle for day-to-day essentials forced many families into constant crisis mode. The Depression shaped the worldview of the boy in his formative years.

Garment district employment simply vanished. According to Stanley, his father also attempted to run a diner, but the operation failed, draining his life's savings.[8] The toll of chronic unemployment wrecked Jacob and Celia's marriage. Stanley, not yet seven, witnessed his parents "arguing, quarreling incessantly." Like a bad record doomed to play over and over, "it was over money, or the lack of it."[9]

The constant bickering only halted on Sunday nights when they gathered around the radio. Stanley loved the programs, particularly ventriloquist Edgar Bergen on NBC's *The Chase and Sanborn Hour* (airing Sundays from 8 p.m. to 9 p.m.). Bergen's wooden sidekick was Charlie McCarthy, a wisecracking, often slyly suggestive mouthpiece. Since radio listeners could not actually see Charlie, the real joy came from Bergen's comedic patter and storytelling.

While Celia cleaned or cooked, Jacob scoured the newspaper want ads. Stanley watched his father venture out each day searching for work. In the evening, he returned despondent and desperate. Jacob, according to his son, sat at the kitchen table staring out listlessly as the family teetered near collapse. Sometimes, Jacob would try to goad his wife into going for a walk in the park. She "hated it," Lee recalled. "They never got along."[10]

Always cash-strapped, Celia had to ask her more well-to-do sisters for money. If begging family members wasn't enough of a humiliation, they also moved into a smaller apartment in the Bronx. Stanley slept on the couch in the living room, situated—like in so many low-rent apartments—in the back of the building. The window looked directly into another building. Stan remembered: "All we could see was the brick wall of the building across the alley. I could never look and see if the other kids were out in the street playing stickball or doing anything that I might join in."[11] The cramped confines and Larry's birth (another mouth to feed) sadly amplified the despair.

★   ★   ★

Dressed in a dark replica of a sailor outfit, complete with a felt tam-o'-shanter hat perched at an angle atop his head, young Stanley sits on an antique desk, leaning on his tiny right arm. This is the kind of popular photography pose that parents forced kids to endure in the 1920s. Although a youngster, the boy reveals dark, mesmerizing eyes and a faraway look that seems to hide the key to some distant mystery.

Too young to fully understand his family's plight, Stanley bounced along, relying on his mother's love to overcome his father's anxiety and persistent rules. His aunt Jean recalled that Jack was "exacting with his boys," demanding adherence to daily routines per his orders: "brush your teeth a certain way, wash your tongue, and so on."[12] Celia, on the other hand, filled Stanley with her hopes and dreams. "She often asked me to read aloud to her," he remembered. "I enjoyed doing that, imagining I was on some Broadway stage reading for a vast, entranced audience."[13] Celia and Jack struggled, but she instilled a sense of greatness in her son. The encouragement was a sea change from the bickering he heard from his parents.

Without the money to attend sleep-away summer camp like his friends and frequently by himself, Stanley turned to reading as a coping mechanism. "It was my escape from the dreariness and sadness of my home life."[14] More importantly, reading empowered the boy's sense of adventure and creativity. "Used to scribble my own comics, as far back as I can remember," Lee said. "Used to draw horizon line and add stick-figure people, telling myself little stories all the while."[15] His mother created a safe environment where a poor kid could spend time reading and drawing, in contrast to life in the city for other immigrants, who had to fight and scrape just to survive. His future cocreator Jack Kirby, for instance, was in a street gang and got into countless scrapes.

In addition to fostering reading, Celia pushed Stanley to excel at school. He was quick-witted and smart, developing a precocious intellect. However, his youth and brightness did not help him socially. "I was always something of an outsider," he remembered. "My mother wanted me to finish school as soon as possible so I could get a job and help support the family."[16] Eager to please her, Stanley skipped grades. He initially found it difficult to establish friendships with older classmates who had been together as they progressed through school. As the youngest in his classes, he was often the first picked on—an easy target for older kids.

In elementary school, Stanley found a role model in Leon B. Ginsberg, a young Jewish teacher. Each day, Ginsberg began class with a thrilling baseball story featuring imaginary slugger Swat Mulligan, connecting with the students through storytelling. Stanley remembered the Mulligan tales as "funny and exciting." Mulligan's heroics made learning fun, a rarity in public education in the early decades of the twentieth century. Stanley found life lessons in Ginsberg's daily tale: "Whenever I want to communicate to others, I always try to do it in a lighter-hearted way and make it as entertaining as possible."[17] The combination of Mulligan's adventures and the radio programs nurtured the boy's imagination and demonstrated the power of storytelling.

The next creative leap came from Lieber's other passion: movies. He loved the way film mixed amusing stories with vivid scenes to create excitement. In the late 1920s and early 1930s, he imagined a bigger-than-life future personified by film icon Errol Flynn. The actor burst onto the scene in *Captain Blood* (1935), which showcased his good looks, flamboyant charm, and athletic grace. Flynn became the industry's top action star, drawing viewers with choreographed fight scenes and swordplay, as in *The Adventures of Robin Hood* (1938), Flynn's first color film. "There on the screen were worlds that dazzled my mind, worlds of magic and wonder, worlds which I longed to inhabit, if only in imagination," Lee later recalled.[18] For a boy creating his own comic stories and devouring books, the movies showed the power in the marriage of visual elements and dialogue.

Despite the Depression, the era's movie houses were grand palaces. Stanley went to Loew's 175th Street Theatre, one of New York's "Wonder Theatres" designed by noted architect Thomas W. Lamb. An elegant hodgepodge of influences, Loew's could have been at home in Spain, Thailand, or India. The inside featured an enormous seven-story-high Robert Morton Wonder organ. Although these organs became obsolete with the decline of the silent film era, they were magnificent artworks with towering, stacked keyboards and ornate paneling that added to the grandeur of the experience. The décor was just as eclectic as the exterior. Interior designer Harold Rambusch gave it an exotic feel with Arabian motifs and Indian sculptures, along with reproductions of styles used by French monarchs Louis the XV and XVI.

Not solely interested in action adventures, Stanley also loved the comedies of the Marx Brothers and Laurel and Hardy. Within a three-block radius of 181st Street, the youngster could pick from five movie theaters. He eagerly anticipated *Tarzan* and his other favorite, *The Jungle Mystery*, the adventures of a man-ape. After the films ended, he met with his cousin Morty Feldman on Seventy-Second Street, where the boys ate pancakes and talked about the movies.[19] Even during the Depression, youngsters could scrape together the nickels and pennies for these small luxuries.

Stanley grew into a self-described "voracious reader." In later years, he often cited Shakespeare as his most important influence, shaping his ideas about storytelling, particularly the "rhythm of words," explaining, "I've always been in love with the way words sound."[20] Stanley took a book or magazine with him everywhere—even the breakfast table—using a little wooden contraption his mother found that held the pages open.

Although he loved reading and film and dabbled with drawing, the boy had no illusions about comic books, which then were largely reprints from newspaper strips (and physically like books or magazines). In the 1920s, black-and-white strips were popular, particularly the slapstick humor of Bud Fisher's *Mutt & Jeff*. "Creating comic books was never part of my childhood dream," Stanley explained. "I never thought of that at all."[21] He did, however, read *Famous Funnies*, widely considered the first modern American comic book, published by Dell in 1934 and distributed in Woolworth department stores. He specifically remembered enjoying *Hairbreadth Harry*, a strip created by C. W. Kahles, featuring the hero in various melodramatic adventures to keep his rival, Rudolph Ruddigore Rassendale, from the heroine, Belinda Blinks.[22]

★ ★ ★

The crushing blow of the Wall Street crash was the way it demoralized the American people. The shocking speed shook the public's faith in the economic system as millions of workers lost their jobs. Construction in New York City, for example, came to a near halt as 64 percent of workers were laid off. By October 1933, the city had some 1.25 million people on relief. Another 1 million were eligible for relief but did not accept it. Some six thousand New Yorkers attempted to make ends meet by selling apples on the streets. But by the end of 1931, most street vendors were gone. Grocery store sales dropped by 50 percent. Many urban dwellers scoured garbage cans and dumps looking for food. Studies estimated that 65 percent of the African American children in Harlem were plagued by malnutrition.

Two years after the crash, some 200,000 New Yorkers faced eviction. Many who were not evicted sold off their valuables in a last-ditch attempt to raise money. Others—like the Liebers—trekked from apartment to apartment. For the small family, the crash had lasting consequences, yet they managed to stay together. On the surface, the obvious impact was that Jacob's profession disappeared. Clothing manufacturers struggled to remain solvent.

The constant money challenges took a toll on the Lieber marriage. As he got older, Stanley found things to keep him out of the house. Unfortunately, his little brother, Larry, suffered more directly. He spent his formative years enduring the stress and strain of a troubled marriage.

Jack's unemployment meant Stanley had to work; any little extra income would help the family avoid misery. When he reached his midteen years, the boy (along with millions of other teens) either worked or continuously searched for jobs. The mix of Celia's fawning support and grade jumping eventually paid off. The enterprising teen—smart and already a budding story-teller and wordsmith—found odd jobs: an usher at a movie theater, office boy at a factory that manufactured jeans, and even writing obituaries of living celebrities filed away for when they died.

Lieber attended DeWitt Clinton High School in the Bronx, a twenty-one-acre campus at 100 West Mosholu Parkway South and East 205th Street. Described as the "castle on the parkway," the all-boys school stood as one of the world's largest high schools, enrolling ten thousand to twelve thousand students (a diverse ethnic population heavily tilted toward immigrants and their children). Many students from Lieber's era went on to great fame and achievement after leaving high school, from champion boxer Sugar Ray Robinson (class of 1938) and graphic novel godfather Will Eisner (1936) to Pulitzer Prize–winning journalist A. M. Rosenthal (1938).

Clinton seemed more like a factory than a school, so creating a reputation was difficult. Yet Lieber's high school years were filled with school clubs and opportunities to exhibit his budding leadership and showmanship traits. The pensive boy who holed up with a book grew into a handsome, tall young man (though rail thin). He joined the public-speaking club and the law society, contemplating a future as a famous courtroom attorney.

Nicknamed "Gabby" due to his charming personality and incessant chatting, Lieber envisaged for himself a dazzling future. His classmates echoed that sentiment. High school friend Bob Wendlinger remembered thinking Stanley was headed to greatness. "You always knew that he was going to be successful," Wendlinger said. "It was a given."[23] Lieber experimented with a variety of personas, first gravitating toward publicity with a job on the business staff of the Clinton literary magazine, the *Magpie*. Despite his own budding writing talents, he confined himself to "publicity director." Part of the Lieber youthful lore is that before a meeting in the tower, the high-ceilinged part of the school where the *Magpie* staff worked, he found a ladder left there by a worker. Showing off, he scurried up, then wrote, "Stan Lee is God," on the ceiling where all his fellow students would be sure to see it. Perhaps unwilling to risk getting in trouble with the maintenance crew or administrators for defacing the building using his real name—or just playing around with a stage name—this was the first recorded use of the moniker that would later travel the globe.

While Lieber imagined numerous careers—including acting—advertising seemed his true calling. He was fascinated by ads. Several of the jobs he held during high school centered on words or selling, including writing publicity materials for a Jewish hospital in Denver, the obituary job, and hawking newspaper subscriptions. Stan recognized his dramatic flair and public-speaking talents. In high school, he also adopted a magician's persona; calling himself the great "Thimbilini," he performed sleight-of-hand tricks with small thimbles that drew crowds of curious classmates (akin to how Johnny Carson first performed as a magician to gain attention and approval).

As a fifteen-year-old, Lieber entered a high school essay competition sponsored by the *New York Herald Tribune* called "The Biggest News of the Week Contest." The paper, owned by Ogden Reid and his wife, Helen, although conservative, pursued local issues in a stylized fashion, focusing on the Big Apple's gritty realism. Lieber claimed to have won the prize for three straight weeks, goading the newspaper to write the boy and ask him to let someone else win. According to Stanley, the newspaperman suggested he look into becoming a writer, which, the boy claimed, "probably changed my life."[24]

Like many tall tales from Lee's life, the story is apocryphal. Research reveals that the young Lieber won a seventh place prize of $2.50 and two honorable mention awards—hardly the rags-to-riches tale that he would identify as the moment he wanted to become a writer. "After all," comic book historians Jordan Rapheal and Tom Spurgeon said, "Lee is a storyteller, and his account of the *Herald Tribune* essay contest certainly made for a good story, even if it's untrue."[25] While the story veers from truth, the prize money made an impression on a poor Jewish kid. A year later, in 1939, the teen worked a total of twelve weeks, pulling in $150 via part-time jobs and whatever work he could muster.[26]

★   ★   ★

Leaving the hallowed halls of the monolithic all-boys DeWitt Clinton High School in 1939, Stanley entered a jittery job market, but it was certainly better than the darkest economic doldrums of 1932 to 1935 when unemployment consistently sat north of 20 percent. President Franklin Delano Roosevelt attempted to alleviate the turmoil, but gross national product actually fell 4.5 percent in 1938 and unemployment climbed to 19 percent. Ironically, Hitler's invasion of Poland several months after Stan's graduation led to increased war planning and thereby helped revive the economy. Prior to the attacks on Pearl Harbor, the United States shipped products to desperate Allied nations while prepping for its seemingly inevitable entry into the conflict.[27]

The economic rebound did not kick in soon enough to aid Stanley. For him, graduation did not equate to launching a career. Although he might daydream about acting or becoming an attorney, his immediate future meant employment, not college. The teen's graduation and subsequent salary might offer the Lieber family a measure of financial stability. He just needed a job to help support his family, as his mother, Celia, had hoped all along.

The young man may have clung to vague memories of life before the crash, but his perspective would forever be shaped by his father's unemployment, shaking him to his core. "The most important thing for a man is to have work to do," he explained. "To be busy, to be needed."[28] The idea molded him—not only to work but to feel needed. "Even when I made a good living, my dad didn't think of me as a success," Stanley remembered. "He was pretty wrapped up in himself. . . . Some of that rubbed off on me. I was always looking at people who were doing better than I was and wishing I could do what they were doing." Sadly, he explained: "Part of me always felt I hadn't quite made it yet."[29]

According to Stanley, the "specter of poverty" cast a dark cloud over his parents' marriage.[30] Fear caused him to privilege work and a steady paycheck. Lee shared this feeling with contemporaries in comic books (like future cocreator Jack Kirby). Many of the early men in comics were also first-generation Jewish immigrants. They knew each other's neighborhoods and had parallel experiences navigating Depression-era New York City. They had seen the breadlines! One writer described these consequences for Lieber—producing a young man "agonizingly sensitive, desperate for approval and easily influenced by others." Highly intelligent, Stanley yearned for a marvelous life that would fulfill his mother's predictions about his future fame and fortune.[31]

Mr. Timely Comics

*R*ising to his feet, Joe Simon stabbed the air with his cigar, then looked down at his desktop, covered with drawings and pencil doodles. The haphazard pages and correspondence littered every square inch. The Timely Comics head writer and editorial director put out his hand, welcoming his young assistant with a hearty shake.

Feeling a little dizzy, star struck, and truly amazed at what he'd just been offered, Stanley vigorously pumped the older man's hand. A steady paycheck—eight whole dollars a week!

For a kid just out of high school, the salary meant that he might help his family regain its footing. More importantly, however, the job gave the teenager security and a shot in writing and publishing. Words appealed to the boy. He dreamed of one day writing the Great American Novel.

But Stanley was a long way from fame and fortune as the next Ernest Hemingway or Margaret Mitchell. He started his publishing career at the lowest rung, plying away the hours as an office boy for Simon and the other full-time Timely Comics employee—artist and writer Jack Kirby. Some days Lieber refilled Kirby and Simon's inkwells or went out for sandwiches while the duo filled the air with pungent cigar smoke and together concocted new superhero stories.

Lieber worked with enthusiasm, even as he swept floors or erased stray pencil marks on finished pages to prep them for publication. The hours of watching and listening proved more valuable than he could have then imagined. He learned at the feet of two of the industry's budding stars. Stanley had a job! His father's fate would not befall him. He set off on a career!

Many episodes in Lieber's early life are still shrouded in uncertainty. How the teenager bounded from Clinton High School to Simon and Kirby's assistant at Timely involves both a bit of mystery and a touch of mythmaking.

Several versions of Lee's comic books origin story exist. One account begins with Celia. Clearly she put her hopes in her older son, particularly since her faith in her husband nearly led the family to ruin. In this account, we have Celia telling Stanley about a job opening at a publishing company where her brother Robbie works. Without delay, the young high school grad shows up at the McGraw-Hill Building on West Forty-Second Street, despite knowing little about the company or comic books. However, given Robbie's influence with Martin, Joe Simon takes the time to explain the publishing business and how comic books are created. Then, again with Robbie's prodding, he offers the kid a job. Basically, he and Kirby are so frantic and overworked, particularly with their new hit *Captain America*, that they just need someone (anyone, really) to provide an extra set of hands. Right place at the right time for the teenager.

Robbie Solomon is also at the center of another version (here the main player), essentially as a conduit between Simon and owner Martin Goodman. In addition to being Celia Lieber's brother, Robbie had married the publisher's sister Sylvia. In running his businesses, Goodman had surrounded himself with family members (despite the imperious tone he took with everyone who worked for him). "His entire publishing empire was a family business," explain historians Blake Bell and Michael J. Vassallo.[1] As a result, getting Uncle Robbie's stamp of approval (and the familial tie) made the boy's hire fait accompli. Allegedly Robbie's job was to be a kind of in-house spy who ratted out employees who were not working hard enough or playing fast and loose with company rules, so he had power. Simon, then, despite what he may or may not have thought of the new hire, basically had to take him on.

While the family connection tale is credible and plays into the general narrative of Goodman's extensive nepotism, Lee offered a different viewpoint, making the episode a coincidence. "I was fresh out of high school," he recalled. "I wanted to get into the publishing business, if I could." Rather than being led by Robbie, Lee explained: "There was an ad in the paper that said, 'Assistant Wanted in a Publishing House.'"[2] This alternative version calls into question Lee's early move into publishing—and throws up for grabs the date as either 1940, which is usually listed as the year of his hiring, or 1939, as he later implied.[3]

Lieber may have not known much about comic books, but he recognized publishing as a viable option for someone with his interests and abilities. He knew that he could write but had no way of really gauging his creative talents. Although Goodman was related by marriage, he did not have much interaction with his younger relative, so it wasn't as if Goodman purposely brought Lieber into the company. No one will ever really know how much of a wink and nod Robbie gave Simon or if Goodman even knew about the hiring, though the kid remembered the publisher being surprised the first time he saw him in the building.

The teen, though bright, talented, and hardworking, needed a break. His early tenure at Timely Comics served as a kind of extended apprenticeship or on-the-job training at comic book university. Lieber was earnest in learning from Simon and Kirby as they scrambled to create content. Since they were known for working fast, the teen witnessed firsthand how two of the industry's greatest talents functioned. The lessons he learned set the foundation for his own career as a writer and editor, as well as a manager of talented, creative individuals.

★   ★   ★

Martin Goodman formed Timely in 1933 to sell cheap, tawdry men's magazines, not great art. Dollar signs drove Goodman. He wanted to make a pile of money in the least taxing manner possible. The publisher focused his attention on magazines. He also kept a close eye on broad publishing trends and demanded that cover art be sensational, revealing, and provocative, particularly when it came to covers of scantily clad women. The titles were also vivid: *Marvel Science Stories* and *Mystery Tales*.

Some of the magazines Goodman and his competitors sold were so salacious they were basically semipornographic and kept behind closed doors. The seedy side of magazine publishing tempted various underworld elements, including the mafia and other gangsters, who viewed pulp magazines as a way to make a quick buck and semilegitimize themselves or their business interests. There is no evidence tying Martin to organized crime, but rumors and formal investigations fingered many of his fellow publishers.

From his expansive office perch in the McGraw-Hill Building on West Forty-Second Street between Eighth and Ninth Avenues, Goodman excelled at scrutinizing what other publishers produced, figuring out which magazines sold, and then throwing the full weight of his company behind the craze. His goal was to keep the company efficient and afford himself a comfortable living. Like all the men who ran pulp publishing houses in that era, Goodman came of age when the industry was rough-and-tumble, filled with stories of horrific bankruptcies and wholesale corruption.

In the 1920s, many publishers had grown rich off the pulp craze. They fed an eager public—with more leisure time to devote to things like reading and the extra money to purchase magazines—via advanced print technology that enabled higher-quality photos and better distribution. Despite the successes Goodman and others enjoyed, they faced criticism due to coarse content and lurid cover images.

In response, many publishers set up false-front companies to play fast and loose with financing. One large company might set up dozens of smaller ones; if any single entity went under, it would not topple the entire empire. Publishers loaded debts onto one entity, which would then go bankrupt, eventually having its assets bought by a secret sister firm at pennies (or less) on the dollar. With little oversight or regulation, the publishers jumped from one fad to the next—from highly sexual adventure stories to true-crime dramas with scantily clad damsels in distress or science fiction. Titles like *Real Confessions* and *Mystery Tales* played to base desires.

The publishers ran wild, and New York City officials responded in an attempt to clean up the industry. First, they went after the newsstand owners, then targeted the distributors. Finally, they got close to the publishing executives with obscenity charges that might land them in jail. Summing up the environment, one writer explained that publishers "managed to follow the letter of public decency laws while selling the most obscenely racist and sadistic sexual fantasies."[4] The publishers kept finding ways to circumvent the rules and stay just inches ahead of fire-breathing consumer advocacy groups and politicians like Thomas Dewey, New York City's crusading public advocate and future Republican presidential candidate.

What Goodman didn't realize right away was that various forces were aligning against the pulps, ultimately causing another format to grasp the spotlight—comic books. Growing out of the cartoon strips in newspapers, comic books had originally just been reprints bound together and sold at newsstands. Most were aimed at children, such as Richard F. Outcault's *Yellow Kid* and Bud Fisher's *Mutt & Jeff*. Later, pulp magazines featured more heroic characters designed to titillate the magazine-hungry masses. Tarzan, Doc Savage, and the Shadow had superhero powers, secret origins, and extraordinary abilities. Millions of readers gobbled these characters up, thereby creating a kind of intermediary publication that stood between explicit magazines and kid-friendly comic books.

In 1929, Dell had published *The Funnies*, the first comic book comprising original work rather than newspaper reprints. The publication lasted only a year but gave rise to other stand-alone comic books. M. C. Gaines, a salesman at Eastern Color, the company that printed the Sunday comics in color for many large northeastern newspapers, experimented with smaller-sized comic books in the early to mid-1930s with a ten-cent cover price. *Famous Funnies No. 1* sold out, and other comics were a hit as giveaway promotions for major corporations like Proctor & Gamble and retailers like Kinney Shoes. Soon comic book sales eclipsed the one hundred thousand monthly sales mark, while the promotional ones reached into the millions. A craze took shape.

The comic book industry in the mid-1930s is full of legendary tales, but the business catapulted from the strange union of two wild, nearly mythical characters: Major Malcolm Wheeler-Nicholson and Harry Donenfeld. Wheeler-Nicholson had an adventure-filled past, including swashbuckling tales of chasing Mexican bandits with the US Cavalry, battling across Europe during World War I, and fighting the Bolsheviks in Russia. After a controversial court-martial and being wounded in an assassination attempt, he ventured to New York City. He wrote nonfiction books about the military, but his fame grew when he began writing adventure stories for magazines in an attempt to give readers a realistic portrayal of the hardships and adventures of warfare.

Donenfeld, a Romanian Jewish immigrant who grew up on the Lower East Side, developed an entrepreneurial mindset amid the gangs who ran the streets in the neighborhood. Later, as he rose through the publishing ranks, Donenfeld benefited from his street smarts, forming ties with mobsters that enabled him to prosper (rumors circulated that he used his publishing network to help the mafia run liquor during Prohibition). Catering to a base audience, Donenfeld published smutty pulp magazines that bordered on pornography, most frequently called "girlie magazines," long before Hugh Hefner created *Playboy*.

The two men's paths intersected when Wheeler-Nicholson agreed to a distribution deal for his new *Detective Comics* line with Donenfeld's Independent News Company. In 1937 and 1938, Wheeler-Nicholson barely remained solvent. Always strapped for cash and facing a large debt to his distributor, he agreed to form Detective Comics, Inc., with Donenfeld publishing the first issue (soon the company would be known simply as DC). Later, Independent News bought Wheeler-Nicholson's National Allied Publications at auction and forced him out.[5]

The comic book revolution required one more spark. That catalyst ignited in Cleveland, Ohio, at the hands of two amateur—but highly inventive and artistic—comic book creators: writer Jerry Siegel and artist Joe Shuster. They struck gold with Superman. After a long march toward publication, the superhero appeared on the cover of the first issue of *Action Comics* hoisting a car over his head and smashing the front end, pieces flying off the vehicle as onlookers fled in terror. No one realized what a blockbuster Superman would become.

Within several months, Donenfeld received the issue's sales figures, which backed up what newsstand owners had reported. The independent Superman comic book launched in early 1939 sold nine hundred thousand copies. Eventually, *Action Comics* sold more than a million copies a month. Sadly, Siegel and Shuster, like so many early comic book creators, sold away their rights, working initially for $10 a page, thus earning a combined $130 for the first Superman story.

The success of *Action Comics* launched a Superman craze, including aggressive marketing campaigns, a newspaper strip, a radio show, and a series of animated cartoons. The radio show drove further expansion; according to one writer, "The comic strip sold to nearly three hundred newspapers by 1941." The publicist hired to promote Superman for Donenfeld claimed "35 million people were following Superman in at least one medium."[6] Beyond the media avenues, there were countless merchandising efforts, including trading cards, buttons, and metal action figures. The merch made Donenfeld rich beyond his dreams.

Donenfeld himself got into the act, reportedly wearing a Superman T-shirt under his tuxedo. Out carousing with friends (and his mistress) at posh bars and restaurants around the Big Apple, people would point at him in awe as the man who published Superman. Never one for discretion, Donenfeld would wait for some minor accident to happen, leap up, and rip open his white tux shirt to reveal the hero's logo underneath.[7]

Reluctant to sit idle while competitors made money, Goodman jumped on the comic book bandwagon. Frank Torpey, a Funnies, Inc., sales manager who had worked with the publisher at Eastern Distributing, urged Goodman to launch a comic book division. They shook hands on a deal for Timely to publish the work of Bill Everett and Carl Burgos, two virtually unknown writers who also did their own artwork. Their superheroes, a term used loosely to describe the angst-ridden Namor the Sub-Mariner and troubled android the Human Torch, served as the centerpieces of *Marvel Comics #1* (August 1939), an anthology published by Goodman. Supremely cautious, the publisher took a wait-and-see attitude toward comic books, outsourcing production entirely to Funnies, Incorporated.[8]

The first issue was a hit, selling eighty thousand copies in September and ultimately ten times that figure, even more than most of Donenfeld's output, and eventually rivaling sales of *Superman*. *Marvel Comics* was renamed *Marvel Mystery Comics*, focusing on its two successful superheroes.[9] Namor and Human Torch became more powerful as the issues piled up—in other words, more Superman-like. As other publishers jumped on the superhero craze, a familiar demand rang out across New York City artist and writing communities: "Find me the next Superman!"

Opting for total control over output, Goodman hired his own artists and writers rather than pay the Funnies, Inc., team. The publisher offered veteran freelancer Joe Simon a position as head writer for $12 a page, much more than the writer/artist had made with Funnies. Simon urged Goodman to hire a young artist named Jacob Kurtzberg, a tough kid from the Lower East Side who had been a gang member like Donenfeld but also became obsessed with writing and drawing comic book heroes. His experience included working in the famous Fleischer Brothers animation house, helping out with *Popeye* and *Betty Boop* cartoons.

Simon and the artist (employing the pseudonym "Jack Kirby") formed a partnership. Initially, they worked on a character Simon created called Blue Bolt. Many creative teams work well on paper, but Simon and Kirby excelled, particularly since each could do each part of the job, from writing and penciling to drawing covers. When people asked about who did what, Simon shrugged: "We both did everything."[10]

Goodman recognized the duo's talents and realized how quickly the comic book market was growing, so he offered Joe and Jack a royalty schedule in addition to page rates. In late 1939, he named Joe Simon as Timely's first editor.[11] Simon then convinced Goodman to hire Kirby at a higher page rate than others earned, explaining that the artist worked so fast that the steady paycheck would more than pay for itself. Simon and Kirby set up a two-man operation to develop new concepts. Goodman purposely kept the comic book division small to see if it remained successful.

Content to not micromanage (though he always obsessed over the cover art and adding new titles), Goodman basically let Simon and Kirby manage the division. There were a couple of misfires, including the Red Raven and the Vision, but Simon and Kirby soon hit their stride. Together they came up with Captain America (though each later disputed their roles and argued over who deserved more credit). The patriotic hero changed the course of Goodman's company and the industry.

Steve Rogers (Captain America's alter ego) got his superpowers from an Army experimental superserum that made him nearly invincible. Realizing they needed a perfect villain, the creative team featured Hitler on the cover of the first issue. As evil Nazi soldiers shoot at Cap in vain, he knocks the German leader off balance with a strong right.

Simon and Kirby's *Captain America #1* appeared on newsstands on December 20, 1940 (the cover date for comic books always ran three months ahead, so the official date is March 1941). The comic book, according to writer Sean Howe, "sold a near-Superman number of one million copies."[12] Simon and Kirby shot to fame after creating Captain America, one of the first really successful superheroes not being published by DC Comics, which put out the industry's two hottest commodities, Superman and Batman.

★   ★   ★

Simon, only twenty-seven years old, and the twenty-three-year-old Kirby grew accustomed to keeping the Timely operation afloat, despite being understaffed and somewhat underappreciated by Goodman. Human Torch, Sub-Mariner, and Captain America were all wildly popular among readers. Lieber, the young, handsome teenager, with a shock of dark hair and endless smile, joined his new bosses in the cramped offices. Although not much older than Lieber, Simon and Kirby were gruffer and acted older, constantly puffing away on cigars, filling the office with smoke.

At first, Simon kept the new employee busy with menial tasks. "I'd fill the ink wells. I'd run down and get them sandwiches at the drug store, and I'd proofread the pages," Lee recalled. "Sometimes in proofreading I'd say, 'You know, this sentence doesn't sound right. It ought to be written like this.' 'Well, go ahead and change it!' They didn't care!"[13]

Stanley agitated Kirby by playing a small flute in the office, yearning to make himself the center of attention. The artist threw things at his young protégé, and Simon laughed as his partner's temper flared. Kirby, the quintessential artist, had a manic—almost obsessive—need to draw and draw fast. He didn't appreciate the kid distracting him from his work.

Simon and Goodman built on Captain America's popularity, creating additional titles to expand the superhero lineup. DC's Batman had a young sidekick—Robin—that comic book creators believed would appeal to younger readers. Batman's success launched a wave of teen partners. Simon and Kirby followed, devising teenage sidekicks: Bucky for Captain America, who got to kick Hitler in the stomach in the second issue, and Toro for the Human Torch, a fire-eating circus performer who could also burst into flames and fight villains.

Kirby and Simon hired freelancers to keep up with demand but still struggled to keep up. Although he couldn't have anticipated it at the time, Simon's next move to ease his burden would change comic book history. The editor wanted to find out if Lieber could write, so he assigned the teen a short Captain America story. Text-based tales qualified comic books for a lower postage rate. They were considered less important than paneled, illustrated stories. Lieber's short story "Captain America Foils the Traitor's Revenge" appeared in *Captain America Comics #3* (May 1941). He signed the piece "Stan Lee," the pseudonym he adopted in hopes of saving his real name for the future novel he planned to author.

Given the publication schedule, the latest Lieber could have written the story is February 1941, but he probably composed it earlier. The date is important because it speaks to Lieber's career development. If he joined the company in late 1939, just after Kirby and Simon (when they were hard at work in developing Captain America), then there probably wasn't much writing for him to do. However, if the more likely time frame of late 1940 is accepted, then Lieber was put to work as a writer fairly quickly, probably because of the chaos Simon and Kirby faced in prepping issues of *Captain American* and their other early creations, as well as editing and overseeing the Human Torch and Sub-Mariner books.

Lee later acknowledged that the two-page story was just a fill-in. He also admitted: "Nobody ever took the time to read them, but I didn't care. I had become a published author. I was a pro!"[14] Simon appreciated the teen's enthusiasm and diligence in attacking the assignment. "Stan Lee," the youngster's new identity, was born.

An action shot of Captain America knocking a man silly accompanied "Lee's" first publication. The story—essentially two pages of solid text— arrived sandwiched between a Captain America tale about a demonic killer on the loose in Hollywood and another featuring a giant Nazi strongman and another murderer who kills people while dressed up in a butterfly costume. "It gave me a feeling of grandeur," Lee recalled.[15] While many readers may have overlooked the text, its cadence and style is a rough version of the mix of bravado, high-spirited language and witty wordplay that marked Stan's later writing.

Villain Lou Haines is satisfactorily evil, but the reader never learns what he did to earn the "traitor" moniker. In typical Lee style, the villain snarls at base commander Colonel Stevens: "But let me warn you now, you ain't seen the last of me! I'll get even somehow. Mark my words, you'll pay for this!" In hand-to-hand combat, Captain America lands a crippling blow, just as the reader thinks the hero is doomed. "No human being could have stood that blow," Lee wrote. "Haines instantly relaxed his grip and sank to the floor—unconscious!"[16] The next day when the colonel asks Steve Rogers if he heard anything the night before, Rogers claims that he slept through the hullabaloo. Stevens, Rogers, and sidekick Bucky share a hearty laugh. The "Traitor" story certainly doesn't exude Lieber's later confidence or knowing wink at the reader, but it demonstrates his blossoming understanding of audience, pace, and style.

In *Captain America #5* (August 1941), Lee wrote his first comics story, a five-page filler titled "Headline Hunter, Foreign Correspondent." Jerry Hunter is a newspaper reporter searching for a scoop in war-torn London. The journalist isn't really a superhero but displays super strength and cunning, all in a snazzy blue suit and red tie, looking a little like Captain America.

In the end, Hunter foils a Nazi plan to steal Navy cargo route maps and even blows up a German munitions plant. "Oh, gosh, it wasn't anything! And besides, boy! Look at the swell scoop I got," Hunter tells the American ambassador as the story ends. The teen language and "golly-gee" tone exhibit

Lee's budding comic book style. Hunter could be an early incarnation of Peter Parker in the way he acts and speaks. The story is decent, particularly for a short piece within the wildly popular *Captain America*, but it is leagues better than "Tuk: Cave Boy," an odd rip-off of Tarzan with exaggerated cavemen, another filler in the same issue. At the time, the comics were sixty-plus pages, so the Captain America parts would take up two-thirds, while fillers increased the page count.

Lee could not rest on the laurels of his first superhero publication. He quickly moved from office boy to writer and editor based on Timely's limited resources. The small crew necessitated that Lee, even though a teen, produce content *and* new characters.

Stan's first original superhero—Jack Frost—appeared in *U.S.A. Comics #1* (August 1941). The story brims with Lee's dialogue and verve. When "the king of the cold" finds a dying man in his "eternal deathly quiet" kingdom, he vows to bring the murderer to justice, exclaiming: "Dead! I have heard that crime flourishes throughout the world, but it has now reached my land. . . . I will avenge this deed and prevent more like it!"

Jack Frost (like many of Lee's later superheroes) is actually a kind of anti-hero, initially misunderstood by the New York City police chief and mocked by the chief of detectives. Eventually, though, Frost rescues the damsel in distress and wipes out a gang of "puny evil-doers." When the police try to arrest him, the story ends with Frost turning against them, exclaiming: "After this sort of reception I've changed my mind—if I can't work with you, I'll work against you—the next time we meet beware!" The idea that would later make Lee and Marvel famous—heroes and villains not fully good or evil—had already appeared in his writing two decades before his voice would change comics forever.

Given his writing for Captain America, it is no surprise that Lee used a similar origin point for a successful character he cocreated (with artist Jack Binder) called Destroyer. Appearing on the cover of *Mystic Comics #6* (October 1941), the superhero is reporter Kevin Marlow, accused of being a spy in Nazi Germany and thrown in a concentration camp (before that phrase was associated with the Holocaust). The tie to Captain America occurs when Marlow is given a superserum that gives him otherworldly strength and turns him into Destroyer, complete with a skull for an emblem. Like Cap, the superhero battles Nazis, wreaking havoc on Hitler's inhuman forces.

The Destroyer never became a household name like Captain America, but sales increased as the character fought in ravaged Europe against Nazi forces that were diabolical, gruesome, and drawn to appear animalistic. To mask his identity, Destroyer donned a costume that featured blood-red-striped pants and long crimson gloves. The costume made Destroyer appear just as inhuman as the villains.

★   ★   ★

One way to look at early comic book history is as a battle for talent. Timely's success led to Simon and Kirby being courted by other publishers with deeper pockets to pay the hot duo. The offers were too tempting, particularly for the perpetually money-nervous Kirby. They took on freelance projects at a hotel room near the Timely headquarters. The entire comic book business seemed reliant on these kinds of backdoor deals. While many creators worked for set page rates, Simon negotiated better paying deals for himself and Kirby.

According to Simon, Lee frequently tagged along with his office mates when they ventured out. One day, the teen chased after them as they snuck off to their hotel studio. Once there, Lee finally realized they were working on comics for DC. Simon says he "swore him to secrecy," despite "my theory that in comics, everybody knew everything. . . . There were no secrets there."[17] Given industry jealousy and publisher collusion, it probably wasn't a surprise when Simon and Kirby were inevitably discovered. In his memoir, Simon remembered working on *Captain America #10* when several of the Goodman clan who worked for Martin—Abe, Dave, and Robbie—crammed into the Timely office to confront Simon and Kirby.

"You guys are working for DC," Abe accused them, complaining: "You haven't been true to us. You haven't been loyal to us. You should be ashamed of yourselves."[18]

Abe then delivered the final blow, announcing that once they finished the current issue of *Captain America*, they were fired. One quasi-member of the Goodman clan was conspicuously absent, Simon explained: "Stan was nowhere to be seen."[19]

As the head writer at Timely, Simon admitted getting fired was "very humiliating," but the dismissal enraged Kirby, known for his short temper. He pinned the firing on Lee, judging that the timing seemed too coincidental.

"Jack always thought Stan had told his uncle that we were working for DC," Simon said. "He never gave up on that idea, and hated him for the rest of his life—to the day he died." Simon did not feel the same. Decades later in his memoir, he threw doubt on Kirby's implication.[20]

The suggestion that Kirby held Stan responsible and held the grudge for the rest of his life adds a new twist to the creative duo's relationship that would later revolutionize comic books. Later in their careers, they would have to get past (or bury) this episode. If they didn't, then the animosity that spilled out in ensuing years as they tangled over credit for creating the famous

Marvel superheroes must have brought Kirby's "hatred" back to the surface with newfound ferocity.

Lee's recollection of the incident is markedly different. He recalled Goodman personally firing the two after finding out they were moonlighting for the enemy. Lee explained: "Unexpectedly, Joe and Jack left Timely Comics! Supposedly it was because they were working on the side for National Periodicals." He then added, "Truth is, I never knew exactly *why* they left. I only knew this: it was suddenly *my* job to be in charge of the comics."[21] Earlier, when describing how "Joe and Jack left Timely in 1941," Lee called their ouster "a surprisingly unexpected development." He also chalked it up to the "luck" that "seems to deal most of the cards in the game of life."[22]

Simon and Kirby's abrupt dismissal is yet another enigmatic episode in Lee's career. Although it would have been underhanded to rat out his mentors, the memories of financial struggle just a few years earlier may have fueled a betrayal. Or it could be as Simon suggests, an open secret that Martin Goodman had to confront. The publisher did not abide disloyalty. Perhaps Goodman believed that Lee or someone else could take over the franchise without much of a loss.

Speculation is one thing, but evidence suggests significant dishonesty on all sides. First, Goodman and his accountants were actually ripping off Kirby and Simon, purposely reporting lower sales figures to reduce their share of the profits they were contracted to receive. On the other hand, Simon and Kirby secretly worked for DC. They covertly negotiated a $500-a-week combined salary with DC but still drew Timely paychecks as they attempted to figure out the transition and continue to make money from both companies.

★   ★   ★

Even a teenager with Lee's advanced imagination could have never dreamed that he would take over the comic book division at such a young age. In addition to his youth, he was hindered by an utter lack of experience managing anything. Luckily, the comics were produced by a small number of creatives and Goodman did not micromanage. Artists Al Avison and Syd Shores continued to draw the red, white, and blue hero, and Lee took over writing duties.[23]

The success of Captain America, though, did exert some extra pressure on Lee. He had little time to contemplate what it all meant—the publication calendar slowed for no one. Kirby and Simon worked on *#10* before they left (dated January 1942), meaning that they probably left Timely in late fall 1941.

Thrust into a leadership role, Lee made a wise decision—he mimicked Kirby and Simon, working himself hard across numerous projects. "I was responsible for all the stories," Lee recalled, "either writing them myself or buying them from other people." The range of work expanded: "Always when I was there—being the editor meant being the art director too, because you can't just edit the stories without making sure the artwork is done the right way so it enhances the stories . . . and the stories have to enhance the artwork. They have to go hand in hand."[24] Suddenly, with Kirby and Simon gone, Lee became head writer, editor-in-chief, and art director.

Stan employed thinly veiled pseudonyms to make it seem to the outside world that many people worked at Timely, including "Stan Martin," "Neel Nats," or other variations on his name. According to Stan Goldberg, who managed Timely's coloring department, Lee served as "the only editor." He also had an assistant named Al Sulman, whom Goldberg remembers not doing much work, and two female administrative aides.[25] On the art side, Lee worked with freelancers to fill the issues in Kirby's absence. Luckily, the youngster had talented artists and writers to draw from, including artist Alex Schomburg, as well as Burgos and Everett.

Under intense pressure to fill pages, Lee produced more than anyone else—and faster—perhaps the writing version of Kirby, always known for being a fast worker. The quality of Lee's writing is debatable. "Lee's early comic book work was hardly groundbreaking," explains comic book writer and historian Arie Kaplan. "His 1940s-era superhero comics were written just as well as anyone else's, but there was little room for innovation or complex characterization under the watchful eye of Martin Goodman."[26] Yet artist Dave Gantz held a different opinion: "I thought he was the Orson Welles of the comic book business."[27]

Goodman may have just wanted the kid to just keep the seat warm until he could find another editor, but Lee proved that he could handle the job. The youngster was the only one left capable of running the division. "I assume he wanted to find someone who wasn't just out of his teens," Lee recalled. "But apparently he had a short interest span and eventually stopped looking." The teen editor thought up a new moniker for himself: "Mr. Timely Comics."[28] Lee began honing his craft as primary writer, editing the work of freelancers, and overseeing the art. He grew up and into the job.

· 4 ·

Winning World War II

$\mathscr{I}$n 1942, the United States lurched toward full mobilization. Army officials estimated that they would need to train and prepare some nine million troops for the Allies to win the war. Pearl Harbor had sent the nation scrambling, but war is never just about battlefields and strategy. Transforming an economy emerging from the Great Depression would take time and immense coordination.

The American effort hinged on near-total mobilization of the industrial base. Corporations and businesses of all sizes had to create an intricate infrastructure to support the struggle. Although this obligation took a toll on the home front—from rationing food and everyday products to full-scale controls on gas, rubber, chemicals, and other essentials—Americans rallied to do what was necessary to aid the troops fighting the war.

Stan Lee, still a teenager, realized he could not stay home and helm Marvel while countless young men were preparing to fight and die. For a person who earned his first publication credit writing about Captain America—the superhero that had punched out Hitler on his debut cover—staying out of the war was unthinkable. Lee enlisted on November 9, 1942. He would still be a teen for seven more weeks—from boy editor to young soldier!

The military needed smart troops and a method for identifying them in an era in which only about 5 percent of American males had college degrees. Planners created the Army General Classification Test to evaluate inductees on intelligence and aptitude and then group them into one of five rankings. The Signal Corps was a plum assignment for highly intelligent trainees based on its intricate technical and scientific work. Just prior to Stan's enlistment, some 39 percent of Signal Corps recruits had tested into Classes I and II, but that figure jumped to 58 percent by 1943. Lee's intelligence enabled him to score high enough to get into the Signal Corps.[1]

Although he knew it was inevitable, Goodman was apprehensive about his editor-in-chief going off to war. Who would run the thriving comic book division? Across the industry—rather than enlist—some artists and writers were waiting until they were drafted. In the meantime, they scrambled to fill pages and prepare comic books. The publisher could hardly question Stan's decision. He certainly understood that no one wanted to be viewed as unpatriotic.

Captain America remained Timely's most popular series. By 1943 there were more than 140 comic books on the newsstands, according to one source, "read by over fifty million people each month," though only about 100 would survive until the end of the year because of paper rationing for the war effort. While regulations on paper usage limited industry growth, demand soared. In 1944, for example, Fawcett's *Captain Marvel Adventures* sold fourteen million copies, up 21 percent over the previous year. Superhero titles drove sales, but publishers also played to changes in what consumers wanted by expanding into other areas, such as humor, funny animals, and teen romance.[2]

Comics were exactly what readers wanted—an inexpensive diversion from the daily intensity of global warfare and full-on mobilization at home. Comic book publishers pumped out patriotic "good versus evil" stories that were reflective of the era. Always following the trail blazed by others, it suddenly seemed as if Goodman had a golden touch. With interest in comic books at an all-time high, he and many other publishers got rich.

★   ★   ★

When Stan decided to volunteer, he had been the editor-in-chief at Timely for about a year. He spent much of that time writing scripts or cocreating new characters, but his primary task was to keep Timely's most popular comics going, particularly *Captain America*. The young editor managed a growing staff of production assistants, artists, writers, and freelancers.

Once Stan signed up for the military, Lee and Goodman had an immediate need: find an editor to replace him while he served. They turned to Stan's friend, artist Vince Fago, who had earned his reputation through work as one of the early cartoon animators on Superman, Popeye, and Gulliver's Travels for Fleischer Studios. Run by the famous Max Fleischer, the animation studio was also one of the places Kirby had worked earlier in his career. The Fleischer firm competed with Disney, a fierce rivalry for America's animation dollars. Fleischer differed from Disney by focusing on human characters, such as Betty Boop and Koko the Clown, rather than talking mice, ducks, dogs, and other anthropomorphic figures. Later, the Fleischer brothers would sell their animation company to Paramount.

"How would you like my job?" Lee asked his buddy Fago. Martin offered him a salary of $250 a week.[3]

Fago knew that Lee and Goodman hired him to keep the comic book division on track, but it wasn't the same company during the war. The fighting overseas was heavy stuff; readers yearned for lighter comedic fare. Disney's popularity and Fleischer's cartoons blew open the children's market. Goodman didn't need anyone to twist his arm; he jumped on the bandwagon. Fago specialized in the type of funny animals that children craved and many adults wanted as a way to put the war on the backburner, if only for a short time.

Goodman used Disney as a model, which had licensed its characters in comic books to Dell. Timely transformed into Disney-lite, putting out a flurry of amusing animal comics, such as *Comedy Comics* and *Joker Comics*. Some of these characters Lee had concocted, like Ziggy Pig and Silly Seal (cocreated with artist Al Jaffee, the future *Mad* magazine illustrator).

The comedy duo—Ziggy was the straight man and Silly was the less intelligent one—battled Toughy Cat, a character in bright-red pants, frayed at the bottom, and mismatched suspenders. Their antics caught on with readers. The popularity of the zany duo and other comics in a similar vein helped Timely thrive during the war years. Ziggy and Silly headlined their own comic until September 1949.[4]

Timely's success meant Fago could barely keep up. He estimated that each comic had a print run of about five hundred thousand. "Sometimes we'd put out five books a week or more," Fago remembered. "You'd see the numbers come back and could tell that Goodman was a millionaire."[5]

Under Fago's editorship, Goodman doubled down, pushing him to entice more female readers. The editor used the patriotic angle, publishing stories about Miss America, a teenage heiress who gained superhuman strength and the ability to fly after being struck by lightning. The superheroine first appeared in *Marvel Mystery Comics #49* (November 1943), an issue with Human Torch and Toro thwarting a Japanese battleship on the cover. In January 1944, Miss America became a lead title character. However, when sales came in lower than anticipated, the next issue was delayed until November and published with the new name *Miss America Magazine #2*. On the new cover, a real-life model portrayed the character in her superhero outfit.

For the relaunch, Fago and his creative team gradually eliminated superhero material in favor of topics deemed more "appropriate" for teen girls. Humor and teen-based topics grew more popular as the war continued, while superheroes slowly waned.

★   ★   ★

While Fago churned out comic books, Stan went off to basic training at Fort Monmouth, a large base in New Jersey that housed the Signal Corps. Fort Monmouth had a storied past and played a significant role in military research. Several years earlier, radar had been developed at the base, as well as the all-important handheld walkie-talkie. In later years, military researchers there would learn to bounce radio waves off the moon.[6]

Army strategists knew wars were often won by infrastructure. The Signal Corps played a key role in keeping communications flowing, an essential factor in modern warfare. Stan's training focused on learning how to string and repair communications lines, which he thought would lead to overseas combat duty.

Despite its talented, intelligent candidates, the Signal Corps could barely keep up with demand. The military division was forced to open additional training centers, first at Camp Crowder, Missouri, and then at Camp Kohler, near Sacramento. By mid-1943, the Corps consisted of 27,000 officers and 287,000 enlisted men, backed by another 50,000 civilians who worked alongside them. In addition to his technical training, Lee performed many everyday tasks, such as patrolling the camp perimeter and watching for enemy ships or planes. Based on Pearl Harbor and reports of sub activity in the Atlantic Ocean, the military feared that Germany might mount a surprise attack in the midst of the cold New Jersey winter. Stan claimed that the frigid wind whipping off the Atlantic nearly froze him to the core.

The oceanfront duty ended, however, when Lee's superior officers discovered his work as a writer and editor. He wouldn't be going to the front lines; instead, Stan was headed back to New York City! The Training Film Division of the Signal Corps was headquartered in Astoria, Queens. He joined with other artists, filmmakers, and writers to create a range of public relations pieces, propaganda tools, and information-sharing documents. His ability to write scripts had earned him the transfer. Like countless military men on the home front, Lee would play a supporting role.

The Army purchased a building at Thirty-Fifth Avenue and Thirty-Fifth Street in Astoria that housed the Signal Corps Photographic Center, the home of the official photographers and filmmakers supporting the war effort. Colonel Melvin E. Gillette served as commander, the same role he held at Fort Monmouth before the Army bought the Queens facility in February 1942, some nine months before Lee enlisted. Under Gillette's watchful eye, the old movie studio (originally built in 1919) underwent extensive renovation. When completed the studio rivaled the major production companies in Hollywood.

Gillette's men had an important role to play in the war for democracy. Their work would aid in educating the troops since education and skill levels varied greatly. With millions of men requiring training on complex weapons, instrumentation, and other advanced technology, the military required easy-to-understand training films and instructional guides. Gillette's division also supervised the highly sensitive and classified materials associated with filming, particularly troop movements and battle footage.

A line of grand columns protected the front entrance of the Photographic Center, flanked by rows of tall, narrow windows. Inside the Army built the largest soundstage on the East Coast, enabling filmmakers to create a variety of military settings. Some of Hollywood's finest directors, cinematographers, and crews would create war movies for the general public from the Astoria Center. The facility opened in May 1942, then served as headquarters for the entire film and photography effort.

Stan described his work among the small group of scribes: "I wrote training films, I wrote film scripts, I did posters, I wrote instructional manuals," Lee said. "I was one of the great teachers of our time!"[7] The Signal Corps group included many famous or soon-to-be-famous individuals, including three-time Academy Award–winning director Frank Capra, *New Yorker* cartoonist Charles Addams, and children's book writer and illustrator Theodor Geisel, whom the world already knew as "Dr. Seuss." The stories that must have floated around that room during lunch breaks!

Lee took up a desk in the scriptwriter bullpen, to the right of eminent author William Saroyan—at least when the pacifist author came into the office. Saroyan, who had won a Pulitzer Prize in 1939 for his play *The Time of Your Life*, found that his fame spread when he rejected the award. While with the Signal Corps, Saroyan spent much of his time working from the Lombardy Hotel, a twenty-two-story Manhattan hotel that had been purchased by newspaper mogul William Randolph Hearst for his leading lady, actress Marion Davies. Later the Army sent Saroyan off to London to work on films. Lee and the others, including screenwriter Ivan Goff and producer Hunt Stromberg Jr., earned the official Army military occupation specialty designation "playwright."[8]

As home-front efforts intensified, Lee and his colleagues were sent to bases outside New York. Stan journeyed to several camps on temporary duty (TDY in military vernacular), essentially crisscrossing the Southeast and Midwest. He made stops in North Carolina, Indiana, and other locations. Each base had a critical demand for easy-to-understand instruction manuals, films, or other public relations materials based on the influx of men surging into the armed forces via the draft or enlistment. Whenever he had to write a script for a film on using certain cameras during combat (or some other subject he knew little or nothing about), Lee worked by a familiar motto—simplify the information. "I often wrote entire training manuals in the form of comic books," he recalled. "It was an excellent way of educating and communicating."[9]

One post took him deep into the heartland—Fort Benjamin Harrison in Indiana, just northeast of Indianapolis—which must have been jarring for a New York City boy who had not seen much of the country or traveled. While in Indiana, Stan worked with the Army Finance Department, which seemed to perpetually struggle to keep up with payrolls. "This was hurting army morale because there would be guys overseas in foxholes who were getting their butts shot off and they weren't getting paid on time," Stan told comic book historian and writer Clifford Meth. Recruits with finance backgrounds were few and far between, but the problem had to be solved quickly.[10]

Watching the wannabe accountants and payroll servicemen marching around the base, Lee noticed that they seemed lethargic. He hoped to pep them up, so he penned a song for them to sing while marching, basically inserting new lyrics over the well-known "Air Force Song." The peppy scriptwriter included memorable lines, like "We write, compute, sit tight, don't shoot." While not Grammy-worthy, the new fight song energized the unit and improved morale.

Stan's songwriting antics were just the beginning of his work with the Finance Department. When the higher-ups realized how long it took to train payroll officers, they asked Lee to rewrite the manuals. Stan added humor and a bit of levity by introducing a cartoon character that helped the officers learn the proper methods in a lighthearted manner. "I rewrote dull army payroll manuals to make them simpler," Lee remembered. "I established a character called Fiscal Freddy who was trying to get paid. I made a game out of it. I had a few little gags. We were able to shorten the training period of payroll officers by more than 50 percent." He joked: "I think I won the war single-handedly."[11] Clearly, Stan realized that using humor would help the men learn the intricate procedures more effectively: "While following his adventures, we were teaching the embryonic officers how to do the payroll."[12]

Lee later moved to another project, which he dubbed "my all-time strangest assignment."[13] He created anti–venereal disease posters aimed at troops in Europe. Sexually transmitted diseases have plagued armies throughout history. American leaders took the effort deadly seriously. Despite implementing extensive education programs and making condoms readily available, the military still lost men to syphilis and gonorrhea. Prevention was critical. For example, the British—less willing to confront the taboo STD epidemic—had forty thousand men a month being treated for VD during the Italian campaign. On average, the US Army lost about six hundred personnel daily due to venereal diseases. Although medical innovations would cut the treatment time greatly, in the early stages of World War II, an STD caused a hospital stay from thirty days for gonorrhea to six months for syphilis.[14]

While overseas, servicemen were given repeated lectures, sometimes up to half a dozen times a month by surgeons, doctors, chaplains, and officers. When they had an overnight pass or were on furlough, each soldier was given a prophylactic kit (referred to as "V-Packettes") that included ointment, a cleaning cloth, and cleansing tissue. Military leaders went to extreme measures to thwart STDs, including authorizing the creation of propaganda posters that showed Axis leaders Hitler, Mussolini, and Tojo deliberately plotting to disable Allied troops via disease.

Many of these images, such as those created by noted artist Arthur Szyk, depicted the Axis leaders as subhuman animals with rat-like features or as ugly buffoons riddled with disease. These illustrations deliberately created an adversarial image, focusing on xenophobic attitudes of the typical Allied soldier. In "Fool the Axis—Use Prophylaxis," for example, Adolph Hitler is riddled with sores, wears a "syphilis" sash, and carries an oversized syringe. Mussolini's image is even worse. He carries an image of a prostitute in place of a syringe, with a skull-and-crossbones symbol on her dark negligee.

Unsure how to combat the scourge, Lee promoted the prophylactic stations the army had established, in Stan's words, "all over Europe." Men visited the small huts when they believed they were infected. Inside, they received a series of rough and painful treatments in hopes of prevention. "Those little pro stations dotted the landscape," Lee said, "with small green lights above the entrance to make them easily recognizable." He wrestled with many different examples, and then he realized that the simplest message would work best: "VD? Not me!"[15] Lee illustrated the poster with a cartoon image of a happy serviceman walking into the station with the green light clearly visible.

Army leaders liked the simplicity, flooding overseas posts with the posters. Ironically, given the sheer number of soldiers, the print may have ranked among Lee's most-seen, yet it was also the most roundly ignored. In contrast to his lighthearted design, most posters were darker in tone and more ominous.

Lee worked on scripts, posters, and brochures for the Army just as he did back in Goodman's Manhattan headquarters: fast and efficient. According to lore, the other "playwrights" couldn't keep up. The commanding officer ordered Stan to slow down.

While it is difficult to fully quantify the importance of the films, posters, photos, and materials the Signal Corps produced, analysts determined that using educational films cut training time by 30 percent. On the home front, Signal Corps efforts also provided from 30 percent to 50 percent of newsreel footage for movie theaters, which kept the public informed about the global skirmish. Photographers were even able to use new telephoto technology to snap pictures at the front and send them home almost immediately. Lee, Capra, Geisel, and the other Army "playwrights" did important work for the war effort. Military historians George Raynor Thompson and Dixie R. Harris note, "The written word, the spoken word, and the art of the motion picture all helped to create the conditions under which high morale flourished."[16]

★   ★   ★

A workaholic with plenty of downtime, Lee used the extra time to keep his fingers dipped in Timely ink and his pockets filled with Goodman's money via freelancing. The added income enabled him to purchase his first automobile while stationed near Duke University in Durham, North Carolina—a 1936 Plymouth. He paid $20 for the beat-up wreck, but it ran. The vehicle had a fold-up windshield that allowed the warm North Carolina wind to blow in his face as he cruised the back roads of tobacco country.

No matter where the Army sent him, Lee received letters from Fago that outlined stories every Friday. Lee then typed up the scripts, sending them back Monday. In addition to working on comics, Lee also helped out with the pulps. He wrote cartoon captions for *Read!* magazine, one of Goodman's adult publications. An example of Lee's short ditties (January 1943): "A buzz-saw can cut you in two / A machinegun can drill you right thru / But these things are tame, compared— / To what a woman can do!" The accompanying drawing shows a plump woman feeding her bald husband, who is chained to a doghouse.[17] The ribald humor fit that era and certainly within the magazines Goodman published, filled with sexist overtones, racy photographs, and plenty of violence.

Stan also wrote mystery-with-a-twist-ending short stories, similar to the ones he had earlier written for Joe Simon in the *Captain America* comics. In "Only the Blind Can See," which appeared in Goodman's *Joker* magazine (1943–1944), the joke is on the reader. What he eventually understands is that a supposedly blind panhandler (who people assumed was a phony) was truly blind. Written in second person so Lee can speak directly to the reader, whom he addresses as "Buddy," one learns that the down-on-his-luck beggar had too much pride to confront those who thought he faked it. He had to get run over in the street by a speeding car before people would realize the truth.[18] These kinds of short stories were the training ground for the science fiction and monster comic books that Lee would write after the war. The voice and style were heavily indebted to the thrillers he had read as a young person and the countless movies he had watched. Like so many people of his generation, the combination of deep reading and films shaped his creative imagination.

Lee's after-hours writing for Timely went largely unnoticed by his superiors, but the freelance effort once got him arrested (in typical Lee madcap fashion). One Friday a bored mail clerk overlooked Stan's letter, telling him his mailbox was empty. Puzzled that he hadn't received anything from Fago, the next day, he swung by the now-closed mailroom. He saw a letter in his cubby with the Timely return address clearly in view.

Not willing to miss a deadline or freelance paycheck, Lee asked the officer in charge to open the mailroom. The harried officer said no, telling Lee to worry about the mail on Monday. Angry, Lee got a screwdriver and gently unscrewed the mailbox hinges, enabling him to get at the assignment. The mailroom officer went berserk. He reported Stan to the base captain who was just as mad that orders had been ignored. They charged Lee with mail tampering and threatened that he could end up in the Leavenworth prison if convicted. Luckily, the colonel in charge of the Finance Department intervened, thus saving Lee's bacon. In this instance, Fiscal Freddy really did save the day![19]

Taking Comics into the Cold War

$\mathcal{S}$igning his name and rolling his ink-stained thumb across the Army discharge paper made it official—Sergeant Lee was a civilian again. Practically before the ink even dried, the twenty-three-year-old jumped into his new car and roared off base. The large black Buick convertible had hot red leather seats and flashy whitewall tires with shiny hubcaps—a noticeable upgrade from the battered Plymouth with the foldaway windshield.

Lee received a $200 bonus (called "muster out pay"), which the Army disbursed so soldiers could jumpstart their postmilitary lives, but Stan skipped the mandatory class that went along with the funds.[1] Instead, he deposited half in a savings account and kept the rest. It was late September 1945, and the Army had allotted him $42.12 to get back to New York City from the discharge center at Camp Atterbury in central Indiana, about fifty miles south of where he had been stationed earlier at Fort Harrison.

A car junkie, especially with sleek convertibles, Lee hit the open road. So excited to get back to the Big Apple, Lee joked that he "burned my uniform, hopped into my car, and made it non-stop back to New York in possibly the same speed as the Concorde!"[2] He wanted to get back to his helm at Timely, which Goodman had consolidated with his magazine operations in a new headquarters on the fourteenth floor of the Empire State Building. Lee zoomed off on the more than seven-hundred-mile trip to the Big Apple.

★   ★   ★

Almost like an animated character careening across the page—all gangly arms and long legs—Stan Lee proved a frenetic blur. He weaved in and out among ambling pedestrians window-shopping along Broadway, dipping and twisting around the sightseers. Stan dashed the two-and-a-half-mile trek south from his new two-room abode at the Alamac Hotel to the Timely office in the majestic Empire State Building. Lee's feet scratched across the sidewalk creating a wild beat matched only by the thoughts bursting in his head and the scripts playing like film scenes in his mind.

The postwar years brimmed with opportunity for go-getters like Lee. After the years of home-front rations and devastation overseas, people viewed the future with enthusiasm. New York shimmered with optimism. Comic book sales had soared during the war. Readers wanted diversions, especially on the front or working on bases at home or overseas. Comics filled a need for easy, quick reading that was fun-filled, exciting, and a distraction from the brutality of death tolls, fierce battles, and innumerable injuries. After the war, industry insiders estimated that 90 percent of children and teens from ages eight to fifteen read comic books on a regular basis.

Stan's return to Timely would be in the midst of a new age for comics and the country. The nation seemed electric. Popular culture, from comic books to Madison Avenue advertising campaigns, burst with vivid new colors, sounds, and images in stark contrast to the rationing and sacrifice necessary during the war. It was a good time to be in publishing.

Lee's new home was the Alamac Hotel on Broadway and Seventy-First Street, a stately nineteen-story dark-brown brick edifice built in 1925. The hotel became a home for many jazz groups in the mid- to late 1920s, as well as an away trip locale for major league baseball teams. The Alamac had some six hundred guest rooms, as well as a handful of shops and a restaurant on the ground level. Later, in the early 1950s, the CIA would use the Alamac as a safe house for German scientists and technicians working for American national defense during the Cold War.

The Alamac provided a steady flow of new friends and acquaintances. More importantly, it gave Stan a forty-block walk to the Timely office. Stan ambled back and forth, his frantic energy keeping his loopy legs loose. Despite his love for hotrods, he walked almost everywhere in the city. Lee embraced the sights and sounds on his daily commute: the thrills of Times Square, towering skyscrapers, and mass of humanity coursing through the streets.

Stan felt like he had a new lease on life: fine apartment, steady (and growing) income, and many dates in the heady, joyous postwar era. Yet there were aggravations, too. "One thing that both irritated and frustrated me," Lee explained, "was the fact that nobody, outside of our own little circle, had a good word to say about comic books."[3] The nagging self-doubts about his future in comics still needled him, despite the millions of copies rolling off presses and filling the nation's newsstands.

The negativity prompted bouts of self-consciousness. Hoping to live up to his mother's predictions, Stan felt predestined for success, something larger than comic books. During the war, he had served with some of the nation's great creative minds; now in his mid-twenties, he was back to being *just* a comic book writer.

★   ★   ★

Although Lee bristled at the reaction he received from people who asked him what he did for a living, he really loved the focus on writing and creating at Timely. Working in the Signal Corps, the young man witnessed firsthand the true value of animation, film, and entertainment as a means to educate. While the nature of writing was often lonely, the team aspect of creating comic books thrilled him. Plus, he was responsible for so many different aspects of the job. The entire organization ran through him, but it wasn't a dictatorship. He enjoyed the camaraderie.

Consumers had more money to spend on pop culture and added free time due to technological advances and the booming postwar economy. America's superpower status propelled the creation of thriving middle- and upper-middle classes. Yet Lee had to reconcile his joy with the sideways glances he received when people found he worked in comics.

Vince Fago's small team had turned out countless comic books during the war, thriving as consumer tastes changed. The popularity of Archie and his teenage gang of friends in *Archie Comics* (first published in 1942) influenced the whole industry and lasted into the postwar years. Reacting to the trend, Lee published comics featuring young female heroines and teen humor.

Ruth Atkinson, a renowned artist/writer, created the smash hit *Millie the Model*, which began its long run in late 1945. As one of the first women in comic books, Atkinson paved the way for others. She also created *Patsy Walker*, a spin-off from the old *Miss America Magazine* series. Lee jumped on the bandwagon, creating *Nellie the Nurse*, another title in teen humor/romance.

Wartime paper restrictions ended in late 1945, enabling publishers to go full tilt. The next year, forty million copies sold monthly. The superheroes remained popular, with Fawcett's *Captain Marvel* and DC's *Superman* and *Batman* selling well, but readers enjoyed other genres too: crime stories, teen romps, and science fiction. Late in 1946, Lee tried to capitalize on the popularity of female heroine stories by cocreating Blonde Phantom.[4] As secretary to private eye Mark Mason, Louise Grant kept her Blonde Phantom identity a secret. At night she donned a bright-red evening gown and mask, fighting criminals with a mix of martial arts skills and a trusty .45-caliber pistol. Blonde Phantom was in the vein of DC's Wonder Woman and Timely's own Miss America. Launched as a solo comic (beginning with *Blonde Phantom Comics #12*), the title lasted about two years.

In another effort to revive superheroes, Lee combined several into a super team, similar to DC's Justice Society of America, which had debuted in *All Star Comics #3* (Winter 1940–1941). *All Winners Comics #19* (Fall 1946) featured Captain America, Human Torch, Sub-Mariner, Whizzer, Miss America, and their teen sidekicks.

Lee's typical cover promised "a complete SIZZLING, ACTION THRILLER!" He hired *Batman* cocreator Bill Finger to script the book. Finger's initial story focused on a villain's attempt to steal a nuclear weapon, but fans were not impressed—*All Winners* proved a shipwreck of All Losers! The title appeared once more before Goodman cancelled it. The publisher also axed *Young Allies Comics #20*, a Simon and Kirby series that had launched in summer 1941.

Stan received his first dose of national publicity in November 1947 when *Writer's Digest* magazine asked him to pen a featured article. Not yet twenty-five years old, the boyish Lee chomped on a pipe in the cover photo in an attempt to look older and wiser. Although he still doubted his long-term future, Lee played up his role as a seasoned editor. "There's Money in Comics!" offered would-be writers advice for breaking into comic books—including how there should be emphasis on realistic dialogue and developing characters. Lee divulged these ideas about writing and creativity in a publication that was read by other scribes as a means to find freelance gigs. The Stan style in the article also foreshadowed Marvel's 1960s voice and cadence.

Publishers continued to test different genres as sales remained strong. Simon and Kirby remained a force in the industry. They created the teen romance genre with *Young Romance* (September 1947), published by Crestwood/Prize. A narrative of "true" stories, *Young Romance* sold millions of copies. Some estimated that the *Young Romance* comics (and various spin-offs tied to the title) sold about five million copies a month for the rest of the decade.[5] The series ran through June 1963, when Crestwood sold it to DC (who then published the series through 1975).

Genres habitually shifted: superheroes gave way to teen comedy, which then morphed into romance titles and next mutated into cowboy comics and true-crime books. With Stan at the helm, Goodman's company stayed among the leaders in sales but never moved into the top ranks creatively. The tried-and-true worked at Timely—follow the trends rather than begin them. Superheroes were cut when Goodman saw sales figures plummet. For example, in 1947 the long-running *Sub-Mariner Comics* morphed into *Official*

True Crime Cases Comics #24, with the latter taking over the sequential order of the superhero title.[6]

Comic books also had a new rival for people's popular culture attention: television. The growing popularity also influenced comics, as film had. Cowboy movie stars—first Gene Autry, then Roy Rogers—sparked interest in Western comics. Rogers, along with his trusty horse, Trigger, and wife, Dale Evans, appeared in popular films like *King of the Cowboys* (1943) and *Home in Oklahoma* (1947). From the early 1940s through the late 1950s, Rogers became the nation's most popular cowboy actor. His groundbreaking licensing agreements put his image and likeness on numerous products, second only to those of Walt Disney. He was the first star to conquer the entire media landscape—from hit recordings to starring in a long-running radio show that later moved to television.

Western-crazed readers also turned to Fawcett's *Hopalong Cassidy*, which sold four million copies in 1947 and eight million the following year, while DC brought out *Dale Evans Comics* in 1948. Goodman published *Wild Western* (1948–1957), starring Kid Colt, but also introducing a rotating group of additional heroes, from Apache Kid to Arizona Annie. Lee served as general editor of *Wild Western*. He wrote some of the stories, and freelancers and staff artists scripted and drew other issues.

In March 1948, Timely launched *Two-Gun Kid #1*, featuring a singing hero just like Rogers and Autry. Five months later, *Kid Colt, Hero of The West #1* hit newsstands, giving a stand-alone book to the popular character—a fast-draw sharpshooter who hunts for and kills the villain who murdered his father, then searches for redemption by becoming a hero, despite being a fugitive. The issue promised "Thundering Guns vs. Crooked Lawmen," with the cover a cornucopia of whizzing bullets and blazing six-shooters. The hero, neither fully good nor fully bad, served as a precursor to the superheroes Lee and his team of cocreators would birth a little more than a decade later.

Lee's favorite new character was Black Rider, a doctor who donned a secret identity to battle criminals, dubbed "The Greatest Gun-Fighter the West Has Ever Known." Goodman had always been fascinated with the covers of his publications, preferring to use photographs, as he did with early *Miss America* comics and many of his pulp slicks. For a *Black Rider* issue, promising "a movie-length Adventure of the Black Rider" in early 1950, Lee donned the ominous black outfit and mask, appearing on the cover holding two six-shooters.

Publishers were notoriously nervous, regardless of sales. Trouble began in 1948, though, with true-crime books. Many were tame, with scintillating stories of gangsters and detectives; others, though, featured lurid stories and explicit violence. For example, the cover of Fox's *Murder Incorporated* (January

1948) showed a buxom female firing a bullet into a man who had cheated at cards. The illustration depicted his gruesome facial reaction as the bullet entered his chest. Although the cover blurb announced "For Adults Only," it seemed the stories were aimed at younger readers.

Adults hated the violence, but the popularity of crime comics increased circulation that year by 20 percent over the previous year and up 50 percent over two years. In 1948, a *Time* article implied some juveniles committed copycat crimes after reading comic books. The piece contributed to a growing nationwide hysteria. Frederic Wertham (an influential author and psychiatrist) fueled the propaganda, organizing a symposium that concluded comic books glorified crime, violence, and sexuality. Once the media fed into the controversy, the comic book industry faced a true crisis.

★   ★   ★

Lee remained extremely busy with boundless energy and an engaging imagination. But he did not seem to possess the entrepreneurial spirit to launch his own project like many other writers and artists had done in the postwar years. Stan's focus was on the steady paycheck, plus he genuinely enjoyed working with the other writers, editors, and artists. However, the quality of the output didn't change much at Timely: "Every few months a new trend and we'd be right there, faithfully following each one. . . . I felt that we were a company of copycats."[7]

In 1947, Stan attempted to break from his doldrums, self-publishing *Secrets Behind the Comics.* The booklet sold for one dollar, a significant investment when comics were just ten cents. Using comic book fonts and illustrations, the publication featured "by Stan Lee" in prominent script on the cover. Stan dedicated the book to his younger brother, Larry, and Goodman's children, Iden, Judy, and Chip.

Ironically, but not out of character, "Secret No. 1" was Stan himself. Here he outlined his career and the book's rationale. With an illustrated headshot—pencil behind the ear and dotted bowtie—the introduction listed his many publications as Timely's "Managing Editor and Art Director." The Lee trademark writing style leaps from the page: "NOW, for the first time ever in the world, Stan Lee will show you exactly how comic strips are WRITTEN!!!"[8] In addition to Lee's "secrets," the book contained blank illustration areas where readers might attempt to draw the Blonde Phantom.

Apparently with Goodman's permission, Stan used other Timely characters, including Captain America and Bucky, its most famous superheroes. Artist Ken Bald illustrated the booklet. The controversial aspect of *Secrets* is the way Stan pandered to his boss, even though Goodman wasn't publishing the tome. Calling Martin "the young brilliant magazine king," Lee gives his boss credit for the idea of Captain America ("I must create a comic character who will represent freedom's battle against fascism.") without mentioning Joe Simon and Jack Kirby. The errant micro-history even ends with a fanciful illustration of Goodman shaking hands with Captain America.[9] The rationale for Stan subverting the truth has never been fully uncovered, but the awful decision would in later years give his detractors fresh ammunition for discrediting him for usurping credit versus his cocreators. And, in the moment, although the book allegedly sold well, *Secrets* did not provide an escape route from comic books. He did not follow up with another book.

Occasionally, though, Lee did edit magazines aimed at adults. Ironically, the pulps were actually more respectable (a *real* career), even the tripe Goodman published. For example, Martin had Stan work on the 1950 celebrity pinup *Focus*. Dubbed a "photo bedsheet" because it measured 10 × 14 inches, *Focus* aimed at male readers with bikini-clad cover models (including future screen icon Marilyn Monroe) and vivid headlines. The following year, the publisher changed it to a small pocket-sized magazine, only 4 × 6 inches. He notoriously fiddled with covers, titles, and physical size, hoping some slight modification might lead to increased sales.[10]

Stan also took on additional freelance work, much of it anonymous since he did not want to get fired or risk upsetting Goodman, who he had seen usher out Joe and Jack for moonlighting. "I ghosted them under other people's names," he explained, everything from television shows and radio programs to advertising copy. However, Lee did sign his name to the popular Sunday *Howdy Doody* newspaper strip (1950 to 1953).[11]

While he gained momentum professionally, Stan's personal life hummed in the energy and revitalized spirit of postwar New York. In 1947, however, his world spun into a different orbit when by happenstance he met English model and actress Joan Clayton Boocock. Lee's cousin had arranged a blind date for Stan, telling him to meet the date at a local modeling agency. However, when he knocked on the door, Joan answered—not the intended woman. Love at first sight! Stan blurted out that he loved her, claiming he had been drawing her face since he was a boy. Rather than run in horror, she laughed at the offhanded exultation. Soon they were an item.

Joan had been working as a hat model but had come to the United States as a war bride (marrying an American officer in Great Britain after a whirlwind romance, a common happening in the war years). The hasty marriage didn't last, so she planned a trip to Reno, Nevada, to get a divorce. (New York state laws made divorce nearly impossible for women.) In the Wild West of Nevada, Joan only had to serve six weeks' residency.

Stan waited nervously. The young model drew several suitors while serving the residency. After Lee received a letter from Joan addressed, "Dear Jack," he threw caution to the wind and embarked on a convoluted, twenty-eight-hour plane trip to Reno. Luckily, when he arrived, the young couple rekindled their relationship. On December 5, 1947, Stan and Joan pulled a Reno special: in one room, a judge nullified her marriage; then they walked next door, where the same judge then married them. In a matter of minutes, Joan Boocock became Mrs. Stan Lee.[12]

The young couple took the train home (much more leisurely than a harried plane ride), arriving during the Christmas holiday season. They moved into a tiny apartment in Manhattan on Ninety-Sixth Street, between Lexington Avenue and Fifth Avenue. They settled in, getting two dogs: cocker spaniels Hamlet and Hecuba.

Stan was always reserved in talking about his parents. He rarely mentioned Celia's death (December 16, 1947), just eleven days after his marriage. As a result of her passing and his father's distant relationship with both boys, Larry, then fifteen years old, moved in with Stan and Joan. Rather than stay in the city, they found a small town on Long Island called Hewlett Harbor. They purchased an eight-room house on West Broadway and bought a green Buick convertible that had been owned by a Blue Angel pilot; the car's novelty, which Stan loved, was "a huge flying female as a radiator ornament."[13]

The couple enjoyed Lee's professional successes (like many men in the late 1940s and early 1950s, he did not want Joan working). In 1951, they and their young daughter, Joan Celia (born a year earlier in 1950, then called "Little Joan," but later "J. C."), moved into a house at 226 Richards Lane in Hewlett Harbor. They adored the charm of the slightly aged home, built about a quarter of a century earlier. The street name may have influenced Lee's decision years later to name the leader of the Fantastic Four Reed Richards.[14]

After moving to Long Island, Stan commuted one hour to Manhattan to meet with artists and get their pages. The daily grind of getting into the city made it necessary to work from home a couple days per week. During warm months, Stan worked outside, putting the typewriter atop a bridge table, creating a makeshift standing desk. He could then act out the stories and type while standing. Joan bought the family a little twelve-foot round plastic pool to splash around in. Lee said that he could "swim" it in a stroke and a half, joking at the office: "Well, I did 100 laps today."[15]

Martin Goodman and his family lived just a few miles away. Publicly, then and later, Lee distanced himself from Goodman, usually portraying their relationship as detached. However, substantial evidence reveals how intertwined they actually were. Goodman's son Iden learned to drive in Stan's driveway.[16] The Lees needed family support in 1953 when their second child (a little girl named Jan) died just three days after birth. Unlike many couples facing tragedy, Stan and Joan managed to overcome their grief, building a stable family for themselves and J. C.

In the office or at home, Stan poured his energy into writing, editing, and art direction. Although prone to wild behavior, like jumping on desks to act out scenes as onlookers sat dumbfounded, Lee was an energetic, encouraging, and savvy editorial director. The creative and support staff liked working with him. His own writing was fast—perfect for the quick pace and relentless publication deadlines. Yet Stan still faced bouts of depression and anxiety, calling this era his "limbo years." He had slipped into a rut: "Go to the office—come home and write—weekends and evenings. Between stories, go out to dinner with Joanie, play with little Joanie, look at cars."[17] The money afforded the Lees a privileged lifestyle, but Stan worked nonstop, dreaming of a future outside comics.

As America moved from postwar euphoria to Cold War fear and the nuclear age, Stan had achieved what most people hoped for: employment, family, and home ownership. But he still felt unfulfilled. While he enjoyed the relationships with his staff and freelancers, the relentless production cycle created a pressure-filled workplace. More importantly, he bristled at the perception that writing for comic books didn't count as *real* writing. Lee yearned for opportunities that might enable him to leap out of the business.

Stan wasn't quite sure what he should do next.

★   ★   ★

Comic books burned!

Across America makeshift bonfires blazed in town squares, church parking lots, and schools. Adults turned against comic books. As the smoke lifted skyward, parents and youngsters sent a message to New York publishers, political leaders, and anyone who would listen: we will no longer stand for this!

"Criminal or sexually abnormal ideas . . . an atmosphere of deceit, trickery and cruelty"—these are the thoughts that comic books ensconced in young readers' minds, according to anti–comic book crusader Frederic Wertham, a grandstanding psychiatrist and author of the polemic *Seduction of the Innocent* (1954).[18] Since the late 1940s, Wertham had been inciting criticism, calling comics a national scourge. He saw comic books as a form of evil that surpassed even the wanton cruelty, murder, and destruction propagated by Hitler. Wertham perceived a direct correlation between juvenile delinquency and the violence, gore, and lurid sexuality in some comics. The future of America's children, in Wertham's mind, hinged on the rejection of comics and the industry's inherent immorality.

For Wertham, the nation's morality stood in the balance.

In 1938, the National Organization for Decent Literature (NODL) had rallied against "indecent literature." A group of Catholic bishops declared that comics and lewd magazines were "printed obscenity" and "an evil of such magnitude as seriously to threaten the moral, social and national life of our country." The bishops claimed such publications "weaken morality and thereby destroy religion and subvert the social order."[19] Subsequent media investigations resulted in a national firestorm. Some local governments even attempted to ban comics. The criticism mirrored other forms of censorship in popular culture, including the reaction to James Joyce's novel *Ulysses* and the Hays Code, which forced filmmakers to adhere to morality standards. In the late 1940s, several prominent media outlets ran anti–comic book pieces, including ABC radio, *New Republic*, and *Collier's*.

Yet the industry fanned the criticism, publishing crime and horror comics with explicit, violent, and sexual content. In 1948, publishers attempted to stave off the condemnation by hiring Henry Schultz as "comic book czar" to lead the Association of Comics Magazine Publishers (ACMP). Over time, the ACMP made inroads, but not all publishers joined. The group disbanded in 1950.[20]

The self-appointed culture police did not specifically target Timely, Goodman, or Lee. While Stan claims to have participated in debates directly with Wertham or one of his minions in the early 1950s, there is little evidence supporting the claim.[21] Whatever his actual interaction with the rabble-rousers, Lee did flagrantly satirize Wertham in *Suspense #29* (April 1953), a story illustrated by one of Lee's closest friends—artist Joe Maneely.

Displaying his bombastic style—and lack of subtlety—Lee titled the story "The Raving Maniac" and wrote himself in an imaginary argument with a Wertham-like figure. After listening to the intruder rail against comics, the editor delivers a blistering freedom of speech soliloquy: "In a dictatorship, people try to change your mind by **force**! You should be grateful you're in a land where only **words** are used!!" The story's twist ending—one of Lee's specialties—is that the intruder is an escapee from an insane asylum. In the final frames, Joan and J. C. greet Lee. He rocks his daughter to sleep, telling a bedtime story about the "excited little man." We don't know if this fictional account ever reached Wertham's desk, but publishing it was huge gamble.[22] "To me," he explained, "Wertham was a fanatic, pure and simple. I never cease to be amazed at the gullibility of human beings."[23] Yet, while Stan and others in the industry might have thought the crisis would pass, it actually gained momentum and threatened to destroy them.

In 1953, as a result of the media glare, the Senate launched a formal investigation into comic books—the Subcommittee on Juvenile Delinquency.

They utilized the power of televised hearings after a similar subcommittee to root out organized crime led by Estes Kefauver produced extraordinary ratings and turned the Tennessee Democrat into a major political operative on a national scale. Robert Hendrickson (R-NJ) led the investigation and established proceedings at several locations (including Denver, Boston, New York, and Philadelphia). Wertham was the government's star witness, ultimately using the publicity to sell more books.

In April 1954, the New York hearings opened in room 110 of the Federal Courthouse. A parade of experts from education, sociology, and child services criticized publishers, but most found the concrete evidence underwhelming. Wertham made the most damning points: "I think Hitler was a beginner compared to the comic book industry. They get the children much younger. They teach them race hatred at the age of four, before they can read."[24] The senators took cues from *Seduction*, never questioning Wertham's authority.

The movement gained power on April 21, 1954, when Kefauver questioned EC publisher William Gaines. In preparation for his testimony, Gaines had stayed up popping Dexedrine diet pills (assumed to be a kind of middle-class wonder drug at the time, prescribed to overcome fatigue). The publisher mistakenly believed that once audiences heard his testimony, they would come to their senses. Kefauver had different ideas.

The Senator patiently waited to strike. Gaines had difficulty keeping up. He later admitted that the Dexedrine wore off, leaving him feeling sick. As if on cue for the television cameras, Kefauver pulled out *Crime SuspenStories #22*, a gruesome illustration of a man holding a bloody ax in his right hand and a blond woman's severed head in his left. Her mouth dripped blood, as did the ax, with her bare legs splayed on the floor. Gaines did not budge, foolishly insisting the cover was appropriate for a horror comic. The exchange proved to be the defining moment for television viewers and a front-page story in the *New York Times*, as well as *Time* and *Newsweek*.[25]

The public uproar had far-reaching consequences. Industry-wide, many publishers folded, while others faced steep sales declines. Goodman's sales plummeted from 15 million monthly in 1953 to 4.6 million in 1955.[26] "Parents everywhere were forbidding their children to read anything that even hinted at action or adventure or any sort of gripping conflict," Lee said.[27] The only sellable genres were the female leads like Patsy Walker, science fiction titles, teen humor, funny animals, and Westerns—anything not hinting at violence. Goodman and Lee published enough to persevere but cut staff and freelancers.

★   ★   ★

The outcry against comics led to the 1954 editorial code adopted by the Comics Magazine Association of America (CMAA), the organization the publishers formed to regulate the industry. The Comics Code obliged publishers to submit comic books to a review board, which determined decency standards, including outlawing some innocuous characters (like vampires) or having the word "horror" on the cover. Issues that passed could print the "Approved By" stamp on the cover.

Goodman again forced Stan to fire staff and freelancers: "The market for comic books disintegrated with artists and writers being fired by the barrelful. I was amazed that Martin kept me on, but then, he had to have somebody to fire all those other people for him."[28] After the carnage, Lee struggled, wracking his brain to conceive a genre that Wertham and his cronies wouldn't attack. "I was the hackiest hack who ever lived," Lee lamented. "Goodman," remembered colorist Stan Goldberg, "left it all up to Stan. . . . I don't think Martin ever came into Stan's office, and I never saw him in the bullpen."[29] Stan and his skeletal crew of freelance artists, colorists, and inkers focused on romance, animals, war stories, crime tales, and Westerns. Quantity categorically trumped quality.[30]

Horror comics weren't breaking new ground creatively, but after the Wertham chaos, many remaining titles were silly to the point of absurdity, featuring somewhat stereotypical characters that engaged in harmless adventures, such as the long-running and benign romance comics *Nellie the Nurse* and *Millie the Model*. "I felt I was a better writer. . . . I shouldn't be wasting my life on this," Stan said. The only positive, however, was that he enjoyed the process of working alongside other creative talents. "I'll stay just a little bit longer," he told himself, "because this is fun."[31]

In the wake of the downturn, Goodman vacated the Empire State Building for smaller offices at 655 Madison Avenue, the heart of the American advertising industry. Most of his Magazine Management, Inc., operations were dedicated to magazines across a variety of genres. Lee settled into a small office and attempted to resurrect comic books. Martin's other editors and writers basically ignored Stan, finding his work appalling at best and at worst utterly depraved.

★   ★   ★

Compounding the turmoil, Goodman made several regrettable decisions that nearly ruined the company. In 1956, he closed his distribution operations, turning to industry leader American News Company (ANC). The move made sense, but behind the scenes, ANC was troubled, waging a four-year battle with antitrust regulators amid rumors of mob connections. Goodman gambled, and his bet turned sour.

Timely was renamed Atlas Comics in the early 1950s, just as the distributor situation worsened. In January 1957, two of ANC's most successful magazines (*Collier's* and *Woman's Home Companion*) folded. Then, its largest client, Dell Publishing, decided to find a new distributor. That year ANC lost $8 million and fired eight thousand employees. Two months later, it was out of business.

The debacle seemed to signal the end. Stan declared: "It was like we had been the last ones to book passage on the *Titanic!*"[32] Many publishers went bankrupt. For Goodman, ANC's collapse not only threatened comic books but also placed his life's work in jeopardy. He had no way to get his magazines into the hands of consumers.

Desperate, Goodman begged rival Independent News (owned by National Periodical/DC Comics) to distribute his whole catalog (magazines and comics). After watching ANC's battle with federal regulators regarding antitrust charges, Independent News executives feared intervention. They signed an agreement with Goodman but with stringent stipulations. Atlas could only publish eight comic books per month.

Overnight, the comic book division again plummeted. Despite the downturn after the comic book scare, Lee had still been publishing sixty to seventy titles monthly. In one fell swoop, though, Independent News neutered its (now dependent) competitor. Martin and Stan resolved to publish sixteen bimonthly comic books, including stalwarts *Millie the Model*, *Patsy Walker*, *Strange Tales*, *Wyatt Earp*, and *Two-Gun Kid*. The backlog of artwork and scripts were put to use, meaning freelancers who had stayed with Lee after the fallout were now out of luck.

Despite his reputation for toughness, Goodman left on a Florida vacation, once again giving Lee the onerous task of firing staff. Venerable artists like John Romita and Joe Sinnott had no new jobs on the horizon. "Toughest thing I ever did in my life," Stan remembered.[33] As a result, many freelancers left the business entirely, opting for stability in advertising or the corporate world.

Lee hunkered down in a cubicle, fearful that Goodman might ax him next. Yet Stan had several points in his favor: he worked fast, he was a family member, and he knew Goodman did not want to miss the next comic book wave when the industry eventually picked back up. The psychological toll was difficult for Lee. He reacted badly to having to fire his friends and coworkers, bouncing between fear of unemployment and continued unhappiness in comics. "I couldn't shake that gnawing feeling of depression," Stan explained. "It was like I was chasing my tail all the time. I could never shake that feeling of vague dissatisfaction."[34]

While the comic book industry suffered, Goodman's publishing machine ultimately rebounded. The magazines were a mix of conventional titles about Hollywood, the burgeoning television industry and its stars (like Jackie Gleason), and romance magazines, along with spicier titles: *Stag, For Men Only, Man's World*, and *Male. Stag* (an *Esquire* copycat) and the others emphasized explicit photographs and content. Yet many first-rate writers worked for Goodman, including Ogden Nash, Graham Greene, and William Saroyan (Lee's old Army office mate).

Stan continued to shift between comics and magazines. At the time, it seemed to him (and adults outside publishing) that a brassy Hollywood pinup magazine like *Focus* was more prestigious than comics, even though the former featured risqué photographs, provocative drawings, and stories heavy on sexuality (such as "I Kidnapped the King's Harem Girl" and "Divorcees Are Dynamite"). Martin's pulps were a far cry from the *New Yorker* but still leagues above writing for comic books.

In June 1958, Stan made a decision that would later change comic book history by calling artists Jack Kirby and Steve Ditko. Both needed the work. Ditko's fluid style and gripping sense of shapes and sizes worked perfectly for the science fiction and fantasy titles. Despite his talents, Kirby was in difficult straits at the time, having burned bridges with the editorial team at rival DC Comics and seeing his partnership with Joe Simon evaporate in the downturn (Simon settled into advertising).

With few assignments and facing reduced page rates, Kirby had limited options. There is no record of how Goodman felt or if there were resentment between them about Captain America profit sharing and the artist eventually being fired. From a similar background as Lee, yet more hardscrabble and poorer as a youth, Kirby developed a manic drive to support his family. Stan assigned Jack monster books to keep him working. Though the art in those comics didn't require Kirby's full skill set, the work provided a paycheck.

At the time, Stan and Jack were more alike than either would have admitted. Both had reservations about comic books. They also shared an overriding concern with their jobs and supporting their families. Although they may have had lingering animosities from earlier in their careers when Jack was Stan's superior, they were united in work ethic and apprehension about the future. Neither was truly happy, yet here they were together again. Jack said he felt "shipwrecked," while Stan nervously felt Goodman was purposely snubbing him. Lee remembered his boss/relative walking past him without saying a word. The silence sent a clear message, Stan explained: "It's like a ship sinking, and we're the rats. And we've got to get off."[35]

What Jack and Steve had in abundance was ideas for ways to rejuvenate comic books. They needed a conduit, though, to get their work in front of audiences. When they crossed paths with Stan, they couldn't have imagined the consequences. He was sick of the old ways and working in a second-rate business. In those fateful early days, little did Lee, Kirby, and Ditko realize that they would soon revolutionize the comic book industry and global popular culture forever.

· 6 ·

New Heroes for a New Age—
The Fantastic Four

$\mathscr{B}$arely glancing at the road in front of him, Stan Lee barrels toward Long Island in a souped-up Buick convertible. Jack Kirby, chewing on a cigar, sits in the passenger seat to Lee's right. John Romita, another one of Lee's favorite artists, grips the back of Kirby's seat. With one eye on the duo in the front and one on the traffic, Romita is a captive audience, fearing for his life.

Lee can't stop talking. Over the onrush of air and booming sounds of the city, he barks out soliloquies about the intergalactic adventures of a quartet of superheroes. Shot through with gamma rays after crashing a spaceship back to Earth, each member has developed a superpower. With their newfound powers, they vow to battle evil together.

Kirby punctuates his ideas with a jab of his stogie. Even in the swirl of wind, he shifts the cigar from one side of his mouth to the other, waiting for Lee to pause. The arguments over plots and scenarios began as soon as Lee's foot stomped on the gas. Jack had done a short-lived comic book similar in feel in the late 1950s at DC, called *Challengers of the Unknown*.

Nonchalant, Lee swerves and jukes between passing vehicles. Kirby focuses on the plot, seemingly unfazed by Lee's daredevil driving. As they bicker over how the stories should unfold, each battling for his particular point of view, Romita realizes that neither is actually listening to the other. "They would both come in with their ideas," he recalled. "They would both ignore each other. . . . I never really knew which way they would go because both of them had a different aspect on the story."[1]

The bickering doesn't end until Lee drops Kirby off at his house in East Williston on Long Island, a bucolic little village of less than three thousand souls. The tiny hamlet is far removed from the great artist's youth on the crime-ridden streets of the Lower East Side.

Such story conferences, whether they took place in a whizzing convertible shooting toward Long Island, over the phone, or in Lee's cramped office in the Empire State Building, came to define the way he and Kirby created superhero stories in the 1960s. Neither the writer nor the artist probably realized it at the time, but these arguments and the countless others they had actually reinvented the way comic books were created.

The new writing style mixed storytelling, plot, and visual representation (later dubbed the "Marvel Method"). Both the writer and artist had a say in how the final product unfolded, rather than the artist merely following a script, as it had been in the past. The new process Lee utilized with artists gave both creators a hand in how the final story unfolded. Taking the creation process one step further, the Marvel Method actually benefited from a *team* of creators, everyone involved in how a character sounded and looked and what colors and fonts leapt from the page.

When readers went nuts for the new superhero team, Lee and Kirby realized that they were at the dawn of a new era. It all began with those gamma rays and the Fantastic Four!

★ ★ ★

From the planet-smashing opening burst of sound to a pistol shot and train churning headlong around a bend and nearly right at the viewer, *The Adventures of Superman* gave television audiences chills up and down their spines. The orchestra blared, while the announcer proclaimed that the hero fought for "truth, justice, and the American way." Tall, with dark slicked-back hair and a broad chest, actor George Reeves brought Jerry Siegel and Joe Shuster's character to life. *The Adventures of Superman* blazed across the 1950s, and television sets across the nation were tuned to the program.

Julius "Julie" Schwartz, the editorial director of DC Comics (Goodman's chief competitor), realized *The Adventures of Superman*'s success with a large swath of television viewers gave DC an opportunity to rekindle interest in superhero-driven comic books. He had been editing Wonder Woman, Flash, and Green Lantern since 1944. Interest might have waned, but he had faith in the characters, despite the ongoing challenges with Wertham's crusades. Television's lure and the interest it created in Superman, he believed, could keep DC atop the comic book industry.

Beginning in 1956, the editor gingerly pushed the company back into the superhero game, bringing out updated versions of the Flash, Green Lantern, Hawkman, and the Atom, among others. Schwartz's efforts paid off when readers tuned back into the characters. One hit led to another. Then the initial success of the Flash led the editor to introduce a superhero team modeled after the Justice Society of America, which had run its course in 1951. The new group, with the slightly different name of the Justice League of America, first appeared in *The Brave and the Bold* #28 (March 1960).[2] Although Superman did not appear on the cover with the superhero team, both he and Batman were soon revealed as members of the supergroup. The combination of the Superman television show and the Man of Steel's inclusion in the new superhero lineup helped National Comics remain at the top of the industry.[3]

Schwartz wasn't the only comic book insider observing the resurgence of Superman and estimating its consequences. As usual, Martin Goodman smelled a trend in the making and wanted to pounce on the moneymaking opportunity. Innovation and originality did not interest him; he only cared about profit. Goodman had a seemingly simple directive: move mountains of paper as fast as possible. Although he had a lifelong affinity for cowboy stories and some interest in science fiction, this was about as complex as he got about magazines and comic books. Both were merely products to sell.

Goodman's fundamental business acumen centered on waiting to see what worked for his competitors and then brazenly copying them, whether this meant setting up a series of shell corporations to prevent any one piece of his publication empire from toppling the rest or latching onto a hot genre being pushed by a competitor. Timely/Atlas had been successful by riding a new fad until the next one appeared. He wasn't alone, however; it seemed as if much of the industry ran on this notion of watching the market leader and then imitating it. Publishing had an incestuous nature. Many of the men who ran comic book houses knew each other well: playing cards and drinking, dining at the same high-end restaurants, golfing, and even vacationing near one another in Miami Beach. Though each attempted to dominate the others on the newsstands, they shared the commonality of comic books and publishing. The razor-thin margins and constant up-and-down cycles turned them into a kind of odd tribe. To top it off, comic books and magazines were hardly seen as reputable concerns. Few prominent business leaders considered publishers titans of industry.[4]

For several decades from the mid-1940s through the early 1960s, Goodman cut every corner possible to make money. Often, he dipped into rather seedy and unscrupulous tactics and content in search of sales. Titles like *For Men Only* and *Stag* appealed to sordid interests (primarily of men), essentially publishing soft-core pornography, horrific crime-scene photos, and pirated movie stills of famous Hollywood stars to heighten the sensationalistic content. Goodman even urged employees of his magazine business and freelance staffers to pose as models for the magazines, which saved him from hiring real models or actors.[5] The bonus for Goodman was that *Stag* and other lascivious magazines were sold for twenty-five cents versus the comic books at just ten cents.

In the cutthroat publishing business, profitability meant keeping costs down and averting risk at all turns. Goodman believed that the people buying comic books were primarily preteen and teenage boys, mainly interested in rock 'em, sock 'em stories with over-the-top fight scenes and action-filled pictures. Another pool of readers was drawn from a large base of dim-witted adults. According to Goodman, they did not give a hoot about quality. Instead, he had his editorial staffers push conventionality. The publisher famously followed in the wake of competitors who launched new trends and genres, exclaiming, "If you get a title that catches on, then add a few more, you're in for a nice profit."[6]

Stan did not have notions of high artistry, and he balanced his internal ideals about quality with Martin's signature on his paycheck. At one time, Lee had dreamed of writing a great novel or getting into movies, but years of work for Goodman knocked those ideas on their ear. He knew the reality—publishing was a moneymaking venture. Stan's foremost priority centered on creating products that would sell. The marketplace determined product in Goodman's eyes. Yet the young editor also realized that there might be more to creating comics than simply generating profits. He understood that comic books could play a more significant role in young people's lives, such as helping youngsters learn to read or even sparking their imagination in ways that would help them later in life.

These different impulses warred inside Lee. The monotony of writing and editing comic books at the relentless pace essential to make Goodman's strategy work pulled at his conscience. He served as the comic book division's editor, writer, and art director but felt like he was spinning his wheels. Am I wasting my life on comic books? he wondered. "I felt we were merely doing the same type of thing, over and over again with no hope of either greater financial rewards or creative satisfaction."[7] In 1960, with basically two decades in the business, Lee hung at the end of his rope. Depressed and desperate, he thought he should travel some other career path—anything, really, to get away from the banal topics, plots, and characters that filled comics.

Still a couple years removed from forty years old, Lee considered other options, but his habitually optimistic outlook was curtailed by thoughts of his own family history. After living through his father's fight with internal demons brought on by chronic unemployment during the Depression, the mere thought of leaving his job sparked his deep-rooted despair. Jacob Lieber had been just a little older than Stan was now when he lost his job. As a man, Stan never forgot how his father's chronic unemployment incited tense fights between his parents. The resulting fallout left his small family in tatters. He wouldn't do that to Joan or J. C.

Stan had a pivotal decision to make. He balanced two conflicting notions: a regular paycheck that provided a stable, happy life for his family on one hand versus the relentless gloom he experienced by grinding out uninspiring comics on the other. As the primary writer and editorial director, Lee spent long days scripting and editing teen romance and humor comics, like *Teen-Age Romance* and *Life with Millie*, and perennial Westerns, such as *Rawhide Kid*, *Wyatt Earp*, and *Two-Gun Kid*. Monster stories featuring surprise or twist endings, including *Strange Tales* and *Journey into Mystery*, also took up much of Lee's time. How could he possibly bring these warring ideas to a point?

Stan added up the pieces and realized that the comic book business seemed doomed. Sales figures that had taken off in the 1950s later plummeted at the end of the decade. Public outcry had hurt the industry and added to his unhappiness. "There we were blithely grinding out our merry little monster yarns," Lee says. "We were turning out comics by the carload, but nothing much was happening."[8] No matter which way he turned, Lee felt pressure: stay in comics for a regular paycheck and keep churning out derivative characters to satiate Goodman's demands, or leave behind the only career he had ever known.

★   ★   ★

In the summer of 1961, Lee took action. He decided to create a superhero team that would put the consistently second-rate publishing house on the map. He immediately got to work piecing the team together. Contrary to the Justice Society and the Justice League, which were formed by disparate individuals, Lee determined that his team would be a family and, like a regular family, would confront the challenges people faced in the real world. The only difference, Lee thought, is that these seemingly typical people would have to deal with gaining superpowers that they never asked for. Lee wondered: how would people who lived next door or down the street react to living through a rocket crash to find that they had abilities that could enrich or destroy the world?

Jack Kirby had been funneling ideas to Stan for new lines of superhero comics, which he felt would save the company. He had drawn prototypes of the characters, putting his amazing artistic skills to work on costumes and action scenes, as well as vignettes that explained what made the characters super. The two industry veterans were both at the end of their wits in terms of creating meaningful work. When they began working together, magic happened. They just needed a catalyst for turning the ideas into reality—a hint that hero-based comics would sell.

"[I wanted to] make the unreal real," Lee said about the new superheroes that would make up the Fantastic Four. "Take extraordinary people, put them in extraordinary circumstances, and then have them behave like ordinary people." He remembered thinking, "No audience of ordinary people could resist." Stan considered the ideas and stories that attracted him when he was growing up, including the books he read and radio programs he tuned in to hear. He planned to mirror the kind of storytelling that had charmed him: "Plop an earthly superhero into a familiar setting, and you've got some classic pulp fiction."[9]

Like a captivating dramatic film, Stan began the Fantastic Four with the love story between Reed Richards and Susan Storm. Then he upped the intensity and interwove family dynamic by adding her hot-tempered younger brother, Johnny. Lee rounded out the new team with Ben Grimm, the group's everyman. When Grimm became the Thing—a monster of rock come to life—the group gained both comedic relief and a sense of humanity. The monster's impenetrable exterior concealed a sensitive soul. The team's interactions—both as superheroes and individuals coping with a new world and one another—served as the jet fuel to send the comic racing. Lee saw that action between the foursome as the central facet: "I like to have characters to work with as though it's a movie or a soap opera, where the characters' own personal lives would help write the dialogue and come up with situations."[10] The quartet would be a loving but dysfunctional family, held together by affection but dealing with a myriad of challenges brought on by their newfound might.

Stan and Jack drew from current events to give the origin story added context. The tale began with the team taking a risky spaceflight "to the stars" in an attempt to beat the Soviet Union into space. The Russians—referred to as "commies," in the parlance of the day—had actually beaten the United States into space, initially with the launch of Sputnik (the first satellite), then in 1960 sending the dogs Belka and Strelka into orbit, so Lee's plot served as a kind of revisionist history. But Stan and Jack knew the science fiction–like plotline would charm readers growing increasingly more familiar with nuclear weapons and their potential for global destruction.

When the group battled Mole Man, its first supervillain, they were already on red alert because the evildoer struck an "atomic plant behind the iron curtain" and a French facility in Africa. These references to reality and lifelike events—even keeping the team unmasked in a nod to the burgeoning celebrity culture of the age—made the team more appealing. The familiar territory and use of common lingo helped readers relate to the plight the team faced.

The partnership with Kirby was a natural decision based on their work together over the past couple of years. *The Fantastic Four* would be an epic, and that was Jack's specialty. He had been dutifully crafting series covers and stories for years. Stan knew talent when he saw it, and Jack was the best in the industry. His visual skills set the tone for Atlas, essentially originating a house style for the company. Kirby excelled at space epics and illustrating action scenes that made readers feel the force of a roundhouse punch or the ground shake as an enormous intergalactic monster shambled through a cityscape. "I didn't discuss it with Jack first," Lee explained. "I wrote it first, after telling Jack it was for him because I knew he was the best guy to draw it."[11] Kirby, according to his cocreator, "has the uncanny ability to visualize unforgettable scenes so clearly in his mind's eye that all he has to do is put down on paper what already exists in his incredible imagination."[12] Moving from the page to the comic panel, Jack used his own intuition, for example, giving Thing a mix of sensitivity and raw emotion. With Kirby's masterful style and story captions that Stan would utilize to write the dialogue, the action came to life in a way that seemed brand new.

A horrifying green monster pushes up through the city pavement, clutching a half-invisible blond woman as a human flame circles in flight. A handful of citizens react in horror. The reader sees another character from behind, a kind of monster, while the fourth seems to have limbs that stretch, loosening ropes that entangle him. A callout box tells us their names and announces: "Together for the first time in one mighty magazine!"

The Fantastic Four have arrived!

Without straying too far from the monster/sci-fi comics that were selling so well, Kirby creates a scene both dramatic and intense. Another feature that really draws the reader's eye is the bold-red fanciful script used to title the series. Taking up a third of the page, the giant "F" leaps from the page, a representation of the atomic age in the early Cold War. Next to the title and just below the Comics Code stamp is a tiny box with a capital "M" atop a smaller "c." Already, Lee and Kirby were thinking "Marvel Comics" as a way to differentiate this book from the company's other titles.

Inside, *The Fantastic Four* comic unfolds in a four-part story that Stan decided to convey in a nonlinear narrative. Although we know from the cover image that the heroes will battle a monster, the reader doesn't actually reach this event until the third act. The first two sections introduce the team and tell its origin story.

Initially, when Richards uses a "4" smoke signal to assemble his teammates, citizens and the police react with terror. Thing is viewed as a monster. The police wonder if this strange being portends "an alien invasion." Reacting to the illogic of what they are seeing, the officers attempt to shoot him, but he uses the city's sewer system to evade a further confrontation. Later, the government launches jetfighters against another member—the Torch—eventually targeting him with nuclear missiles. Mister Fantastic saves Johnny—and the city—as he "hurls the mighty missile far from shore where it explodes harmlessly over the sea."

The next section begins with an argument between Reed and Ben over the safety of the experimental rocket and the possible consequences of flying through "cosmic rays." Although he doesn't want to pilot an unsafe ship, Susan manipulates Ben by invoking the dreaded "Commies" as rationale for potential danger. Then, when he still refuses, she infers that he is a "coward." Soon after, decked out in dark plum-colored spacesuits and blue helmets, the team sneaks past a guard and into the rocket. In what might be Kirby's strongest panels in the entire book, the rays pulse through the ship, causing Ben to collapse and Johnny to combust. You can almost smell the teen's flight suit go up in flames.

After the ship crashes back to safety on Earth, the team emerges from the wreckage dazed and angry. Susan is the first to be impacted. She slowly turns invisible as the others look on in horror. "Wha—What if she never gets visible again?" her brother asks in amazement. Next, as Ben and Reed start to get angry, the former turns into the Thing, an orange-skinned monster, like a giant rock pile gone amuck. He reveals his secret longing for Susan, exclaiming, "I'll prove to you that you love the wrong man, Susan," and swings a tree trunk at Richards. The latter eludes the violent outburst by stretching his body and neck. Then, using his newfound ability, he wraps Ben up using his arms as ropes, demonstrating incredible flexibility and strength. Finally, Johnny bursts into flames, which starts a brush fire.

As four individuals, they realize the power of using their collective powers to help humankind. As a group, they determine: "We've changed! All of us! We're more than just human." Speaking for them all, Ben declares they "gotta use that power to help mankind." In a moment of incredible lucidity, they band together under the "Fantastic Four" moniker.

The final two sections of *The Fantastic Four #1* find the team—donning their purple jumpsuits—tracking a mysterious threat to "Monster Isle." There, they battle a flying three-headed monster, a giant rock monster, and various other gargoyles, including the green giant last seen on the issue cover. Using Torch's immense heat, they thwart the leader of the underground monsters: Mole Man. Ultimately, the team entombs the evildoer and the monsters underneath Monster Isle. They fly away in a private jet, grimly facing the future.

Stan and Jack may have created a partnership that brought the Fantastic Four to life, but neither had grand expectations for its success. "Okay, that's it," Lee figured. "I'm going to get fired. I got that out of my system."[13]

Yet Stan was also proud of the epic tale and his own willingness to go out on a limb to produce a comic that he would want to read. However, neither he nor Kirby had the luxury of waiting to see if *The Fantastic Four* would sell.

Comic books were actually released about three months prior to the month printed on the front of the book. Then it took another handful of months for the sales figures to trickle in. Moreover, it wasn't as if Stan and Jack didn't have a lot more work to do. There were ten to twelve issues that had to be produced within the stipulations of Goodman's punitive agreement with the DC Comics distribution arm, which included the next issue of *The Fantastic Four*.

As Lee and his creative staff pushed to meet the tight printing and distribution deadlines, they experienced something totally different when it came to the new series—they got mail. Almost immediately after the premiere issue of *The Fantastic Four* hit the newsstands, an avalanche of fan mail poured in. Readers were crazy for the new superhero team. According to Lee, getting any mail at all was virtually unprecedented. Previously, fans only wrote to them when an issue had some mechanical defect or a reader wanted a refund. "We were swamped with it," Lee recalls, "and it just kept growing with each new issue."[14]

Rather than face Goodman's wrath or get fired, Kirby and Lee had struck gold. The sales figures that came in months later reiterated the comic book's popularity. The success took Lee and everyone else associated with the book by surprise: "I never realized it would sell that well."[15]

In response to the mail, Lee started answering fan letters within the pages of the comic and writing up a chatty column that let readers in on insider information about Marvel and its staff. On the surface, the jokey, easygoing interaction with fans seemed frivolous. Over time, however, it became an important link in establishing Lee as the central public persona of not only Marvel but the comic book industry. Lee seemed like every reader's favorite uncle, always willing to share a wisecrack and some insider gossip going on behind the scenes at the company.

The play between reader and writer/editor turned many young people into lifelong fans. Readers felt as if they were there in New York City with Stan and his "bullpen" collaborators, whom they imagined they knew based on the colorful nicknames the editor gave them and the way he touted both their skills and quirky personalities. A born showman, Lee used the space at the back of the comics to express his newfound happiness. His personal gamble in creating the Fantastic Four paid off.

Although *The Fantastic Four* sold well, Marvel did not list the title among its 1961 sales figures since it had been released so late in the year.[16] If the comic was the company's best-selling issue that year, though, one can infer its sales exceeded *Tales to Astonish*, which ranked fortieth with about 185,000 issues sold. In comparison, *Uncle Scrooge* (published by Dell) ranked first in 1961 with more than 850,000 in paid circulation, while DC's venerable *Superman* stood at 820,000. Based on how publishers reported circulation, *The Fantastic Four* would not appear on the official roll until 1966, when it placed nineteenth for the year at 329,000 copies. The first place finish for *Uncle Scrooge* reveals the dual nature of comic books at that moment—divided between titles obviously aimed at younger children versus books like *Superman* and *Tales to Astonish* for teens or older.

The combination of fan enthusiasm and the mountain of mail streaming into Marvel's Madison Avenue offices served as an indication of the watershed moment in Lee's career. In 1961, DC's *Justice League of America* won the Academy of Comic Book Arts and Sciences (Alleys) comic book of the year award. The next year, however, *The Fantastic Four* won the award. The Marvel revolution had begun.

★   ★   ★

Although years later Kirby and Lee would contest who deserved credit for creating the Fantastic Four, thereby setting the Marvel Age ablaze, they each brought special talents to the process, like all great creative duos, whether musicians, filmmakers, or athletes. Without Kirby's inimitable artistry, the superhero team would not have burst off the page, generating so much energy and action that a reader could almost feel the void of deep space or what it felt like for a man's arm to stretch hundreds of yards or another to burst into flames. Lee is all words. He delivered a distinct dialogue and narrative style that left his own unique mark on the team and its thrilling collection of archenemies.

The fact of the matter is that by 1961 both men were seasoned professionals, having spent their entire adult lives in the comic book business. Soon they would become legends. It is easy to forget, too, in the generations of praise they have received since they created the Fantastic Four, that Kirby and Lee each felt personally and professionally stuck at that time. Both had been deeply unsatisfied. They felt anxiety and fear regarding the future for themselves and the industry they had dedicated their professional lives to building. Later—particularly as Lee's career shot skyward and Kirby felt jealous and used—a personal cold war enveloped the duo. But when *The Fantastic Four* hit newsstands for the first time, the two barely looked up . . . the writer from his one-finger, clickety-clacking typewriter and the other from his well-worn drawing table. They did not realize that they were creating a masterpiece. For them, it was just another product, one among many that kept them chained to the business.

Headstrong and talented, Stan and Jack were also intense workaholics and deeply driven. They had divergent personalities, but the combo worked on a mix of fear, concern, pride, and passion. Clearly the Marvel Method perfected by Lee and Kirby was successful because of the skills each willingly put on the table. Here were two extraordinary talents who came together at a watershed moment and put their futures on the line—together. And let's not forget the many other hands that it took to produce the series. Stan and Jack are "cocreators," yet they did not operate in a vacuum. Finally, no discussion of the company's accomplishments is complete without examining Lee's role as editor-in-chief. If observers and critics want to blast him for the color-by-number nature of the pre–Fantastic Four comics Timely/Atlas produced under his watch, then he should be praised for the risk in creating the new superhero team and its ultimate triumph. Stan had the final say for the comic books produced. In other words, to use the Truman era saying, "The buck stops here." He approved every aspect of every series, and if a page, cover, or bit of dialogue didn't meet his standards, it was changed. Martin may have requested a new superhero team, but it was Stan's job to make the wish reality. That responsibility separates him from Kirby because he had the added weight of the organization on his shoulders.

There are lasting hints and glimpses of how Kirby and Lee worked together, from penciled pages with Jack's notes on the action to interviews with the two creators and others who were on the scene back then. These archival pieces have served as fodder for comic book historians as they argue about who deserves credit for Marvel's successes. From my perspective, there is an important distinction between the micro- and macro-level discussion of *creation* as a concept. Ultimately, from the minutest perspective, we will never fully identify where one creator's vision began and another's ended. It was only years and decades *after* the success that people began to parse out who did what. From a macro-viewpoint, one has to make a decision that is comparable to the chicken-or-the-egg brain puzzle: what came first, Jack's or Stan's ideas or the fact that Stan had ultimate decision-making responsibility for what the company produced? Kirby worked for Lee. In the advertising world, it would be clearer—Lee's onus for organizational achievement and financial success (like a creative director) would mean that any accomplishment under his editorship would be primarily his. Yet this doesn't seem quite fair either.

The only method to truly assess the cocreation would have to be based on notes from discussions at the moment of creation when the two brainstormed and then later as the superhero team developed. Looking at the evidence from others who saw them argue and talk through the creation, it seems as if they were true collaborators—teammates using their individual talents for the collective good because of their individual dedication to professional achievement and its financial reward. The ultimate success of the Fantastic Four blurred memories over the subsequent decades, making the creation a more intense line-in-the-sand moment for Stan and Jack. Yet, in that moment, they were toiling under Goodman's demand for something to mimic what he saw going on at DC. In response, Stan turned to his best artist and thinker to throw things at the wall until an idea emerged that could be a winner, all within the larger framework of that week's production schedule.

Years ago, Lee stumbled across his original two-page synopsis of *The Fantastic Four #1* and shared it with *Alter Ego* magazine editor Roy Thomas, Lee's onetime protégé and later replacement as Marvel editor-in-chief. One of the surprises the manuscript uncovered was that Lee had obviously run some parts of the story and its characters by the Comics Code Authority. Directly in the origin story, for example, Lee informs Kirby about the Human Torch character, passing along that the CCA warned that he "may never burn any-one with flames, he may only burn ropes, doors, etc.—never people." Thomas speculated that Lee cleared the character prior to writing the overview because he feared potential outcry that might delay the comic.[17]

This episode also reveals two sides of Lee's work as writer/editor. While Lee experienced joy in creating a new kind of superhero team, he had to be businesslike and strategic in getting the Code censors' approval, particularly when time and deadlines played such an important role in his work. Talking to an early interviewer about "King" Kirby, Lee praised his partner for mix-ing storytelling and visualization like no one else in the business. He explained that Kirby often plotted the comics himself, admitting, "We're practically both the writers on the things."[18] The King also took on the role of unofficial art director, training new artists in the company style, which really was just his own style applied to Marvel's superhero lineup.

Lee's budding showmanship grew and his confidence increased as a result of the superteam's increasing popularity and sales. By the third issue, when the Fantastic Four took on the seemingly invincible Miracle Man, Lee took the brash step of tattooing the phrase: "The Greatest Comic Magazine in the World!!" just below the series title. From issue four on, a slightly altered slogan appeared above the title: "The World's Greatest Comic Magazine!" No one could miss the blaring letters, essentially daring the reader to disagree. The publicity generated by the tagline increased the notoriety, which Lee antici-pated. Always willing to go out on a limb to spark sales, the writer explained, "I figured a line like that would certainly get attention, if only for its flagrant pretentiousness."[19] Lee knew that he took a risk, but no one could really prove or disprove his claim. Like a great fastball pitcher or rock-and-roll guitarist, the declaration drew a line in the sand and told competitors: "We're the best comic book company in the world." Lee's "flagrant pretentiousness" became a public persona that his fans loved.

The success of *The Fantastic Four* served as a hurricane-force wind thrust-ing Lee and Kirby deeper into the psyches of their hero team. Lee remem-bered that, after ten issues, "we had both gained new insights into the FF and their ever-menacing antagonists." These were more than comic book creations, Lee explained: "Reed, Sue, Ben and Johnny seemed like part of our own families by now." For the longtime writer, "I felt comfortable writing their scenarios. It was increasingly easy to imagine what they would say or do in almost any given circumstance, for they had become as familiar to me as my own friends."[20] The family saga intensified as the Fantastic Four continued saving the world and dealing with the strains this effort caused them as individuals and a team. What Stan called "scenarios" were mainly phone calls with Jack or brief meetings to go over the macro-level plot points. Like today's e-mails, no one thought to save notes from these discussions (even if that were possible) so we can't fully fathom or appreciate what they meant to the cocreation process. There were witnesses to some of the talks, including John Romita Sr. and Marie Severin, who recalled what they saw as both men mixing it up regarding ideas and storylines.

For many fans, Ben Grimm/Thing was the group's go-to hero. Kirby modeled the hero after himself and added many of the tough-guy characteristics he had acquired himself as a kid on the Lower East Side battling among gang members. According to Lee, Grimm epitomized what he hoped to create with the superhero group: "I realized there was no monster, no funny, ugly guy who's a hero. . . . When this guy becomes very powerful, he also becomes grotesque. It had a touch of pathos."[21] Thing's creation later became a point of contention between the artistic duo, but these competing ideas reveal how they melded impressions (Lee's "pathos" with Kirby's modeling on himself) to invent a superhero that is better than either imagined. Should Jack and Stan give a cocreation credit to Robert Louis Stevenson based on Jekyll and Hyde?

The creative duo also specialized in inventing supervillains evil and nasty enough to cause the reader anxiety. For example, they brought back Bill Everett's Prince Namor, the Sub-Mariner, as a misunderstood, majestic villain who just wanted his underwater kingdom to be left alone—that is, until he determined that Sue should rule the seas by his side, thus giving Reed constant fits as Namor moved in on his fiancée.

Doctor Doom proved even more interesting and despicable, a criminal genius and physically powerful foe who caused global mayhem from his home base in Latveria, an imaginary Eastern European kingdom that Lee concocted. In one of their sometimes dazzling and often argumentative story conferences, Kirby and Lee talked about a villain that would put the superhero team to the test. Lee latched onto the name "Doom," but Kirby was skeptical. Still, they found a way to work through their differences, despite having strong opinions. Lee recalled, "Whenever something is really right, it never takes long to put it all together. Each little idea led to another, more exciting one."[22]

Making Doom as sinister as possible, Kirby sketched him in a suit of armor, with his face hidden behind a cold gray steel mask. The villain first appeared in *The Fantastic Four #5* with a short origin story that would later be given a fuller treatment. The issue begins with one of Lee's soon-to-be famous in-jokes—Johnny Storm reading the new issue of *The Hulk*, which in reality had just reached the newsstands. Johnny teases Ben, "I'll be doggoned if this monster doesn't remind me of the Thing." In dysfunctional family fashion, Ben sets off after Torch, resulting in a broken table. Reed and Sue have to intervene, with Sue dousing her little brother with a fire extinguisher, while Reed ties Ben into knots. Reed laments, "What's the matter with the four of us? Whenever we're not fighting some menace to mankind, we end up fighting among ourselves!" Lee's heavy-handedness may be showing, but fans loved seeing the superheroes fight and bicker just like in their own living rooms.

After Doctor Doom ensnares the team in its skyscraper headquarters, Reed recognizes that their masked foe is actually his college classmate Victor Von Doom, "a brilliant science student . . . only interested in forbidden experiments" in "black magic." Doom takes Sue hostage and then whisks the whole team to his fortress. Using a time machine of his own devising, Doom sends the three male members back in time to capture "Blackbeard's treasure." The teammates draw on their superpowers to battle the overmatched pirates and seize the treasure. Instead of giving it to Doom, however, Reed realizes, "If Doctor Doom wanted it, there must be some dangerous power which it possesses, and we've got to see that he never gets it!"

Ben, who the pirates believe is Blackbeard, decides he likes being the outlaw and orders his crew to turn on Reed and Johnny. Moments later, though, a tornado rips apart the ship, nearly causing Johnny to drown. Later, Reed and Johnny discover Ben washed up on shore. He apologizes, "I musta got carried away by being accepted—as a normal man—even if it was only by a band of cutthroat pirates! I—I just lost my dumb head for awhile!" Ben gives Lee a new way to tell stories in comic books. The monster who just wants to be human keeps the tension high because he always yearns to give up his superpowers. Ben's internal struggle and how it plays out publicly when he appears as a monster adds to the pervasive sense of conflict at the heart of *The Fantastic Four*.

When Doom brings the men back to his castle through a time portal, he understands that they tricked him. Locking the team in a vault, the villain starts to cut off the oxygen. Sue, however, is able to turn invisible and stop the attack, thereby saving her teammates. The heroes escape Doom's fortress, but they cannot capture him. He rockets away using a portable jetpack.

By allowing the villain to escape, Lee and Kirby veered from the traditional comic book plot, refusing to neatly wrap up the story at the end of the issue. Essentially, the creative duo invented a comic book that read like a serial or soap opera, revealing more about the protagonists in each episode, while also benefiting from the continuity that episodic entertainment provides. Using these methods, Kirby and Lee infused *The Fantastic Four* with context and a history that fueled future issues. The level of suspense would remain high and, accentuated by Jack's extraordinary artwork, literally take the comic book medium to new heights of artistic achievement. As with the launch of *The Fantastic Four #1*, fan mail about Doctor Doom piled up in Lee's office almost immediately. In short order, Lee and Kirby realized that Doom was "probably Marvel's very top villain, in appearance, in power, personality, and plain sheer reader appeal."[23]

The image of Reed angrily storming away and the seemingly incomprehensible notion of Doctor Doom as part of the team graces the cover of *The Fantastic Four #10*. Despite this intriguing setup, what readers could not have overlooked is the appearance of Lee and Kirby in the lower left-hand corner with their backs to the reader, actually commenting on the issue.

Inside, three team members have to deal with their growing celebrity, each avoiding fans who either want a piece of them or think they should be reined in somehow when they attempt to answer Thing's distress signal. Arriving at the apartment of Ben's blind girlfriend, Alicia, they realize that he is not in trouble. However, the mention of Sub-Mariner causes an argument between Reed and Sue. She blurts, "I'm not even sure of my own feelings." Just then, the story cuts to Kirby and Lee at Marvel's Madison Avenue offices, adorned with images of Hulk, Thor, and other superheroes, as the creative team attempts to create another supervillain.

Suddenly, Doom walks into the office. He removes his mask, causing Lee and Kirby to recoil in horror. Doom then threatens their lives, saying, "You are searching for a story—well I shall give you one! Here, phone Mr. Fantastic—say what I tell you if you value your lives!" He shoots a ray out of his index finger, destroying Lee's ashtray as a show of force. Doom waits for Reed to arrive and then ambushes him with sleeping gas. Next, Doom teleports with Richards to his secret lab.

Using knowledge he acquired from an advanced race of space aliens called the Ovoids, Doom transports his brain into Richards's body with telepathy, while Richards is stuck in the Doom armor. Tricking the Fantastic Four into helping him, Doom is able to lock Richards away in an underground chamber that only has an hour's worth of air left. Ultimately, Reed escapes but is knocked unconscious by Sue at Alicia's apartment. When the rest of the team (minus Doom in Reed's body) shows up, they realize that he might actually be telling the truth. Johnny and Thing trick Doom into showing his true colors, and in a moment of weakness, Reed and Doom are transposed back into their own bodies. Doom is accidently hit with a shrinking ray that makes him so small that he vanishes. Thus, Doom is thwarted again.

Drawing themselves into the comic and actually playing a role in the story may have seemed like a farce, but the issue helped further establish that Marvel books would be categorically different than the competition, especially the staid do-gooder superheroes at DC Comics. Just as important, the issue introduced them to readers as heroic figures, able to engage with their creations at will, even being more than a little scared of Doom, just as one would be in real life. Suddenly, the names adorning the issues—"Stan Lee & J. Kirby"—had meaning for eager audiences. And, as Lee explained, fans called out for the distortion, which he called "perhaps the first super hero take in which our featured players are aware that they are characters in a comic book. It was produced in response to many, many letters requesting such a story, and it was a real hoot for me to script the yarn."[24] Blurring the line between real and imagined showed Marvel readers the playful nature of the company and its primary writer/artist duo.

★   ★   ★

Just shy of Lee's thirty-ninth birthday, *The Fantastic Four #1* appeared on newsstands. Created with Jack at a watershed moment in both their lives, *The Fantastic Four* seemed almost a last-ditch effort, as if their careers really did hang in the balance. After the tumultuous 1950s and public backlash against comic books, many people thought the entire industry might collapse, including the two cocreators. And, based on their deep emotional yearning to *provide* for their families, they must have faced intense mental and emotional anguish. The cyclical nature of the business made the possibility that it could fall apart a reality. How many more of these boom-and-bust periods could one take?

Instead of his personal swan song, however, Lee found himself inundated with fan mail, which had never happened before. Usually, the only gauge for a comic book's success was sales figures, which wouldn't be reported for many months after a comic book launch. As Lee examined the letters, he realized that readers in the twelve- to fifteen-year-old age group had stumbled on the title and dug the angst they found inside. They begged for more, which bolstered Lee's flagging spirits. After producing titles in bunches without much interaction from fans, the outpouring of support gave Lee what he needed at exactly the right moment.

Ever the curmudgeon and cautious, Kirby reacted with less enthusiasm, not willing to jump on the emotional roller coaster he had been on with so many other "hit" comics in his career. He continued to write and draw, always churning out pages at an astonishing clip. Lee viewed the letters and cards he received as vindication of his idea that if he just created a comic book that he would enjoy as a reader, others would enjoy it too.

That moment in time—JFK's Camelot, the baby boom coming of age, and the depths of Cold War fears—brought out Stan and Jack's greatness as a creative duo. *The Fantastic Four* did more than set the stage for Lee and Kirby to conceive more superheroes—it rejuvenated the entire comic book industry. After a career built on creating knockoff titles as quickly as possible, Stan realized that he could assume a different role: trendsetter. He trusted in his instincts, his ability to tell stories that readers enjoyed, and Kirby's phenomenal artistry. Together, Jack and Stan changed the trajectory of their careers, the industry they devoted their lives to, and eventually popular culture across the globe.

Imagine the *real* power of those gamma rays . . .

· 7 ·

Spidey Saves the Day!

$\mathcal{B}$ursting from the page and seemingly swinging right into the reader's lap, a new superhero is all lean muscles and tautness. He is masked: only alien-like curved eyes reveal human features; no mouth or nose is visible. His power is alarming—casually holding a ghoulish-looking criminal in one hand, while simultaneously swinging from a hair-thin cord high above the city streets. In the background, tiny figures stand on rooftops, looking on and pointing in what can only be considered outright astonishment.

The superhero is off-center, frozen in a moment, as if a panicked photographer snapped a series of frames. The image captures the speed, almost like flight, with the wind at his back. The hero's deltoid ripples and leg muscles flex. Some mysterious webbing extends from his elbow to waist. Is this a person or creature from another world?

The answer is actually neither. Looking at the bright-yellow dialogue boxes running down the left side of the page, the reader learns the shocking truth. This isn't a grown man, older and hardened, like Batman or Superman—one an existential nightmare and the other a do-gooder alien. No, this hero is just a self-professed "timid teenager" named Peter Parker. The world, he exclaims, mocks the teen under the mask but will "marvel" at his newfound "awesome might."

Spider-Man is born.

★　★　★

The 1962 debut of Spider-Man in *Amazing Fantasy #15* happened because Stan took a calculated risk. He trusted his instincts, honed over decades of working in the chaotic comic book industry, which often seemed to run on trial and error more than logic. On the long path from the publisher to the newsstands, sales determined what was offered. Fickle comic book fans frequently switched interests, leaving editors like Lee scratching their heads and trying to predict the next fad. Stan had taken the same kind of risk in publishing *The Fantastic Four*. He made Goodman's wish come true—create a superhero team to draft on the success of rival DC in rekindling interest in superheroes. To everyone's amazement, the series took off, driving sales to new heights and changing Marvel's status in the comic book industry.

Despite the recent triumphs, however, rolling the dice on a new character also meant potentially wasting precious hours writing, penciling, and inking a title that might not sell. Time was the comic book creator's most precious commodity. No one wanted to waste time on a dud when that same stretch could be used on more profitable books. In an industry driven by talent and always against the clock, good artists and writers couldn't spare time for an underperforming series. The business side constantly clashed with the creative aspects, forcing fast scripting and artwork to go hand-in-hand. The creative teams always raced against stringent monthly deadlines.

In more than two decades toiling away as a comic book writer and editor, Lee had watched genres spring to life, and then almost as quickly, readers would turn their attention to something different. War stories might give way to romance titles, which would then ride a wave until monster comics became popular, and then those would be superseded by aliens. In an era when a small group of publishers controlled the entire industry, they kept close watch over each other's products in hopes of mimicking sales of hot titles. His partnership with Jack Kirby on *The Fantastic Four* had given Stan some autonomy and breathing room, but the pressure did not abate.

Lee called Goodman "one of the great imitators of all time." Goodman dictated what Lee wrote after ferreting out tips and leads during golf matches and long lunches with other publishers and distributors. If he heard that Westerns were selling for a competitor, Goodman would visit Lee, bellowing, "Stan, come up with some Westerns."[1] Every new fad meant immediately switching to ride the wind created by another company's successes in the marketplace. This effort wouldn't soothe the soul of creators hoping for originality, but it worked in favor of Marvel's bottom line. Goodman saw dollar signs in those trends.

The versatility necessary in this environment played on Lee's primary strengths: swift writing and the ability to plot many different titles nearly simultaneously. Lee had been working under these conditions for so long that he had mastered techniques for easily creating multiple storylines and plots. He would use gimmicks and wordplay to remember names and titles, like recycling the gunslinger Rawhide Kid in 1960 and making him into an outlaw or using alliteration, as in *Millie the Model*. Adding to his editorial efficiency, he had a team of freelancers who had long experience working for him. They understood the demands and pressures and responded to Goodman's wishes.

When certain comic genres sold well, Martin gave Lee breathing room, but when sales dipped, he exerted pressure. A conservative executive, Goodman rarely wanted change, which irked Lee. The writer bristled at his boss's belittling beliefs, explaining, "He felt comics were really only read by very, very young children or stupid adults," which meant "he didn't want me to use words of more than two syllables if I could help it. . . . Don't play up characterization, don't have too much dialogue, just have a lot of action." Given the precarious state of individual publishing companies, which frequently went belly-up, and his long history with Goodman, Lee admits, "It was a job; I had to do what he told me."[2]

Despite being distant relatives and longtime coworkers, the publisher and editor maintained a cool relationship. From Stan's perspective, "Martin was good at what he did and made a lot of money, but he wasn't ambitious. He wanted things to stay the way they were." The publishing industry remained highly competitive, but most American business executives were not cutthroat captains of industry. Goodman pushed Lee, but the writer recalls: "He hired a good friend of his to be his business manager, and they would spend two or three hours a day in Martin's office playing Scrabble."[3] Joan Lee shared her husband's basic feels about Goodman as a businessman, viewing him as "not particularly generous," but enjoyed his friendship and family ties. "I loved Martin and thought he was a wonderful man—a gentleman of the old school, a self-made man."[4] By exerting a bit of pressure on Stan and keeping his eyes and ears on industry trends, Goodman had created a publishing empire that clearly didn't tax him but did necessitate the formation of a machine running at full throttle. The work fell to Lee and the other editors across Goodman's string of publishing entities.

Riding the wave of critical success and extraordinary sales of *The Fantastic Four*, Goodman gave Lee a simple directive in line with his general management style: "Come up with some other superheroes."[5] For the publisher, the order made sense: superheroes seemed to be the next big genre to catch on, so that would be his new direction. Yet *The Fantastic Four* subtly shifted the relationship between editor and publisher. With sales doubling based on the new superhero team, Goodman looked away a bit, which enabled Lee to wield greater influence and authority. From the publisher's perspective, the popularity of superhero books meant simply jumping on the trend until it died out. Lee, though, used some of the profit to pay freelance writers and editors more money, which then offloaded some of the pressure he felt in writing, plotting, editing, and approving the company's limited number of monthly titles. Launching *Spider-Man*, however, Lee did more than divert the talents and energy of his staff. He actually defied Goodman.

For months, Lee grappled with the idea of a new kind of superhero in the same vein as the Fantastic Four, with realistic challenges that someone with superpowers would experience living in the modern world. As he discussed ideas with artists Jack Kirby and Steve Ditko, a character began to take shape. Later, Jack would claim that he invented the superhero based off an earlier character he invented, an assertion Stan denied.

While the original inspiration might be disputed, what is clear is that Lee wanted the new character to be "a teenager, with all the problems, hang-ups, and angst of any teenager." Stan came up with the colorful "Spider-Man" name and envisioned a "hard-luck kid" both blessed and cursed by acquiring superhuman strength and the ability to cling to walls, sides of buildings, and even ceilings, just like a real-life spider.[6] He knew Spider-Man would be an important superhero for the company and its efforts to build out the genre. Yet Stan had to get the idea approved by his publisher, despite his gut feeling that the team had created a really compelling character.

Lee recalled going to see Goodman: "I did what I always did in those days, I took the idea to my boss, my friend, my publisher, my cohort." In an attempt to sell Martin on the teen superhero, Stan even embellished the story of Spider-Man's origin by claiming that he got the idea from "watching a fly on the wall while I had been typing."[7] Lee presented the full character and the gripping rationale that he believed would entice readers: teen, orphan, angst, poor, and intelligent, along with additional traits the young hero would possess. Lee thought Spider-Man was a no-brainer. To his surprise, Goodman hated the character. He forbade Stan from publishing it as a stand-alone comic book.[8]

Martin had three major complaints: "people hate spiders, so you can't call a hero 'Spider-Man'"; no teenager could be a hero "but only be a sidekick"; and a hero had to be heroic, not a pimply kid who isn't popular or strong.[9] To Goodman, a hero who isn't a hero or even particularly likable sounded like a "comedy character." Irritated, he asked Stan, "Didn't [he] realize that people hate spiders?"[10] Given the litany of criticisms, Lee recalled, "Martin just wouldn't let me do the book."[11]

Goodman thought featuring a teenager would also make both him and his company a laughingstock among other comic book publishers, a concern that the executive worried about incessantly. No matter what the company's success, Goodman felt the ups-and-downs of the industry too keenly, so he pushed back on ideas that he thought would fizzle. Martin hated everything about Spider-Man. He usually took a hands-on approach only during down-turns, but when Lee brought him the new character, the writer opened himself up to Goodman's insecurities and fears regarding status in the marketplace and among competitors.

Realizing that he could not completely circumvent his boss, Lee made the executive decision to at least give Spider-Man a try in as low risk a manner as possible. The best case for the experiment would be to place the character on the cover of a series that had bombed up to that point—*Amazing Fantasy*. The comic-buying public simply had little interest in the *AF* run, which usually featured thriller/fantasy stories by Lee, accompanied by surreal art created by Steve Ditko, Marvel's go-to artist for styling the macabre, surreal, or Dali-esque. At one point, Lee even put the word "Adult" directly into the title, hoping that *Amazing Adult Fantasy* would get readers interested. Facing Goodman's disdain and the woeful *AF* sales figures, it seemed as if there were already two strikes against the teen wonder.

Despite these odds and his boss's directive, Lee remembered that he kept coming back to the obvious strengths of the nerdy superhero: "I couldn't get Spider-Man out of my mind."[12] He worked up a Spider-Man plot and handed it over to Jack Kirby. Lee figured that no one would care (or maybe even notice) a new character in the last issue of a series that would soon be discontinued. Based on their partnership on *The Fantastic Four*, Stan thought Jack was perfect for the assignment, despite that Lee leaned on the artist so heavily across the company's titles.

In this fast-paced environment, where Lee served essentially as Marvel's managing editor, writer, copyeditor, and overall creative director, he turned to artists that he trusted because they needed little direction and worked quickly. Often, Lee would dictate a story line and then the artist would take that plot and begin to draw the issue. Later, the writer would add the dialogue and extra information, allowing time to edit or add in what the artist might have overlooked. There were always last-minute changes, too, perhaps a stylistic point, like a background that didn't quite gel or scenes that needed to be bolder or more action-filled. Stan had to make these decisions and then find solutions to the challenges.

When Stan saw what Jack did with Spider-Man, he realized that Kirby had missed the mark. His early sketches turned the teen bookworm into a mini-Superman with all-American good looks, like a budding astronaut or football star. With little time to pause and think about what was essentially a throwaway character, Kirby turned to other projects and Lee put Ditko on the character. Jack was certainly busy enough, so the decision wasn't that difficult. Ditko created the art for *Amazing Fantasy* anyway. Plus, Stan thought, Ditko's style was better suited for drawing an offbeat hero. The penciler had been experimenting with tension and drawing emotion-laden characters for years, all attributes that seemed perfect for Peter Parker/Spider-Man.

The gamble paid off! Ditko nailed Spider-Man. Stan could not have been happier with the artist's version of the teen hero. He explained: "Steve did a totally brilliant job of bringing my new little arachnid hero to life."[13] Ditko's power was in drawing a figure that was totally believable as a teen nebbish *and* as a budding hero filled with angst. The frail Peter Parker, picked on and bullied, actually seemed able to transform via Steve's stunning visualization. Lee and Ditko finished the two-part story, running it as the lead in *Amazing Fantasy #15*. The only challenge Stan faced was the cover art. This was an area where Kirby repeatedly shined, so when Stan had doubts about Ditko's version of the cover, he commissioned Jack for the task, with Ditko inking the piece. The result was a cover that would eventually go down in history as one of the greatest ever created.

Revealing both the busy, all-hands state of the company and their limited expectations when launching a new title, Stan recalled, "We more or less forgot about him."[14] As happy as Lee and Ditko were with the collaboration and outcome, they could never have imagined that they were about to spin the comic book world onto a different axis.

★   ★   ★

Stan's writing style—clearly a critical attribute of *The Fantastic Four* but developed over decades—established a distinctive voice for Spider-Man comic books and the company as a whole. Breaking down the invisible barrier between writer and reader (commonly referred to as the "fourth wall") on the first page of the initial Spider-Man *AF* debut reveals how Lee established a friendly, homespun voice that also gently guided the reader on the hero's journey. This second-person method stood in stark contrast to the more formal, distant language of other superheroes, primarily the competitors at DC—Superman, Batman, and Wonder Woman.

From the start, Stan reveals a secret, explaining that "confidentially," people in the comic business call superheroes "long underwear characters" and say they are "a dime a dozen." Yet the reader is also informed that this new character is "just a bit . . . different!" At about one hundred words into the story, then, Lee has already formed a relationship with the reader and created the context for Spider-Man as something new versus other superheroes and other comic books. The tongue-in-cheek tone emphasizes how "different" this hero will be in a deliberately easygoing style.

On page 2, Lee introduces more characters, demonstrating how adults generally like Peter Parker, including his surrogate parents, Aunt May and Uncle Ben, as well as his teachers, who are "fond" of the "clean-cut, hardworking honor student!" Yet, as quickly as the reader realizes that Parker is a good guy, Stan shows us how his classmates alienate him, particularly in contrast to school stud Flash Thompson. Parker asks a girl out and she refuses, turning instead to "dreamboat" Thompson (a scene brilliantly drawn by Ditko). As the popular gang speeds off in a red convertible, they laugh at him for suggesting that they go to a science exhibit rather than more typical teen fun spots. "You stick to science, son. We'll take the chicks," one of his classmates sneers. In the next frame, Parker is crying as he enters the science lab, declaring, "Someday they'll be sorry!—Sorry that they laughed at me!"

The elegance in juxtaposing Peter Parker as a regular guy versus the "in crowd" makes the teen tacitly sympathetic. Readers are instantly able to relate to Peter and the teen drama as it unfolds because every school has a Flash Thompson who basks in the attention and seems especially gleeful in pushing the smaller, frail Parker aside. Again, Lee addresses the reader directly, saying: "Yes, for some, being a teenager has many heart-breaking moments." The writer establishes that Parker has feelings and that being an outcast hurts. As readers, we can feel for the character, especially because we have seen this happen in our own lives or experienced it ourselves.

The cast-aside teenager melodrama is now a central facet of American storytelling, but in the early 1960s, it was still being developed. Certainly, Peter Parker's tale has echoes of J. D. Salinger's *The Catcher in the Rye* (1951) and his many short stories, which had become staples in high school and college curriculums in the ensuing decade. Spider-Man's thought bubbles are filled with Holden Caulfield–like soliloquies on power and guilt. The similarities are offset by many differences, but the wave of teen angst that Salinger masterfully plucked out of the postwar/Cold War zeitgeist is at least part of the clay that molded Peter Parker/Spider-Man.

Rather than simply hinging the story on Peter as an outsider, Stan exposes the young man's full range of emotions, forcing the origin story into areas darker and more foreboding. Once the atomic-powered spider bites the teen, he stumbles into his newfound power blindly, eventually entering into a professional wrestling contest to test his strength and make some quick money. Parker's lack of confidence causes him to put on a mask to avert the possibility of being a "laughingstock," but he challenges the muscled bruiser Crusher Hogan anyway, who calls the boy "a little masked marvel." Lee's wordplay, using "marvel" here and on the cover, subconsciously creates an association between the character and the future company name, which the writer/editor had been contemplating.

Almost immediately adults search for a way to exploit the teen's powers. A "TV producer" promises the masked Parker a "fortune" via an appearance on the era's immensely popular *Ed Sullivan Show*. Under the tutelage of the TV producer/agent, Spider-Man becomes a sensation, inhaling what is described as the "first sweet scent of fame and success." As the reader can imagine in a burgeoning celebrity culture, the fame is too much for the youth to handle. When the boy has the opportunity to stop a thief that a policeman is chasing, he instead does nothing, despite his extraordinary powers. He could have apprehended the villain without any real physical exertion, but the key is that he made the mental decision to not intercede. As Lee demonstrates through narration and Ditko draws so fluidly, Peter has physical strength and amazing abilities but does not have the wisdom to transform into a real hero.

Later, when the now-familiar story of Uncle Ben's death unfolds, Peter loses his cool, becomes Spider-Man, and utilizes his abilities to hunt down the fugitive. In the only frame in the entire comic that shows his pupils through the mask, Spider-Man realizes that the thief is the same one he could have stopped earlier. Yet the rage-filled teen does not kill the criminal. Instead, he dangles him from a web and lowers the villain to the police below. Simultaneously, Lee was able to depict the anguish the teen suffered and his acceptance of the burden of his actions. In the final frame, Stan wrote the famous line that sums up Spider-Man: "Aware at last that in this world, with great power there must also come—great responsibility!"

Finally able to apply his innovative ideas about voice and style directly to the new superheroes, Lee captured the reader's attention by formulating a character that had genuinely human traits. Peter Parker, a wallflower kid picked on by his peers for being different, actually grew out of Lee's own feelings of being bullied as a kid, accentuated by Ditko's similar ideas. "Because I was the youngest and the thinnest, I was never the captain or leader, and I was always the one getting pushed around," Stan remembered. As a result, when searching for Peter's voice, Lee explained, "I figured, kids would relate to a concept like that. After all, most kids have had similar experiences. Turns out I was right."[15] Lee put the *AF* issue to bed and scurried off onto the next title that demanded his attention.

★   ★   ★

The hectic pace of the comic book business did not allow anyone to slow down, let alone stop to contemplate how the public might react to a particular title—which may account for why "Spider-Man" is listed in *AF #15* both in its correct spelling and alternatively as "Spiderman" and "the Spiderman." Lee and his small crew of artists were already off onto new titles, working against the relentless deadlines.

Although the sales figures would be unavailable for several months, Lee realized that Spider-Man had found an audience when letters from readers poured into the office by the satchel, just as they had a year earlier when the

Fantastic Four debuted. Lee recalled getting about one hundred fan letters a day and sometimes more, which he dutifully read and answered. Anticipation grew as the missives from readers piled up in Stan's office.

The fateful day sales figures finally arrived, Goodman stormed into Lee's office, as always awash in art boards, drawings, mockups, yellow legal pads, and memos littering the desk.

Goodman beamed: "Stan, remember that Spider-Man idea of yours that I liked so much? Why don't we turn it into a series?"[16]

If that wasn't enough to knock Lee off-kilter, then came the real kicker: Spider-Man was not just a hit; the issue was in fact the fastest-selling comic book of the year and indeed that decade. *Amazing Fantasy*, perpetually at the bottom of the sales charts, skyrocketed to number one with issue *#15*, due to Lee's efforts to bring the character to life and Ditko's spot-on creation of the superhero's artistic look and feel.[17] Although it had been months since Steve and Stan had created Spider-Man, the overwhelming popularity meant that the creative team would need to begin work immediately to turn the character into a series.

Despite Goodman's initial negativity and the indifference Kirby had about drawing Spider-Man, the success of *Amazing Fantasy #15* elevated Lee and Ditko, since the new character would soon become the keystone of Marvel's superhero-based lineup. More importantly, the combination of the Fantastic Four and Spider-Man transformed Marvel from a company run by imitating trends of other publishers to a hip and relevant hot commodity.

Because of the long lag in obtaining sales figures and the length of the printing and distribution system, it wasn't until six months later that the new Spidey comic book debuted. To make way for the new title, Lee had to drop one, since the distribution agreement with Independent News only allowed Marvel to carry eight titles, regardless of number of pages. Thus, a little less than a year after its debut, *The Incredible Hulk* ceased publication based on its less-than-stellar sales. In March 1963, *The Amazing Spider-Man #1* burst onto newsstands.

★ ★ ★

When *The Amazing Spider-Man* finally arrived, comic book fans could not believe their eyes. On that initial cover, the teen superhero seemed suspended in midair and encased in clear tubing. He had been captured by none other than Lee and Kirby's supergroup, the Fantastic Four. The Human Torch blazes up to eye level as if checking on the captured hero, while on the ground the Thing shakes his powerful fists, eager for a fight.

The appearance of Marvel's other breakout heroes—the Fantastic Four—as major characters in Spider-Man's debut reveals how Stan hedged his bets.

He had the smart idea to boost sales by bringing the company's two hottest commodities together in one book. This idea seemed to carry over from the final issue of *Amazing Fantasy*, when Lee told readers to look forward to the next issue, even though the comic book faced cancellation. Stan always left the door open to possibilities, probably because he had experienced so much change in the industry over the preceding two decades. Goodman's sales figures showed just how popular Spider-Man promised to be, but using the Fantastic Four as reinforcement made good business sense and spurred a new creative form along the way.

For the cover image of *The Amazing Spider-Man*, Lee once again turned to veteran Kirby, which worked well, particularly since he was the artist and cocreator of the Fantastic Four. The difference between Kirby's cover and Ditko's work in the rest of the issue is immediately noticeable on the splash page. Here, Spidey seems slightly less muscular and truer to his creature namesake—sinewy and sleek, rather than bulky and muscle-bound. A crowd led by publisher J. Jonah Jameson calls out: "Freak! Public Menace!" as the hero retreats to a web, gripping a tendril for balance. Lee's callout to the audience is full of hype and hyperbole: "There's never been a story like this one—because there's never been a hero like—Spider-Man!"

The first *Amazing Spider-Man* issue included two separate stories, which was not uncommon in comic books of the era. The tales were connected but had different purposes. The first focused on recounting the hero's origin story, a much-needed rehashing for fans that might have missed the *Amazing Fantasy* issue but eagerly awaited the character's debut in a stand-alone title. The second half of the book brought Spider-Man face-to-face with the members of the Fantastic Four and introduced the first villain the teen hero would face.

The first Spider-Man story underscored his transformation from teen to hero, recounting the challenges Peter and Aunt May face with no money. It accentuates his desperation and the lengths the boy goes to in order to support them. His efforts are thwarted, however, when (as Spider-Man) his manager writes him a check for his "town hall" show and the bank won't cash it without the masked man identifying himself. Then Jameson publishes a headline labeling the hero a "menace" and lectures around town, declaring, "Spider-Man must be outlawed! There is no place for such a dangerous creature in our fair city." The newspaperman offers his son, test pilot John Jameson, as an example of a real hero as he is about to orbit Earth in a space capsule.

When the orbit mission goes awry, Spider-Man springs to action, even though the pilot's father is the source of his inability to make money performing. When the older man calls Spidey out for being a "publicity-seeking phony . . . trying to grab a headline!" the hero responds in Lee's smart-alecky style, saying, "Instead of flapping your lips, mister—just watch and see what

I can do!" Within minutes, Spider-Man is hanging onto the shooting missile and replaces a control unit that enables Jameson to land safely.

Rather than celebrate the heroics, the newspaper editor resumes the fight, explaining that the difficulties were a "plot by Spider-Man to steal the spotlight . . . sabotaging the capsule." Later, Parker is shown listening to a crowd of workers demanding that the hero be "run out of the country" and reported to the FBI. Even Aunt May turns against Spider-Man, and the episode ends with Parker nervously wondering if becoming "a menace" is the "only course left for me."

In the second story, Peter is still desperate for money. He decides to show off his powers to the Fantastic Four in hopes they will invite him to become a member of the superhero team, which he assumes will offer a steady paycheck. Showing off, he breaks into the group's tech-laden headquarters, the Baxter Building. When the super group picks up his arrival by camera, Johnny Storm quips, "Why didn't he phone for an appointment, like anyone else?" Thing answers: "Cause he's a teen-age cornball show-off, just like the Torch."

Later, the group squares off with the teen, trying to contain him. They basically battle to a draw; then Spider-Man announces his plan, exclaiming, "I'm worth your top salary." Sue Storm tells him, "We're a non-profit organization," while Reed Richards explains, "We pay no salaries or bonuses! Any profit we make goes into scientific research!" Johnny, like Parker a sarcastic teen, says, "You came to the wrong place, pal! This isn't General Motors!" Lee's ear for teen-specific dialogue captures the cadence and sarcasm of the era.

Meanwhile, Spider-Man is about to face his first supervillain—the Chameleon—a highly intelligent criminal who can disguise himself as anyone, even the teen hero. Chameleon orchestrates a plan to frame Spider-Man by stealing secret missile defense plans. The real Spidey escapes from the police and slingshots himself across New York to catch the villain's helicopter. He speeds out in a motorboat to a waiting Soviet submarine, uses his webbing to keep its hatch from opening, and then takes control of the helicopter.

Chameleon employs several tricks to escape momentarily, including impersonating a policeman and forcing the real police to grab Spider-Man. The police realize the ruse, but the hero scampers up a wall "in a fit of white-hot fury" and vows to let the officers catch the criminal rather than try to help. As Spider-Man flees the scene, he tears up, thinking, "Nothing turns out right. I wish I had never gotten my super powers!" The members of the Fantastic Four return to the forefront, shown wondering if Spider-Man may eventually turn evil. The ten-page story ends with Lee's narrative: "And the whole world will have to wonder—until our next great issue! Don't miss it!!"

★   ★   ★

Over the course of the next year, Lee and Ditko introduced almost every one of Spider-Man's most significant supervillains, from Vulture and Electro to the Lizard and Doctor Octopus. While battling these criminals provided the series with the requisite action of a superhero comic book, it was the large supporting cast around Peter Parker that propelled the stories. Peter's interactions with Aunt May, Jameson, and a series of love interests made the youth seem more convincing as an angst-filled teen who stumbled into his role as a superhero.

As a comic book author, Lee used Spider-Man to introduce several innovations that separated him from other writers. Besides narratives directed at the audience, Lee also pulled the reader deeper into the story via thought balloons. As Lee explains, they "let our readers know what a character was thinking as often as possible . . . and add a whole additional dimension to the story."[18] These advances in style and narrative voice shouted at the reader to pay attention, while simultaneously making them aware that a *person* existed within the pages. Lee's easygoing manner let you know that he was a friend and just as excited as you were about what you were reading.

The compelling dialogue melded with Ditko's angsty art. "Steve and I worked beautifully together," Stan said of their partnership. "As far as I was concerned, he was the perfect collaborator. His artwork was superb." According to Lee, Ditko's "story sense was brilliant. . . . You thought you were watching a motion picture from panel to panel." That sense of action and motion—the might of Ditko's artistic style—really set the tone for Spider-Man.[19]

Another Lee and Ditko novelty centered on utilizing New York City as Spider-Man's stomping grounds. Readers could relate to the teen living in a cramped Queens apartment with his surrogate parents. Jack and Stan had done the same with the Fantastic Four, plopping them down in Manhattan, but while they jetted around the globe and universe, Spider-Man stayed central to the city, bringing it alive on the pages. For readers familiar with New York, the stories came to life at the mention of Manhattan or the Brooklyn Bridge, while others could imagine Spidey swinging through the steel and concrete canyons created by the city's massive skyscrapers. "Instead of living in a fictitious Gotham City or Metropolis," Stan explained (taking a swipe at his DC Comics competitors), "[Spider-Man] has his digs in good ol' New York City and . . . might be found running after a taxi anywhere from Greenwich Village to the Upper East Side."[20]

Tactically, from a business perspective, using NYC as the setting for its two hottest titles tied the comics closer to America's largest consumer base. There were more newsstands selling Marvel comics in New York than anywhere else on the planet and more youngsters willing to drop their nickels, dimes, and quarters. For readers outside the city, New York was a place they could imagine or had seen on television or in movies. New York had always been America's city, its primary backdrop and national dreamscape.

Placing all his heroes in and around the Big Apple enabled Lee to accurately depict the setting in his native city and gave him another innovation—having superheroes casually (or not so coolly) run into one another. Beginning with *AS #1*, the guest-starring notion kept comic book audiences thrilled at the idea that Spider-Man could engage with (and potentially battle) the Fantastic Four, the Hulk, or other characters.

The webslinger's growing popularity also enabled Lee to use him as a means of introducing new characters or sprucing up existing ones that needed a sales boost. Fans could not get enough of the teen hero, so Lee and Marvel pushed the limits. For example, Spider-Man appeared in *Strange Tales Annual #2* (September 1963), a seventy-two-page crossover between him and the Human Torch. And in *Tales to Astonish*, which had moved from odd, macabre stories to superheroes, Spidey guest-starred in #57 (July 1964), which focused on Giant-Man and Wasp. When *The Amazing Spider-Man Annual #1* appeared in 1964, with Lee dubbing himself and Ditko "the most talked about team in comics today," it featured appearances by every Marvel hero, including Thor, Dr. Strange, Captain America, and the X-Men.

Spider-Man stood at the center of a comic book empire. Stan could not have written a better outcome, even if given the opportunity. He had a direct hand in shaping American folklore and culture.

All this from a risky run in a dying comic book!

· 8 ·

The Marvel Universe

"*A* monster!" Martin Goodman turned on his heels, shaking his head as he walked away.

The creation of superheroes wasn't done in a linear fashion, and ideas and characters were bounced around. Looking back on the crucial months after *The Fantastic Four* debuted, let's jump back in time to a moment when Spider-Man was still being planned and Marvel's future was still unclear.

Goodman sensed a trend in the making and wanted Stan and Jack to create another superhero team. When Stan told him that he had a different idea, a solo book centered on what he described as an "offbeat" monster, Goodman looked incredulously at his editor and audibly sighed. The notion of not following up on the popularity of the superhero team with another one—derivative or not—seemed ludicrous. Lee watched his boss leave the room, while dreaming of the powerful behemoth that he and Kirby had been kicking around.

"I had been wracking my brain for days, looking for a different superhero type, something never seen before," Lee remembered.[1] The new character had to have super strength but not mirror the Thing or the competitor's venerable Superman. What would make the character different?

Mountains of fan mail had poured into Marvel's Madison Avenue office in support of the Fantastic Four. But the insatiable fans also begged and pleaded for a new superhero. Although he had created or cocreated many comic book characters over the previous two decades, Lee agonized over a follow-up to the hit supergroup. A victim of his own success, Lee felt the pressure to keep up the momentum. He and Jack would have to come up with something completely new and different.

Stan pulled ideas and imagery from classic stories and familiar narratives. Like other great artists in the early 1960s, whether Bob Dylan reimagining old folk songs into protest anthems or novelist John Updike transforming the Peter Rabbit story into a 1960s existential everyman named Rabbit Angstrom, Lee turned to his deep reading of classics and thought back to the early films he loved so much as a kid. He would give fans what they wanted: an almost invincible monster as antihero. Lee created the Hulk out of traces of Mary Shelley's *Frankenstein* and Robert Louis Stevenson's *Dr. Jekyll and Mr. Hyde.* Then, to add to the dramatic tension, he contextualized the comic with heavy doses of Cold War anxiety.

These were impulses that Jack felt too and served as a foundation for his creative wellspring. "I began to learn about the universe myself and take it seriously," the artist explained. "I began to realize what a wonderful and awesome place the universe is, and that helped me in comics because I was looking for the awesome."[2] As the world wrung its hands about the potential devastation of atomic technology, Stan and Jack made nuclear weapon testing the cataclysmic event that turns a brilliant young scientist into a rampaging behemoth. The creative team introduced the Incredible Hulk, a brooding—somewhat terrifying—monster and convoluted antihero, to the growing superhero family.

With the Hulk, Lee and Kirby took another intellectual leap forward, deducing that fans would gravitate to the giant's failures and frailties, just as they had with the squabbling family they created with the Fantastic Four. Although the monster/hero was drawn from extant pop culture influences and ideas centuries old, Hulk felt new to readers increasingly searching for something different than the staid vibe from Batman and Superman. *New* was the key idea that Jack and Stan latched onto at precisely the right moment in American culture. They were able to bring the era's sensibility to comic books.

Stan and Jack had been working together for four or five years, but suddenly they hit on characters, dialogue, and imagery that was distinctly of its time, a contrasting blend of wild-eyed enthusiasm and dire situations. Who could have imagined, say, the elegance and charm of JFK's Camelot in the public spirit versus the Bay of Pigs disaster or world-on-the-brink Cuban missile crisis? How do two comic book creators tap into this vibe after more than two decades in the industry? Yet here they were—the foundational success of the Fantastic Four and then the quick introduction of Hulk, Thor, and Iron Man (and their archenemies and other heroes)—setting off a two-year run that changed the way people across American culture looked at comic books and their creators. Lee and Kirby became celebrities. Lee gave them monikers that readers would adopt: Jack "King" Kirby and Stan "the Man" Lee.

As a creative duo, Lee and Kirby caught a star as it shot skyward, able to bring dazzling characters to life and contextualize their stories with content drawn from what was happening in the real world around them. The new superheroes were different from the past or those of the competition—they spoke differently and inhabited a world that seemed authentic and right outside the reader's window, all the while turning on episodic plots and strong visuals.

Lee no longer had to simply kowtow to Goodman's request to copy the superhero team concept. But he still had to turn out new concepts to keep Goodman at bay. Under this pressure but finally being allowed to create the kinds of comic books that he had imagined doing over the years, Lee and his artist cocreators churned out a succession of superheroes that captured the attention of rapt fans and turned others into first-time readers (the pile-on nature of pop culture ensured that being *in* and *hip* would result in vastly larger circulation figures). Stan now headed the hottest comic book publisher in the business, and he grew into the voice bringing those superheroes to readers around the world.

Lee felt flabbergasted when fans started writing in after *The Fantastic Four* debuted. Subsequently, he read the letters and put admin staff on the task of writing back. Taking the notion of using fans as a kind of focus group, Stan also asked them to write more in the pages of the comics because he knew that he could use the insight later in developing new characters and finding which type of story lines stuck.

Many of those letters, Lee remembered, screamed for "more innovative characters." When he sat down and stared at a blank piece of paper in his typewriter, he considered these missives. He drew on what he considered the craziest idea possible. "Think of the challenge it would be to make a hero out of a monster," he prompted himself. "We would have a protagonist with superhuman strength, but he wouldn't be all-wise, all-noble, all-infallible."[3] That monster would have elements of Frankenstein's creation but turn the idea on its ear by making the townspeople chasing him the real monsters, while the monster would turn heroic, though always misunderstood. Jack and Stan had worked on countless monster comics in the previous decade, which they used as primary reference for the new green-skinned behemoth.

Readers picking up *The Incredible Hulk* #1 could get a sense of the character on the splash page. Kirby drew massive, tree-trunk arms but faraway, almost pleading eyes, capturing the Hulk's pathos and internal strife. A few pages later, when brilliant but meek scientist Bruce Banner endures gamma bomb rays and transforms into the Hulk for the first time, the monster bats young Rick Jones away, demanding, "Get out of my way, insect!" Via Kirby's masterful artwork, Hulk (initially with gray skin) seems to burst from the page, charging at the reader. Where is the line between man and monster? "Lee had come up with the perfect vehicle for exploring the notion of what it would be like to possess super powers in the real world," one comic book historian explained. "Kirby's chunky, monster style art" gave the hero/monster energy and also added to the existential angst and inner id that Hulk represented.[4]

This single panel embodies the essence of the character, as well as the achievement of its creators. Readers almost feel like they are inside the art, watching Jones's feet lift off the ground as the monster shrugs him off. In terms of capturing the giant's bewilderment, Lee decided to use the word "insect," which provides deep insight into the Hulk's strength and feelings about "normal" human beings. He shreds the wall of a military base to escape, then demolishes a jeep that runs into him in his escape. "Have to go! Have to get away . . . to hide," Hulk murmurs as he "storms off, into the waiting night."

Just six months after the debut of *The Fantastic Four*, *The Incredible Hulk* shot out of the gate in May 1962 yet struggled in ensuing months. The idea was fresh and exciting, but readers lost interest, perhaps giving some credence to Goodman's criticism. However, Stan was also limited by the awful distribution deal the publisher was forced to accept. With a limited number of titles available to ship, there wasn't much room for allowing a title to gain momentum. During those crucial months, the circulation numbers revealed how popular Spider-Man was. Stan had to cancel a title to make room for the new teen superhero, which was a certified hit. Hulk was cut to make room for the first issue of *The Amazing Spider-Man* in March 1963, less than a year after the rampaging hero had debuted.

The failure of the Hulk book also highlighted the incredible pressure on Lee. Goodman reviewed the sales figures and wondered what was going on with the book, always urging his editor to cancel titles that undersold. In only six issues, Lee and Kirby had made wholesale changes to Hulk: he transformed into the monster at nightfall, then later when angry; next, they modified the character's intelligence, sometimes making Hulk imbecilic and other times having him keep Banner's supergenius capabilities. The strangest Hulk occurred in the final issue when Hulk transformed but kept Banner's human-sized head. This version had to don a Hulk mask to keep his identity secret. When he faces off against Metal Master, he exclaims: "Don't look so surprised, peanut! Everyone on earth isn't a puny weakling!" Clearly, the character had gone off the rails, and Stan and Jack took the revisions into absurdity.

The distribution restriction forced Stan to come up with creative methods of getting characters space, especially when fans demanded more of them, which was the case with the Hulk. In October 1964, Lee brought the green goliath back in *Tales to Astonish #60*, one book featuring two separate superheroes: a renewed Hulk and Giant-Man. Since early comics were anthologies containing several different stories, like the ones Stan worked on early in his career with Simon and Kirby, he kept that idea going with the team books. From the reader's perspective, it almost seemed as if these comics were de-livering more action than a solo title—two or more superheroes for the price of one!

Hulk would star in the *Tales to Astonish* comic book series and play a role in other titles, including *Spider-Man* and *The Avengers*. Stan and Jack ably produced crossover after crossover, which fueled new story lines and greater reader curiosity. When the draconian distribution deal finally ended and Marvel's popularity surged to the point that the company could launch books at Lee's whim, he had the new *The Incredible Hulk #102* take over the *Tales* numbering in March 1968. It had taken years, but one of Marvel's premier superheroes would now carry on the existential mantle and grow more popu-lar as he appeared across varying media, such as animated television, and on lunchboxes, T-shirts, and other licensed materials.

★   ★   ★

Realistic superheroes were Marvel's strength, but dating back to the late 1930s and Superman's tremendous impact, the industry revolved on near-invincible characters that possessed almost unimaginable powers. Lee understood that he needed a superhero "bigger, better, stronger" than his creations to date. After dozens of failed attempts, from outlandish concepts like "Super-God" to mountains of discarded doodles and sketches in his left-handed scrawl, Lee figured, "since we were the legend makers of today, we'd simply take what had gone before, build on it, embellish it, and come up with our own ver-sion." Instead of "God," Stan focused on Norse mythology to create a "god" with a small "g" that would unfold the "continuing saga of good versus evil—god-wise," just the kinds of stories that human beings had been telling for centuries.[5]

The Norse god that Stan and Jack birthed would be named Thor and powered by the magical Uru hammer. The hero debuted in *Journey into Mys-tery #83* (August 1962), which would replace *The Fantastic Four* in its former slot as a bimonthly book when the superhero team moved up to monthly status. Thor and other new creations debuted in existing anthology books rather than bursting onto the scene as solo efforts. In contrast to how Stan had launched Hulk, the new superheroes were given some space in the team-up books, which allowed him to gauge fan interest prior to committing full-time resources to them. In round-ups and letters to fans in the back pages of the books, Lee frequently asked his rabid fan base to write to him about new series and characters.

Given the unrelenting publication schedule and somewhat limited title range, Stan had to switch back and forth between the teen, Western, and superhero titles. In response, he searched for other writers to fill in the gaps. For Thor, he gave the scriptwriting duties to his younger brother, Larry Lieber (who kept the family name), a trained artist in his own right. "Stan would give me a plot, usually typed," he remembered. "Then he'd say, 'Now, go home and write me a script.'" Initially, Lieber worried about his ability to write because he "thought like an artist." However, Stan "did teach me [to write]" and provided his younger brother with on-the-job insight about how to make stories positive and exciting using strong language. "Everything he said was much better than what I wrote," Lieber explained. "I worked and I learned a lot from him."[6] Lieber became a valuable asset as the company expanded, first teaming with Kirby on Thor, then moving onto Westerns when Stan had a need for him there. Those titles remained extremely popular, even in the superhero age.

Thor is one of the characters that troubles today's fans and observers when they attempt to assess how Stan and Jack worked together. Earlier in his career, Lee had written full scripts and plotlines and given them to artists to bring to life. In addition, he had to change roles in varying degrees to then oversee the process and production as editor-in-chief. With the new superheroes, Stan and Jack both brought plot ideas to the initial discussions, but the artist had much greater leeway than in the past, essentially taking a few lines of direction and creating what he wanted from it. With Jack's caption notes and the action on the page, Stan added in the dialogue and assessed the quality overall from his vantage as editor. This intensely collective practice set the norm for how Marvel superheroes were published.

Both men were also interested in Norse mythology and epic tales. Writing *Thor* enabled Stan to draw from his study of Shakespeare, which he had read out loud as a kid. Other sources, like Edgar Allan Poe and the swashbuckling works of Alexandre Dumas, allowed him to try different dramatic voices to give the Norse god added depth. From a lifetime of watching and analyzing film, he recognized the significance of rhythm and pacing and applied it to his budding superhero writing style.

Stan also looked to Arthur Conan Doyle's Sherlock Holmes, concluding that the sleuth epitomized the ultimate superhero because "a superhero should be believable. There was never a more believable character than Sherlock."[7] Many of Lee's creations were implausible, but their torment and anxiety appealed to the growing number of high school and college readers. Each Marvel superhero that Stan cocreated had some deep wound that gave a natural storytelling rhythm to the comic books. The gulf between the character and the superhero persona gave Marvel comics a complexity that seemed new and innovative.

★   ★   ★

When Lee told Goodman about his desire to create a superhero who was also a handsome tycoon and weapons manufacturer modeled after Howard Hughes, Goodman said flatly, "You're crazy."[8] Ridiculously—or wholly rationally from his perspective—Stan supposed that Goodman hadn't said no, so he co-created Tony Stark/Iron Man with artist Don Heck, Kirby (who created the cover, done prior to the interior pages), and his brother, Larry, who took over scripting. While Stan perceived the mega-capitalist to be similar to Hughes, Heck thought more about the swashbuckling Errol Flynn hero.

With the Cuban missile crisis still fresh on people's minds, as well as former president Dwight Eisenhower's harsh words and warning about the massive growth of the military-industrial complex in his farewell address to the nation, Lee thought Stark should be the antithesis of other superheroes: wealthy, suave, and handsome, a weapons dealer seemingly without a care in the world.

Stan drew from real-world topics, contextualizing the stories, especially when creating a new character's origin story. If it seemed somewhat believable, then the team had added perspective to plumb as the character evolved. As a result, the Hulk embodied the nation's conflicted ideas about science and the potential negative costs of innovation. For Iron Man, Lee would again draw on technology but also place the hero's origin story in a little-known nation on the other side of the world called Vietnam (long before anyone really knew much about the Asian nation). Iron Man, the metallic alter ego of industrial titan Stark, first appeared in *Tales of Suspense #39* (March 1963).

Iron Man peers out from the cover in gunmetal gray and looks stiff, more robotic than human, with no distinguishable facial features except slits for eyes and a mouth slot. The robotic feel is Kirby-esque, homage to the countless covers he did in the heavy sci-fi 1950s. Littered with Lee's typical excitable tone, the reader is asked to speculate about "the newest, most breath-taking, most sensational super hero of all." By this time, Stan is frequently breaking the fourth wall, explaining that the new character comes from the same "talented bull-pen" where the other famous Marvel superheroes "were born." In early 1963, trust was already a defining matter for Marvel readers. Lee asks them to have faith in the new hero (and essentially Lee's role as leader of this flock). He wants the audience's decision to read Marvel to mean something to them, so he makes the relationship between himself and them personal.

Stark is a scientist (like many Lee characters) but also a "glamorous play-boy, constantly in the company of beautiful, adoring women." Much of the plot (created by Lee but scripted by Lieber) unfurls in flashback and traces Stark's transition from Hughes-like industrial leader to armored superhero. The tale centers on a jungle booby trap that fells Stark and his military protec-tors, which allows him to be captured. Later, at the "guerrilla chief's headquar-ters," the reader learns that Stark lived through the ordeal but expects to soon die because a piece of shrapnel from the explosion is lodged near his heart. The enemy leader Wong-Chu determines that he will trick the American inventor into creating bombs until the moment he dies from the steel moving closer to his heart.

Realizing that he has limited time to act, Stark declares: "This I promise you. . . . I shall build the most fantastic weapon of all time!" He immediately begins crafting an iron suit designed to keep his fragile heart safe and exact re-venge on Wong-Chu's forces. With the help of Professor Yinsen, a renowned physics professor imprisoned for not agreeing to build weaponry for the guer-rillas, Stark devises the Iron Man suit utilizing his powerful transistor design. Yinsen fits the suit on the American just in time, and Stark stirs back to life just as the guerrilla's forces kill Yinsen. Iron Man declares he will avenge the professor's murder and flies into the building's shadows to hide until he can concoct a plan.

Finally confronting Wong-Chu, the powerful hero tosses him aside and then uses a transistor design to reverse the trajectory of the soldiers' bullets. Realizing their weapons are no match against Stark's technology, the soldiers run off into the jungle. Wong Chu, however, fights back, dumping a heavy metal cabinet on top of Stark, forcing the hero to use an "electrical power" to extricate himself. Next, Iron Man shoots a stream of oil at an ammo dump that the leader tries to reach. When Stark lights the oil stream with a torch, Wong Chu is blown up along with the armory. Iron Man frees the other prisoners and walks away, covering himself in a long brown jacket and fedora. The su-perhero ponders his new fate as Iron Man, asking, "Who knows what destiny awaits him? Time alone will provide the answer! Time alone . . ."

The collaborative partnership that brought Iron Man to life centered on Heck learning and adapting to Lee's new storytelling mode, which seemed foreign for many artists who had worked at other comic book publishers. As a matter of fact, when Heck first got a story synopsis from Lee, he balked at the process. Later, though, he grew to enjoy the creative freedom and trust that the Marvel Method effected. "Stan would call me up and he'd give me the first couple of pages over the phone, and the last page," Heck remem-bered. "I'd say, 'What about the stuff in between?' and he'd say, 'Fill it in.'"[9] Stan's approach was twofold: first, find a practice for creating comic books that spread the work across creative teams so that he personally had more time to manage the operation as a whole. Second, adopt a methodology that worked so well in Hollywood: utilize many smart minds to tackle a concept and script *after* the central idea has been established. From idea to publication, the many creative fingers that touched the end product each added depth and nuance. While some artists found it difficult to adjust, Heck and many others flourished.

★   ★   ★

When Lee finally had comic books that readers were eager to buy, he created tactics for additional superhero stories to get into their impatient hands. Rather than just load up each issue with filler and old monster tales, he decided to add more superheroes to the mix in the handful of stories necessary to complete the book. For example, the Fantastic Four's Human Torch became the primary star of short pieces that ran in the anthology *Strange Tales*, a leftover title from Marvel's monster era. Lee's intuition paid off, and sales shot through the roof.

Steve Ditko brought Stan a new character in the form of a five-page filler story, which Lee utilized as a companion piece to the Human Torch. The character's distinct voice benefited from Stan listening to a radio program called *Chandu, the Magician* as a kid, but really centered on Steve's surrealistic vision of a superhero centered in dark magic. The hero became Dr. Strange, and his story was filled with Ditko's psychedelic imagery and magical portrayal of the enchanted world. The character's origin story centered on Stephen Strange, an arrogant surgeon who suffers a debilitating injury to his hands, rendering him unable to operate. After hitting skid row, he journeys to visit the "Ancient One," a mystical healer and wise man. After studying with the wizard, he transforms into a supreme sorcerer and returns to set up shop on Bleecker Street in Greenwich Village. Unknown to the world at large, which views him as a fraud, Dr. Strange battles the dark arts. The interesting angle is that Strange saw the dark arts everywhere—the real view of the world that others can't see all around them.

Since Dr. Strange is essentially a magician, Lee and Ditko had him speak in an elevated tone rather than in the corny stage magic "hocus pocus" banter of pulling a rabbit from a hat. Lee reveled in the character and the new words Dr. Strange used. "I can lose myself completely while putting them together, trying to string them on a delicate strand of rhythm so they have a melody all their own," he explained. "When it came to Dr. Strange I was in seventh heaven. . . . I had the chance to make up a whole language of incantations."[10] Reading the comic, one can immediately hear Lee's cadence and voice in

Strange's interesting speech peculiarities and catchphrases, such as "by the hoary hosts of Hoggoth," always alliterative and beguiling.

It did not take long for older teens and college students to catch on to Lee's words and Ditko's groovy artwork. Many tried to dissect Dr. Strange's odd cadence and assess its literary origins. Lee recalled later that he didn't have the heart to tell them that he made most of it up. If it was derived from anything, it was the phrases and symbols that came from Lee's reading science fiction greats while growing up.

When Ditko abruptly left Marvel in 1966, Lee continued writing the series, working with artists Bill Everett, Marie Severin, and Dan Adkins. The mystical sorcerer attained an important place in the Marvel universe. Dr. Strange took on villains that embodied evil itself, such as the dreaded Dormammu and the Living Tribunal. In occupying this dark realm and battling the world's terrifying evildoers, a case could be made that Stephen Strange was Marvel's most powerful superhero.

★   ★   ★

The Fantastic Four surprised everyone when it became a hit and changed Marvel's trajectory, so Goodman never let go of his notion that Stan should create another superhero team. If one group of heroes sold well, then the natural inclination would be to add more to the roster. Finally able to exert a bit of influence with DC's distribution arm, Goodman reworked the deal, allowing Stan to publish more titles per month. Yet we can't give too much credit to Goodman. The deal was primarily a financial decision by Independent News. They planned to capitalize and cash in on Marvel's popularity, even though rival DC owned the distributor.

No one thought that Goodman and Lee would actually catch up to the market leader, so the thinking was that merely allowing a few extra titles a month would just make everyone a little more money. Some of the men who ran Independent probably thought that they were pulling the ultimate irony over their golf buddy/competitor Goodman: the better his comics sold, the more money made by his staunchest rival. The arrogant DC execs would never have envisioned they were essentially letting the fox into the henhouse.

Just as the fan letters had given Stan insight into the popularity of the Fantastic Four, he gathered information from mail that poured in asking for him to create teams of Marvel's heroes. Again, with DC's Justice League of America in mind, Lee determined that the Marvel group would consist of its most powerful characters. Since Kirby drew so many of the heroes in their other comics, Lee tapped him for *The Avengers*, composed of Thor, Ant-Man,

Hulk, Wasp, and Iron Man. Finally, Lee had the roster of superheroes that could form a potent counterpoint to DC's group.

Stan and Jack gave the Avengers an aura of superiority, as if this supergroup were the best-of-the-best in the Marvel universe. Yet, following Lee's playbook on character disposition and attitude, they added the touches of realism that had pushed sales skyward for other comics. Similar to the Fantastic Four, the members of the Avengers wouldn't always get along or agree on how to solve challenges. They too resided in New York City, in a building donated by Tony Stark. Stan viewed these critical plot points as the "fashioning of a world for the characters to live in," which resulted in a "mood of realism to be created so that the reader feels he knows the characters, understands their problems, and cares about them."[11]

While Jack had begun drawing the superhero group, Stan realized he needed an assistant to keep up with the demand of the growing comic book line. He hired Flo Steinberg, who would play a pivotal role in keeping Stan operating effectively. She saw firsthand how the two creatives worked: "Jack would come in and sit around and talk, then he'd go into Stan's office and they'd go over plots, make sound effect noises, run around, work things out."[12] Steinberg's reminiscence of how Jack and Stan hashed out stories in the early days at the birth of the Marvel universe demonstrates their close partnership.

When *Avengers* #1 (September 1963) appeared on newsstands, the action jumped out from Jack's distinctive cover—Thor's swinging hammer, Ant-Man and Wasp swooping in, and Hulk and Iron Man prepping for a fight. The reader only sees Loki, the "god of evil," in a glimpse from behind, as if a camera had taken a snapshot over his right shoulder. The perspective makes it seem that you are there viewing the confrontation firsthand. Thor and Hulk look like they could be first cousins (based on the way Jack drew character faces), but the layout provided a brilliant Technicolor introduction to the new superhero team.

Within the issue's pages, Loki unleashes a sinister plan to draw out his brother Thor using the Hulk as bait. Stan used the Fantastic Four members briefly in a guest-starring role, making them unavailable when a distress call comes in from Rick Jones's Teen-Brigade. Eventually, the heroes find Hulk, who has disguised himself as Mechano, a superstrong robot performing in a traveling circus (the monster is in an odd brown jumpsuit and orange shoes and has white makeup around his mouth). Thinking that Hulk derailed a passenger train, they try to stop him. Meanwhile, Thor returns to Asgard to confront Loki. After fighting Loki and thwarting a series of traps, Thor brings Loki to Earth, revealing the plot to the other superheroes. When the god of evil turns radioactive, it seems he will fight Thor again, but Ant-Man and Wasp swing into action, trapping the evildoer in a lead-lined container designed for trucks to "carry radioactive wastes from atomic tests [and] dump their loads for eventual disposal in the ocean."

After stopping Thor's evil brother, the group decides to band together, even convincing the Hulk to join. Lee's final panel announces "one of the greatest super-hero teams of all time! Powerful! Unpredictable! . . . A new dimension is added to the Marvel galaxy of stars!"

The second issue of *The Avengers* begins with Thor criticizing the Hulk, who threatens him in return. Here Stan placed the supergroup directly within the realistic confines of his other characters. Thor and Hulk itch to fight one another, placing Iron Man in a mediator role. At the other end of the spectrum, Wasp pines for Thor, whom she calls "adorable" and "handsome." Their foe, the Space Phantom, can take the identity of others, so he replaces the Hulk and starts a fight with the others inside Stark's mansion. Hulk escapes but is later confronted by his teen sidekick, Rick Jones, who mistakenly tells him that he can turn back to "Doctor Don Blake when you want to!" (a Lee slip-up that demonstrates the fast pace of comic book production since Blake is Thor's secret identity). Summoning the Norse god, the Avengers defeat the Space Phantom, but in the melee with Hulk, they reveal their suspicion of the green goliath. As a result, he quits the Avengers and leaps off into the future.

Despite being only two issues into the series, Stan had already changed the team (also adding Giant-Man) significantly to add drama to the character interaction, including portraying Hulk as a nearly indestructible force. Over the next several issues, the group continues to battle Hulk when he teams up with Sub-Mariner. Later, the Avengers find Captain America and bring him into the fold. In a callout box, Lee trumpeted the return of the red, white, and blue supersoldier, telling the reader that Kirby had drawn the original and that his first story was a Cap tale: "Thus, the chronicle of comicdom turns full circle, reaching a new pinnacle of greatness!" Lee also urged fans to "save this issue," more or less pushing the notion that comic books could be collector items, explaining, "We feel you will treasure it in time to come!"

The Lee/Kirby creative team set 1963 ablaze with quirky superheroes that seemed quite like real people. Yet, with their newfound, tremendous powers, they were forced to deal with the ramifications. As their comic lineup expanded, though, Stan and Jack needed to introduce new superheroes that didn't solely fit the Marvel mode.

Fearing that readers might get tired of so many accidental heroes, the creative duo broke the mold and thought up a team of individuals who were born with "unique abilities." This group, Stan recalled, would be "mutants . . . an aberration of nature." They created two groups—one good and one evil—which Lee viewed as "an air of freshness and surprise."[13] He stumbled on the word "extra," as in the extra powers the characters possess, after Goodman shot down his original title: "The Mutants" (the publisher thought the idea would be above the heads of young readers). However, he did agree to "X-Men" (as if that made more sense), so Kirby and Lee sat down to brainstorm, plot, and plan.

The world that Stan and Jack created centered on the idea that human beings continued to evolve and some people were born with special powers that came to light when the person hit puberty. They reasoned that teenagers with amazing powers would delight young fans, while having a large cast of heroes and villains would give the stories inherent action and suspense. Such mutants, like Cyclops, who shot laser beams from his eyes, and Jean Grey, who had telekinetic powers that enabled her to move objects at will, attended Professor Charles Xavier's School for Gifted Youngsters. There they learned to harness their abilities and build on them for the good of humankind.

The *X-Men* series enabled Stan to explore the alienated feelings that many teens experienced, while also providing the group with kinship via their relationship with Professor Xavier, who proved to be a father figure for the outcasts. The school turned into an extended family for the youths, many of whom had faced discrimination for having abilities that "regular" humans did not understand. Their powers were a blessing and a curse. Only the wise counsel of Professor X and their experiences battling evil as a team could provide them with a semblance of normality, which always seemed fleeting.[14]

Running from 1963 to 1970, *X-Men* never really generated strong sales, despite the high hopes Stan had for it, but it was a reader favorite, particularly among older fans. He and Kirby faced tremendous pressure to work on the comics that sold well, so when the artist asked for a replacement, Lee granted his request. Later, the writer moved himself off the book to concentrate on better-selling titles. The title would be revived in the mid-1970s by writer Len Wein and artist Dave Cockrum. Their work would take *X-Men* to new heights and ensure its long-term success.

★   ★   ★

Once the superhero lineup took off, Lee created a system that centralized his control over nearly every aspect of the creative side of the comic books division. Some of these work responsibilities were the continuation of what he had been doing in art, editorial direction, and general management, but other aspects grew out of necessity, since Marvel grew as it became more popular. Lee may not have been trained to be a manager or talent scout, but his years in the business honed these skills.

Lee not only knew when to move an artist onto a different piece of work, like the critical decision to replace Kirby with Ditko on the early Spider-Man efforts, but he also respected the freelance artists who served as the backbone of the comic book world. He recognized talent and assembled a crew of artists to infuse Marvel with a new spirit. The superhero comics married the art and writing in a way that the business hadn't seen before. Strong freelance artists served as visual partners for the snappy dialogue and personality traits that Lee and other writers used to differentiate the company.

Lee's unique ability was to mirror the voice and style of the early 1960s and bring them into comic books. As a result, Marvel readers get the humor and satire that actor Peter Sellers brought to *The Pink Panther* (1963) and *Dr. Strangelove* (1964) while also appreciating the full-throttle heroic characters, like Ian Fleming's James Bond, whose action-packed films like *Goldfinger* (1964) encompassed a mix of sophistication, violence, and superhero-like deeds. Popular culture was changing. Lee found a groove with realistic superheroes who balanced great power with existential angst, an idea surging through mainstream media. He explained: "We try to write them well, we try to draw them well; we try to make them as sophisticated as a comic book can be. . . . The whole philosophy behind it is to treat them as fairy tales for grown ups and do the kind of stories that we ourselves would want to read."[15]

As editor and art director, Lee guided the voice and style of the company by working with artists and writers he trusted. When he found a person who possessed first-rate abilities, Lee deliberately indoctrinated the artist or writer into the company's distinctive process. For example, Stan had valued the beauty in the artwork of George Tuska since the 1950s. He was a stylist who some insiders believed had the most unique ability in all of comic books. Tuska had been the full-time artist on the nationally syndicated *Buck Rogers* newspaper strip from 1959 through 1967, a golden age for sci-fi in American culture.

Tuska remained one of Lee's favorites, so when the artist planned his post-strip moves, the editor brought him back to Marvel. By the late 1960s, Tuska would become an invaluable part of the artistic team. According to *Daredevil* artist Gene Colan, "Stan always would hold [Tuska's] work up as the criteria of how he wanted the other artists to draw." Lee's management style enabled Marvel to be distinctive yet also gave his artists a template that emphasized the kind of work he needed done quickly.[16]

In a publishing world often cold and ruthless, Stan cultivated talent. He had little choice since Marvel lagged well behind DC, its rival perched at the top. He needed talented freelancers that could fulfill his vision of producing quality comic books that people would hold to a higher standard. He had to take chances, whether it was utilizing someone he had worked with in the 1940s and 1950s or giving a young writer or penciler a chance to shine. Stan's management style was in contrast to how many comic book creators described their experiences at the main rival. Moreover, Lee's ability to hone and employ artists and writers was rewarded by their loyalty to him and the Marvel movement.

At the start of his career, for example, Colan could not get into DC, which had locked down its talent and ignored newcomers who yearned for a shot. For the venerable industry leader, he simply did not have enough experience. At Marvel, though, Colan received a completely different treatment: "Stan could see something in my work that no one else could see. . . . That's what really got me started, Stan's faith in my ability. Although it wasn't completely there at the time, I was too young and had a lot to learn."[17] The other harsh reality staring Lee in the face was the relentless publishing schedule that placed a real premium on not just speed but efficient speed. What Stan saw in Colan would later be repaid as the artist did high-profile work reviving the X-Men franchise.

For artists who expected to get committed to a specific script (or were used to that treatment at other comics and magazine firms), Stan's style changed their outlook. Colan remembered Lee giving the artistic team "such unprecedented freedom," which translated to happier artists. "I'd talk with Stan about a plot over the phone, and I'd tape record his whole idea—it'd just be a few sentences." Lee would explain: "This is what I want in the beginning, the middle, and what I want in the end. . . . The rest is up to you." For Colan and the other trusted freelancers, this kind of interaction and collaboration created an entirely new process. "I had all the characters work for me, what they looked like was up to me—except those that were already established. But whatever I did, I could do."[18]

Despite a growing public persona that turned him into the face of comic books, the day-to-day Lee as editor-in-chief understood the volatility of the market and its consequences. As a result, many artists grew into huge Stan supporters. The camaraderie that developed had important ramifications: the artists and creators worked long hours to meet the company's needs, but Lee rewarded them by keeping steady work coming their way. Colan, for example, spoke about the grueling hours necessary to produce two complete pages a day, which translated to about two full books per month. Maintaining this schedule took much longer than forty hours per week. Stan's faith in them filled their bank accounts, and in return they provided the voice and visual style he needed to keep the organization humming. Jack remained the artistic role model for the team, as well as being idolized for his prodigious work ethic. He churned out beautiful artwork faster than anyone else in the business.

The core group of freelance writers Stan took under his wing received a master class in comic book writing. Dennis O'Neil, a former journalist who started his comics career as a staff writer at Marvel and later became widely known for his work on *Daredevil, Batman*, and *Green Lantern*, explained, "That first year working for Marvel, my job was to, in effect, imitate Stan." For the young writer and his colleagues, the message was clear-cut and unequivocal: "Stan's style really was Marvel."[19]

For O'Neil, Roy Thomas, and the other writers, Lee served as commanding general but with a benevolent aura that most driven leaders did not possess. Given that he was the boss and decades older than many of the writers, Stan didn't spend a lot of free time mingling. Yet their admiration for him ran deep. The group became the first of Stan's "true believers." According to O'Neil, "I learned the basics. I learned the basics by imitating Stan, and he was, by a huge margin, the best guy to imitate back then." O'Neil and many others under Stan's tutelage viewed themselves as doing revolutionary work under the guidance and training of the industry's pioneer: "the best comic book writer in the world."[20]

Lee's eye for talent, though, was clear, particularly assessing the heights the writers and artists he commissioned would later go on to achieve. Marvel's ascension on the foundation Stan, Jack, and Steve created later developed into a kind of comic book university. They taught the next generation of creators how to build and expand what would become famously known as the "Marvel Method."[21]

Yet, at the same time, the company's achievements with the superhero lineup upped the pressure on everyone in the creative process to perform at a faster rate. Stan and Jack set the pace, but even they neared the limits on how quickly a person could write or draw. At one point, Stan had allegedly hired three secretaries so that he could dictate stories to them in order, running through one as the other two typed out the notes. As the momentum and success grew, each moment escalated in importance.

"In the beginning, I was writing almost all of the stories for Marvel," Stan recalled. "I couldn't keep up." Comic book production demanded that all the various creators be kept busy at all times. For the freelance artists, the need was much more basic: if you aren't drawing or writing pages, you aren't getting paid. Ever inventive, Lee developed a way to keep them active. He remembered seeing the freelancers pacing around the office after they dropped off their current work, always wanting more. Too often Lee simply had no way to keep up with the demand, so he transformed the writer/artist process: "I couldn't stop what I was doing. . . . [Instead] I would tell him generally what I wanted. He would go home and draw it any way he wanted, bring the illustrations back to me, and then I would put in the dialogue and the captions."[22] Actually, the new methodology had been utilized by advertising agencies for the previous forty years and in Hollywood production studios for even longer.

Without fully conceiving a new system for creating comic books before he implemented it, Stan came up with the "Marvel Method," or as he explained, the practice "happened purely through need." The process played on the strengths of Lee's freelance artists. He explains: "These guys thought like movie directors. They were really visual storytellers." As a result, Stan could give them lots of latitude to interpret what he wanted from a quick story conference or brief phone discussion. "When I would give them a plot, they knew how to break it down—how to begin it, how to end it, where to put the interesting parts." When the artists missed the mark, Lee could amplify the artwork with sound effects or extra dialogue. "It started as an emergency measure—it's the only way to keep these guys busy—but I realized that you get better stories that way."[23]

★   ★   ★

The unimaginable successes Marvel experienced in the early 1960s took place as Stan and Jack cemented their creative bond—placing Marvel's future directly on their shoulders. The most logical and straightforward aspect of their relationship centered on mutual respect. They didn't have to hang out socially or get together with their wives. Both were professionals and respected one another in that fashion. Later, however, their relationship grew convoluted. There were inherent difficulties, certainly, even as they worked on the characters that would serve as the foundation of the Marvel universe. In the 1960s, Kirby worked for and reported to Lee, even though he had been Lee's boss when the writer/editor started as a teenage office boy. Though their roles were reversed, the truth was they were dependent on each other. Without Jack's ideas, Marvel could not thrive, and without Stan's voice and power as editor-in-chief, Jack had no way to get his work into the world. The partnership could not have worked without each of them giving every bit of themselves to the effort.

Perhaps even more pointedly, neither realized the immense frustration the other secretly possessed. Each detested many facets of the comic book industry, particularly its seemingly endless boom-and-bust financial cycles. Stan and Jack were friends and had a long professional history, but their friendship did not carry over to the point where they would share intimate details about their hopes and dreams. If either had actually opened up to the other in this fashion, it might not have changed the way their relationship evolved, but it might have enabled them to see that they had more in common than they ever believed.

Clearly they needed each other as professionals. After decades of keeping the comic book division of Goodman's empire alive, Lee recognized talent and knew Kirby was one of the best artists in comics. As editorial and art director, he decided that Kirby's approach would serve as the company's signature style, just as his own writing became the de facto voice. Artist Gil Kane, who worked for Marvel on and off for decades, most memorably drawing many of their covers in the 1970s, recalled:

> Jack's point of view and philosophy of drawing became the governing philosophy of the entire publishing company and, beyond the publishing company, of the entire field. . . . They would get artists, regardless of whether they had done romance or anything else and they taught them the ABCs, which amounted to learning Jack Kirby. . . . Jack was like Holy Scripture and they simply had to follow him without deviation. That's what was told to me, that's what I had to do. It was how they taught everyone to reconcile all those opposing attitudes to one single master point of view.[24]

The entire Marvel line revolved around the Kirby graphical worldview. For example, Jim Steranko passed the Marvel employment test by inking two of Kirby's penciled pages for *S.H.I.E.L.D.* He then worked with Kirby on three Nick Fury issues as a kind of professional apprenticeship. According to writer Chris Gavaler, "Becoming the Marvel house style seems to have required Kirby to regularize his layouts, presumably so they could be more easily imitated. Variation and innovation are not qualities easily taught, and they do not produce a unified style across titles."[25] Yet Steranko built his later reputation on irregular page layouts, which introduced art deco, postmodernism, and new wave impulses into Marvel's pages. The belief in talent that permeated the company via Stan's leadership enabled an artist like Steranko to initially thrive under the Kirby-infused artwork but then later develop his own artistic vision.

All DC could do, despite its iconic superheroes, was try to keep pace. By the time DC recovered—sort of—by producing its own colorful, exciting covers (essentially mimicking their upstart competitor), Marvel's creative leap had laid the foundation for Goodman's firm to eventually take over the top spot in the comic book business. In the battle between Marvel and DC, fans were voting with their nickels, dimes, and quarters.

As a result, an innovative, colorful, and exciting character like Metamorpho, created by DC mainstays George Kashdan and Bob Haney in late 1964, seemed like a Marvel clone rather than a new superhero. The Metamorpho cover (*The Brave and the Bold #57*) mirrored the kind of language that Lee popularized, exclaiming: "See the amazing powers of the world's most fantastic new hero." The book also used dynamic imagery and colors, yet Marvel had already created a beachhead in the war over what the comics fans would deem "hot." It took some time for the upstart to displace the market leader, but few doubted the excitement that Stan and Jack had created down on Madison Avenue. Once Marvel had a couple of hit titles, Lee wanted to add to its roster to keep the forward progress. "I was like a crapshooter rolling one great pass after another," Lee said. "You just don't stop when you're on a winning streak."[26]

In the back of his mind, however, Stan never fully accepted that the superhero boom would not eventually crash, just like all the other cycles he had experienced in the previous two decades. As a result, he moved fast to generate new titles and new characters to capitalize on the trend. He kept his freelancers hopping, driven by his own seemingly endless supply of optimism and energy. Under relentless publishing deadlines, Lee had to live and breathe the constant balance of creativity and commerce, artwork versus commodity. Under his leadership, the company and its creators would spend the rest of the decade solidifying and expanding its empire into the Marvel universe.

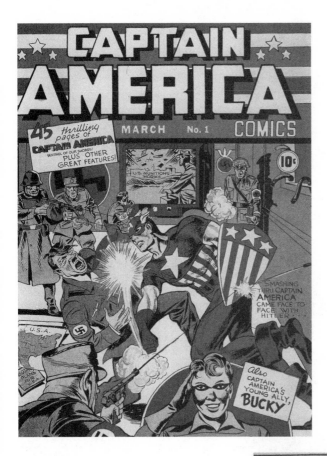

Captain America Comics #1 (March 1941) created by Joe Simon and Jack Kirby, with the hero punching Adolf Hitler. © 1939–2022 Marvel Characters, Inc.

Captain America Comics #3, Lee's first publication. © 1939–2022 Marvel Characters, Inc.

"I'm sorry, Haines, but there is no place in this army camp for the likes of you. You have lied, cheated, spied, and stolen. Your conduct is no longer tolerable and I'm giving you a dishonorable discharge. Now get out!"

Private Steve Rogers, doing sentry duty nearby, was watching the scene interestedly. He had never seen Colonel Stevens so angry; and Lou Haines, too, was threateningly mad. The muscular giant shook his enormous fist at the Colonel.

"O.K. Colonel," snarled Lou, "I'll get out. But let me warn you now, you ain't seen the last of me! I'll get even somehow. Mark my words, you'll pay for this!" Haines walked toward the camp gates, muttering insults under his breath.

Suddenly Haines felt a strong hand grasp his arm. He looked around into the flashing eyes of Steve Rogers! "I wouldn't act like that if I were you," murmured Steve, softly, "you were insulting a man in the uniform of the United States Army! Here are the camp gates; now beat it!"

Haines left, but there was a look of hate in his eyes which Steve could not help but notice!

* * * * *

Later that evening, Steve Rogers was sitting in his tent playing checkers with his young side-kick, Bucky, the camp mascot. Bucky looked disappointed.

"Gosh, Steve," wailed Bucky, "don't you EVER lose a game? I've forgotten what it feels like to win."

Steve smiled cheerfully. "I'll tell you what, kid: suppose you borrow a book on 'how to play checkers' and read it. That'll give me a chance to get some shut-eye. You don't know how tired it makes me to beat you all the time!"

Steve ducked just in time to dodge the pillow that Bucky threw at him. "Why, you little squirt," he grinned, "I ought to put you over my knee!"

"Oh yeah, you big palooka? You and what other army?" Bucky picked up another pillow and was holding it ready.

Suddenly Steve's smile left his face and he put his fingers

Destroyer, a superhero Lee cocreated with artist Jack Binder. © 1939–2022 Marvel Characters, Inc.

Army portrait of Lee, a "playwright" in the Signal Corps' Training Film Division, 1943. Courtesy of Stan Lee Papers, American Heritage Center, University of Wyoming.

Lee during World War II with a copy of *Terry-Toons Comics #25* (October 1944) on his desk and a sketch of his famous "VD Not Me" poster over his left shoulder. Courtesy of Stan Lee Papers, American Heritage Center, University of Wyoming.

Lee with wife, Joan Boocock Lee, late 1940s. Courtesy of Stan Lee Papers, American Heritage Center, University of Wyoming.

Stan Lee as the Black Rider on the cover of *Black Rider #8* (March 1950). © 1939–2022 Marvel Characters, Inc.

Lee at his desk typing, circa 1950. Courtesy of Stan Lee Papers, American Heritage Center, University of Wyoming.

Lee at his editor desk, reviewing comic book copy. Courtesy of Stan Lee Papers, American Heritage Center, University of Wyoming.

The Marvel universe began with *The Fantastic Four #1* (November 1961), cocreated by Lee and artist Jack Kirby. © 1939–2022 Marvel Characters, Inc.

Jack Kirby's iconic cover of *Amazing Fantasy #15* (August 1962). © 1939–2022 Marvel Characters, Inc.

Stan Lee's most famous quote from Spider-Man's origin story, in *Amazing Fantasy #15.* © 1939–2022 Marvel Characters, Inc.

Lee and Kirby confronted by Doctor Doom in the pages of *Fantastic Four #10* (January 1963). ©
1939–2022 Marvel Characters, Inc.

The first solo issue of *The Amazing Spider-Man #1* (March 1963). © 1939–2022 Marvel Characters, Inc.

Iron Man debuted in *Tales of Suspense #39* (March 1963). © 1939–2022 Marvel Characters, Inc.

Stan Lee circa 1965. © 1939–2022 Marvel Characters, Inc.

Marvel merchandise page, 1968. © 1939–2022 Marvel Characters, Inc.

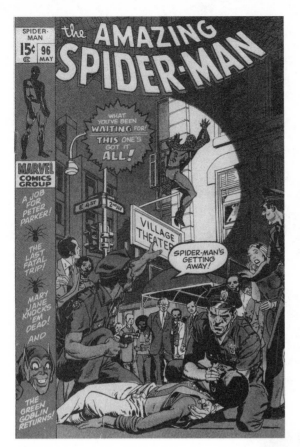

The *Amazing Spider-Man #96* (May 1971), published without the Comics Code Authority stamp. © 1939–2022 Marvel Characters, Inc.

Luke Cage, Hero for Hire #1 (June 1972). © 1939–2022 Marvel Characters, Inc.

Lee posing with his book *The Origins of Marvel Comics*, 1974. Courtesy of Stan Lee Papers, American Heritage Center, University of Wyoming.

Lee in front of a bookcase full of Marvel products, including *Marvel's Greatest Superhero Battles* (1978). Courtesy of Stan Lee Papers, American Heritage Center, University of Wyoming.

Jack Kirby. © Suzy Skaar.

Lee with Spider-Man, 1994. Courtesy of Stan Lee Papers, American Heritage Center, University of Wyoming.

Artist sketch of Lee as a character on *The Simpsons*, episode "I Am Furious Yellow" (2002). Courtesy of Stan Lee Papers, American Heritage Center, University of Wyoming.

Lee greets fans in 2010. © Pinguino K.

Stan Lee and Chris Evans, July 2011. © Frederik Hermann.

Stan signs a fan's comic books. © Gaviin Nansoong.

Stan Lee greets the crowd at the Phoenix Comicon (2014). © Gage Skidmore.

Lee leads the crowd in a cheer of "Excelsior!" (2015). © Gage Skidmore.

Lee at the Cincinnati Comic Expo, September 24, 2016. Courtesy of Suzette Percival.

· 9 ·

The Superheroes

"*F*ace front!"

Not subtle or paternal yet still in his playful, engaging voice, Stan Lee's demand that readers snap to attention kicked off the "Marvel Bullpen Bulletins," a feature page that ran in the back of all the December 1965 issues. It replaced the "Merry Marvel Bullpen Page," which had debuted earlier in August. Filled with "news" and "gossip," along with a checklist of current issues for sale and brief synopses, the yellow shadow boxes quickly became a familiar mainstay for Marvel readers.

No matter where a comic book reader lived or whether they could even envision what the Marvel headquarters might look like, the Bulletins made them feel like a part of the family. Some readers might gravitate to the insider perspective to see who inked a particular issue or to find out the latest scoop on an artist's personal life. Others yearned for the merchandise offers, like the Spider-Man or Dr. Strange T-shirt that a kid could get through mail order for just $1.50. Certainly more than a few young readers viewed the missives as personal letters from Lee, the coolest guy in the country.

Regardless of why comic book buyers loved the Bullpen Bulletins, the page gave Stan the chance to fully embrace his new, hip persona. On one hand, the notes gave him a place to really craft his voice as the main Marvelite. At the same time, the columns demonstrated his savvy strategic sense: he knew that strengthening audience engagement would result in greater dedication to Marvel's books. After receiving and reading thousands of letters from readers, the editor recognized that his direct interaction with them increased sales. He was giving them more than an update—it was a personal experience.

The voice that emerged became a hallmark of Marvel comics in the 1960s. "It was a little thing," Lee said, "but it was trying to give a feeling of warmth, a feeling of friendliness. . . . It seemed to work." For teens and college-aged fans, the wink-wink, tongue-in-cheek tone spoke to their antiestablishment notions and seemed discernibly different from the voice they were used to hearing from adults. "It was all spontaneous," Lee remembered. "When I was writing a story, I'd think of something. So I'd throw it in."[1] His success with superheroes and their angst-ridden personas proved that if he trusted his instincts, good things would happen. The imagery and look of a character might come to life at the end of a pencil or brushstroke, but the words stuck, whether it was Peter Parker lamenting a lack of money to pay the rent or Stan talking to the reader in the editorial pages. The voice fused into a Marvel style that cemented loyalty to the company and its heroes.

As the baby boomers got older and had more disposable income than any generation in American history, the chance to buy Marvel merchandise drew many to the soapbox pages. The cost was fairly meager at a buck or so, which seemed just within their reach. Just how many days of lunch money did a kid need to secretly stash away in order to afford that Dr. Strange T-shirt? Others gravitated to the list of new members of the Merry Marvel Marching Society fan club to see the names of kids from all over the country who shared their same interest.

Most important, Lee's Bullpen Bulletin gave him a forum to speak directly to all Marvel readers. He described the thriving relationship as "part of an 'in' thing" or "sharing a big joke together and having a lot of fun with this crazy Marvel Universe."[2] The insider perspective turned Lee into the comic book nation's favorite uncle. Like all movements, this one needed a leader— Stan stepped into the spotlight.

With this singsong, chatty style, Lee turned up the wattage on his own celebrity status. The "Stan the Man" or "Smiley" voice and personality came through in the dialogue of the comics and in the editorial content: "If I got a kick out of it, maybe a reader would, too," Stan reasoned. "Even in writing the credits, I'd try to make them humorous, because I enjoyed doing that."[3] While today's consumers might think the cheesiness went a little overboard, kids in the 1960s lapped it up. Who else but Stan could award select fans that wrote intriguing letters or otherwise caught his fancy a "Marvel No-Prize," literally no prize, for their effort? He then sent them an empty envelope, mockingly stamping "Handle with Care" on the outside. The sillier he acted, the more fans gobbled up the shtick.

In essence, Stan was perfecting a marketing strategy that continues to work into the twenty-first century: give the consumer a product that elevates them among their peers while also seeming exclusive to them alone. Let them scream, "I'm part of the tribe; I, too, am a Marvel reader," while providing the unique experience of engaging with one's "favorite" heroes or characters on an intimately individual level. Simultaneously, Lee set Marvel up versus DC and satirized the competitor, which turned the growing legion of readers into rabid fans. They wanted to declare their allegiance to Marvel's characters, which Stan intensified with the militaristic, joking language, ordaining himself as leader of the troops. Most important for a company relying on selling a product, circulation figures soared.

Stan also introduced the bullpen members on a first-name basis and gave them personalities, which translated into a deeper familial feeling for fans. Lee is often "Smilin' Stan Lee" in the updates, a slightly wacky, permanently overworked editor, who is keeping the whole place running by the seat of his pants. He explained the goal: "Give our fans personal stuff, make them feel they were part of Marvel, make them feel as though they were on a first-name basis with the whole screwy staff. In a way, I wanted it to be as though they were getting a personal letter from a friend who was away at camp."[4]

Talking about the otherwise mundane process of creating comics and the people behind the scenes provided readers with a mental image of themselves sitting down next to the famed comic book chief as he regaled them with stories of Jack (King) Kirby or (Jolly) Joe Sinnott. Marvel filled readers' dreams with visions of the Hulk and Iron Man, while the news from the bullpen made readers and creative staff seem like long-lost friends. That tone gave kids in small towns across the nation the feeling that Lee was their comrade and that Marvel's superheroes—despite a reader's better judgment—might just be real. You could see them there in New York, doing exciting work and creating these many superheroes—simply magical!

★   ★   ★

Lee's mad dash over the previous four years resulted in a superhero frenzy and total repositioning of Marvel in the publishing industry. The company—as well as its editor—stood at the epicenter of cool. This was rare air, usually reserved for magazines, like a previous era's *Saturday Evening Post* or the 1960s *Esquire*, *Rolling Stone*, or *Tiger Beat*. As young baby boomers came of age (and there were a lot of them), they re-created the "teen" market because they had money to spend. The American hype machine went into overdrive, and purchasing power was its epicenter, grabbing onto everything from concert tickets and new clothes to hip magazines. Teen culture and celebrity culture fused into a powerful entity based on hero worship, idolatry, and envy. Stan and Jack were real people, just like the members of the Beatles—both would appear within the pages of Marvel comics. The same people reading those issues were the ones that created the Monkees hysteria, watched California surf movies, and bought 45 singles and played them until the grooves wore out.

As part of the burgeoning culture, superheroes were emulated and became one of the hottest pop culture influences in America. Suddenly, it was Marvel that other publishers wanted to imitate. They attempted to jump aboard the superhero wave, including Charlton Comics (who hired Steve Ditko after he left Marvel and granted him almost complete editorial control over his conservative Ayn Randian creations) and Tower Comics (which doled out work to high-profile artists such as Wally Wood and Gil Kane) and even the venerable Archie Comics (which launched its own group called the Mighty Crusaders). Other new publishing houses entered the marketplace, attempting to capitalize on Marvel's popularity, but often merely put out derivative content and cover art. They might try to emulate Lee and Kirby, but without the real thing, many of the publishers seemed simply eager to make a fast buck. Few childhood bubbles burst as painfully as when a family member or parent said they bought some comic books, then pulled from the bag a collection from a knockoff publisher, not *Spider-Man*, *Astonishing Tales*, *Iron Man*, or another Marvel title. These ones were relegated to the bottom of the pile, fodder for trading to some gullible kid who didn't know the difference.

In 1965, Lee and his creative gang began a series of changes and slight modifications to the hero genre, which enabled them to build a more cohesive, unified cosmos while simultaneously solidifying their growing fan base. For the next several years, the goal would not be to expand the universe by leaps and bounds but to increase depth, nuance, and context. Lee believed that intensifying the relationships between characters and intertwining the superhero worlds would enable future growth and, more importantly, create stronger bonds between the characters and readers.

Marvel's existential heart continued to center on the authentic, daily challenges presented as ordinary people gained larger-than-life powers. Stan quickly utilized the most human of human problems—the trials and tribulations of romantic relationships—and such an approach was relatively organic to the creative staff, at least at the upper level. Both Lee and Kirby had long histories in teen romance comics. Kirby and partner Joe Simon basically invented the genre in 1947, creating *Young Romance*, a title DC was still publishing in the 1960s. Lee also had deep experience, serving as the primary writer for *Millie the Model*, as well as its many offshoots. Indeed, *Millie* quite possibly stood as the most successful nonsuperhero title Marvel ever produced.

The romantic interlude that drew the most interest was the marriage of Reed Richards and Susan Storm in *Fantastic Four Annual #3*. Kirby dazzled readers with the oversized issue, which also contained reprints of two popular earlier issues. The cover featured a free-for-all: nearly every hero from the Marvel cosmos attended the star-studded event, which also attracted countless villains hoping to crash the festivities. While the two sides battled, a glum

Sub-Mariner watched over the proceedings, his heart clearly broken. Inside, Stan called the issue "the most sensational super-spectacle ever witnessed by human eyes!!"

As the wedding draws nearer, the Baxter Building is surrounded by adoring fans (including teen beauty Patsy Walker, another longtime Marvel character) but also faces constant attack. Thing tries to ward off the bad guys but needs the help of Nick Fury, the X-Men, Dr. Strange, and a host of others. Eventually the groom has to intervene to save the day, and the story ends with a wedding kiss ("No mere words of ours can truly describe the tenderness of this moment . . . so we won't even try," Stan wrote). As the episode ends and wedding bliss hangs in the air, two interlopers in top hats and stylish overcoats attempt to crash the reception; Fury and his men stop them. To the reader's surprise, the trespassers turn out to be Stan and Jack, seen from the back, their faces hidden. Not even the Fantastic Four creators could get into such a lavish celebration.

Also that year, Mary Jane Watson first appeared in *The Amazing Spider-Man #25*, but Ditko strategically hid her face, only allowing other characters to exclaim: "She's a friend of Peter's? She looks like a screen star!" Readers wouldn't actually see her for years. At the end of 1965, blond beauty Gwen Stacy debuted. As with M. J., it would take the hapless Peter Parker years to begin dating her. When they initially meet, Parker is so wrapped up with Aunt May and keeping his Spider-Man persona secret that he basically ignores her.

Marvel creative teams used storytelling tactics from across different media channels, whether that meant utilizing episodic plots like soap operas or mimicking the interior dialogue that worked so effectively for novelists. These elements were essential in deepening the ties between the characters and comic book readers. Since Lee's superheroes were intentionally more realistic and similar to regular people, the notion that they were entangled in difficult relationships and other real-world challenges intensified the connection. The emphasis on teams of heroes and the extensive crossover magnified this bond, since the team setting inevitably led to internal strife as individuals came together to confront universal challenges.

In addition to guiding Marvel's art, writing, and production with a small team of full-time staffers and a growing cadre of freelancers, Stan also deliberately spent more time working to expand the company's brand. There were simply too many competing things to grab people's attention, ranging from the overtly commercial, like the national sensation caused by the arrival of the Beatles, to the wholly political, like Martin Luther King's 1965 civil rights march in Alabama and the growing presence of American troops in Vietnam. Comic books might have a difficult time competing with these enormous issues, but the flip side was that they could be marketed as a pleasant diversion from the real-life hardships.

Given the growing sophistication of marketing, advertising, and public relations in the mid-1960s—evolving rapidly since the start of the twentieth century—Marvel pushed to increase profitability. A 1965 flyer aimed at comic book distributors used Stan's amped-up patter in a direct appeal to prospective dealers: "When fans EYE them, they BUY them!" We do not know for certain whether Stan wrote that headline or others like it, but existing notes from the era reveal that the line between editorial/creative and marketing was blurry. The editor certainly reviewed the copy and played an increasingly larger role in marketing strategy, especially as Marvel grew in popularity. The grizzled newsstand owners might have overlooked the exaggerated language, but they couldn't have missed the dramatic sales increase. In 1960, Marvel sold about 16.1 million copies, but that number grew to 27.7 million in 1964, and the company expected to top 35 million the next year.[5]

The marketing brochure underscored pretty much what company insiders knew about Marvel's successes: the superhero "secret formula" that Stan and his team created vastly expanded the Marvel audience, thus reaching a greater number of older readers, including college students and adults. One of the critical aspects of Marvel's reach, according to the flyer, centered on superheroes "bringing in a brand new breed of reader. . . . Marvel Fan Clubs are springing up at every COLLEGE and UNIVERSITY from coast-to-coast." Although Marvel's marketers assumed that newsstand operators would be duly impressed with that information, the company boasted of already having fifty thousand members within the handful of months after its launch.[6]

With sales booming and the end of restrictions on how many titles Marvel could publish each month, Stan sat atop a company with dozens of titles coming out on a monthly or bimonthly schedule. When the lineup expanded, editorial director Lee had to commit to writing a new series or find someone to take it over when there really wasn't a university pipeline of young talent. Consequently, he tapped into alternative sources—writers from fan magazines, talented journalists, and some people who were Marvel readers and just persisted in pushing until they got the editor's attention.

All along, however, Stan continued to refine and hone the unique scripting style that had become a Marvel trademark. The relentless pace and increased number of titles forced the development of new processes to cope with the pressure. Writer Denny O'Neil discussed how the combination of the company style and tight deadlines came together in July 1966, when Marvel upped production to take advantage of the surge in superhero popularity based on the *Batman* television series. "I did *Daredevil #18* because Stan got into a deadline bind," he recalled. "Romita had done the art and put notes in the margins, but Stan didn't have time to do the script."[7] According to O'Neil, Lee worked harder than the writers he hired, putting in countless hours writing to bring the Marvel universe to its eager fans. His role grew along with the company because he had so much to write himself and he was responsible for controlling the editorial and artistic direction from his editor's perch.

Lee's work effort and persistence became part of company lore and inspired the writers he hired to put in similar grueling hours. For example, even a citywide blackout could not stop Lee from completing his allotted pages. During rush hour on November 9, 1965, New York City and parts of seven nearby states plunged into darkness in one of the largest power failures in American history. The city ground to a halt, with eight hundred thousand people trapped underground in the subway and countless others in buildings, in elevators, and on trains. Given the haplessness of the situation, O'Neil and assistant editor Roy Thomas gave themselves the night off. While they walked through the darkened city, Lee was reportedly at home writing by candlelight. "The pages had candle wax dripped on them," O'Neil remembered, though it's difficult to know whether we should take him at his word or if this is yet another Stan legend.[8]

The idea of plotting as writing has been a sticking point for comic book historians and aficionados. The main challenge is that the Marvel Method was created specifically to eliminate the need for lengthy scripts or plot overviews. Like texts or e-mail today making written memos nearly obsolete, the creative teams were doing much of the work by telephone and in-person conversations. The goal was to take as little time as possible in plotting to give the artist added time to think, imagine, and draw.

From existing eyewitness accounts, plotting took little time for Stan. After all, he had been writing comic books for decades and overseeing the production of all the titles during that period. By his own account, during the superhero boom he charted out the different books—perhaps ten to twelve a month—then gave them to the artists to build out and draw. When the artist delivered the work, Lee sat down and created the dialogue. However, Lee's various roles necessitated that he also keep an eye on the art and covers. "While I was putting the copy in," he explained, "I'd be making notes on changes that the artist should make in the artwork." Sometimes, Lee said, he had to deviate from the original plot because the artist took the story in a different direction. Kirby, for example, would change the plot to suit his needs, and Lee would piece together the dialogue, which he likened to completing a "crossword puzzle."[9]

From Stan's perspective, creating the narrative and dialogue made him the *writer*, just like coming up with an idea for a superhero made him the *creator*. The controversy over credit was fundamental as the superheroes became more deeply embedded in American culture. The point centered on how a creator specifically assesses one's role in the product. In an interview, Stan later outlined this rift, explaining that he told Steve Ditko, "I think the person with the idea is the person who creates it," but Ditko's response countered that notion: "Having an idea is nothing, because until it becomes a physical thing, it's just an idea."[10] Stan was an idea person, foremost and fully—he privileged the *idea*. Both men (as well as Jack Kirby) were 100 percent positive that they were the creators of the Marvel universe because they all believed wholeheartedly in their convictions and subjective definitions.

★   ★   ★

The popularity of Marvel's offbeat superheroes turned it into the hip 1960s comic book house, but DC still controlled the industry if sales figures were the sole measure. The ongoing competition between the publishers loomed large, and each focused on outdoing the other. DC counted on the long-standing heroes in its stable—Batman, Superman, and Wonder Woman—while Lee and Marvel countered with the hip Spider-Man, Thor, and Fantastic Four. The popular current seemed to tip toward Marvel, but then the ABC television series *Batman* debuted in January 1966. In a unique programming move, the show aired two nights a week—Wednesday and Thursday—in half-hour segments.

The success of the Batman television series made an immediate impact on the comic book industry, enabling DC to regain some of its swagger. With actor Adam West as the Caped Crusader and Burt Ward as his youthful sidekick, Robin, the TV show perfectly mixed camp and action in a way that appealed to 1960s audiences. The program served up a steady stream of one-liners and jokes and plenty of "POW," "BAM," and "ZONK" to delight audiences across age groups. Targeting younger viewers, Batman delivered words of advice, like the importance of doing one's homework and wearing seatbelts.

Batman focused on the parts of the culture that most appealed to young people. For example, music boosted the show. The soundtrack featured a mix of 1960s pop-infused songs mixed with Batman-specific tunes that were catchy and stuck in listeners' heads like an earworm. West put out a pop-and-country-infused song, "Miranda," that he would perform live while wearing the Batman costume. Like his campy dialogue on the show, the song had cheesy lyrics filled with double entendres, such as: "Ask me to do anything for you, Miranda." Burt Ward's entry into the music scene was a true testament of the era: the song "Boy Wonder, I Love You," which had been written by legendary gonzo musician Frank Zappa. Ward's corny rap/spoken word as Robin was backed by a pop background beat that is both satirical and perfect for the era. While the musical tie-ins played a central role in the show, *Batman* also took advantage of the color television craze, using bright color schemes to bring the comic book characters to life. The dramatic visualization of the femme fatales in vivid Technicolor and the sleek, black Batmobile enticed older viewers. The bright pastels and dark hues also reinforced that adults shouldn't take the show too seriously (it was okay to laugh), while at the same time giving younger viewers a heroic figure to admire.

After half a decade of searching for the magic decoder ring that would open an inroad to Marvel readers, DC seemed to finally depict the voice and tone that Lee brought to comics. *Batman* captured the nation's growing fascination with superheroes, especially in its satirical quality, which Lee had brought to the medium. In many respects, the snarky banter of the two heroes seemed closer in alignment to Spider-Man or the Fantastic Four than anything DC had recently produced. Adam West's semiserious prognostications (delivered with a knowing smirk) and tongue-in-cheek banter with various supervillains were an imitation of Stan's dialogue.

DC benefited as television grew pervasive during the mid-1960s, but its popularity really raised sales across the board. All the major publishers saw sales jumps, and they responded with new characters. Harvey Comics introduced superheroes *Spyman* and *Jigsaw*, while Tow Comic brought out *Dynamo* and *Noman*. Marvel attempted to counter *Batman* to some degree by beginning Thor's solo run in March 1966. The more lasting contribution was debuting the Black Panther, the first African American superhero, in *The Fantastic Four #52* (July 1966).

Although introducing a black superhero was in line with the era's civil rights movement, Stan and Jack worried about political backlash. When he appeared on the *Fantastic Four* cover, for instance, he was fully masked, so the hero's race was unidentifiable to the casual viewer. In contrast, Sue Storm and Reed Richards were fully identifiable as white. Stan cautiously used Black Panther as a guest star in various series over the next couple of years. He wouldn't become a primary player in the Marvel universe until early 1968 when the superhero became part of the Avengers.

Stan and Jack did not let the Bat-mania thwart their efforts to further develop Marvel's interwoven characters and storylines. They introduced a three-part trilogy in *The Fantastic Four #48–50* (March–May 1966) that had the original supergroup battling Galactus, an omnipotent superbeing who sustained life by devouring the energy from entire planets. The epic trilogy pitted Marvel's most powerful villain against Earth's powerful superhero team. A comic book arc would have trouble competing head-to-head against a popular television series, but Marvel hoped to at least increase sales and entice more readers to pick up the books.

Lee's aggressive antics to expand the comic book marketplace started to draw in a broader range of readers, but the change took place gradually. As late as July 1967, almost six years after *The Fantastic Four* debuted, *New York*

Times reporter Leonard Sloane, who covered the advertising industry, correctly deduced that millions of people read comic books. Yet he took potshots at the medium. Sloane referenced the way advertisers thought of the average comic book reader: as members mainly of "special audiences . . . children, servicemen and semi-adults (. . . those over 18 who may not always think at the same level as their chronological age)."[11] Whether this elitist attitude truly reflected how the adult world felt about the industry or was simply Sloane's opinion, Marvel's letter pages and the mail stacks were filled with articulate, passionate messages from educated readers from across the nation that countered the story's message.

Contrary to many other organizations and entities capitalizing on the growing youth market, comic book publishers did not have a handle on monetizing their intellectual property in the 1960s. They were unable to articulate how reader demand might translate to revenue gains to either the mainstream media or large advertisers or the advertising industry. As a result, comic book back pages were filled with strange products, and licensing agreements continued as they had in the early days of comic books rather than innovating with the times.

In the mid- to late 1960s, comics, unlike other consumer-focused magazines, still generated most of their revenue from circulation rather than advertising. Few insiders seemed to realize how significant advertising revenue could potentially be, particularly since comic books had slim profit margins. The publishers won by sheer volume, yet advertisers didn't have faith that comic book readers were their target audiences. Sloane used DC as an example, reporting that it published forty-eight titles a month and sold seven million copies. Despite that enormous figure—equating to eighty-four million comics sold annually—advertising income remained relatively flat, only increasing from $250,000 to $500,000 between 1962 and 1966. Comic book executives usually claimed that their selectivity kept the ad revenue down. However, many companies, including Marvel, decided to run small print ads for a variety of products, from novelty toys and mail-order gimmicks to hobby kits.[12] Many large corporations would not run ads in comic books, so publishers attempted to make up for the lack of direct advertising revenues by licensing the characters to other companies.

In contrast to DC, Marvel's monthly circulation hit about six million, according to Sloane. It attempted to upgrade ad revenue by launching a campaign to run ads for products targeted at older audiences, like shaving cream. Lee equated the quality of the stories and the artwork with the class its audiences expected, explaining: "We editorialize. We try to back the soldiers and try to tell the kids not to drop out of school. We stand for the good virtues."[13] The decision to intentionally target older readers had been Lee's primary concern for years. A little more than midway through the decade, his determination started to pay dividends.

If advertisers were reluctant to move into comic books, Stan would turn his efforts toward merchandising and licensing opportunities. These strategies became more significant after *Batman* debuted on television. Reportedly, DC licensed the character to ninety companies, which would pull in about $75 million in sales; some tagged it as high as $150 million.[14] As the popularity of the books grew, Lee's tasks multiplied, but Goodman was determined to keep a relatively small staff around his star chief editor/art director. Stan could see how the industry was transforming based on television's popularity and the expanding consumer culture.

Although he grew up in the film and radio era, Lee clearly understood the growing significance of television and believed that superhero sagas would be a perfect fit in that medium. In the past, Goodman had stumbled and bumbled with Marvel licensing, so it did not really surprise anyone when he basically gave away the company's animation rights. Figuring that the production part of the company should be run by someone young, he turned over that aspect to his son Charles (Chip) Goodman to use as a proving ground for the heir's eventual ascension to the top position at the family business.

Audited circulation figures revealed that Marvel comic books jumped from eighteen million in 1961 to about thirty-two million in 1965. The surge in popularity attracted television executives, who attempted to determine the company's secret appeal to young audiences. No one could put their finger on it exactly, usually pointing to the combination of the antihero themes and Lee's ability to correctly gauge the pulse of the youth market. These weren't people who had grown up reading comics, so they believed the common assessment about the base nature of the medium.

The TV execs were smart enough to understand Marvel's circulation figures and the importance of the youth market, particularly in animation. In September 1966, *Marvel Super Heroes* debuted, featuring a rotating set of stories based on the heroics of Captain America, Thor, Iron Man, Sub-Mariner, and the Hulk. Ads for the show ran in all the company's comic book titles the next month, listing the twenty stations carrying the cartoon, including big media market stations in New York City, Chicago, and Los Angeles. Later, close to fifty stations carried the show, including overseas channels in Brazil, Puerto Rico, and Venezuela.

Produced by Grantray-Lawrence Animation, the cartoon version used color photostat reproductions of the actual comic books—rather than original animation—which created a seven-minute chapter that could then be played back-to-back or chopped up and fitted into other children's television programming. In total, the company generated 195 segments for the initial syndication effort stretching from September to December 1966.

The crude method of using the comic book panels reduced the animation aspect of *Marvel Super Heroes* but did showcase the exquisite artwork of Kirby, Ditko, and the rest of Lee's talented team. In each shot, there is usually only one object animated. Sometimes it is Captain America's shield looping through the air, while other times it is the character's eyes blinking or lips moving as they speak. The *Marvel Super Heroes* theme song provided a brief overview of each character and then led into the next segment, with voices merrily singing, "The Marvel superheroes have arrived."

Hanna-Barbera Productions launched a second animated television series, *The Fantastic Four*, which first aired on ABC in the fall of 1967. The show began with a bang: a signal arching into the nighttime sky and then bursting into a vibrant "4" that called the superheroes to their New York City headquarters. The minute-long introduction took the viewer through a condensed version of the group's origin story and then showed them battling a variety of bad guys. Aimed at an audience of young viewers, the program emphasized the superstrength of the heroes and turned the villains into dangerous but somewhat campy versions of how they appeared in comic books. The writers aped some of Lee's style, showing its early infiltration into mainstream popular culture, as well as the sustained influence of Adam West's gonzo Batman.

While these many achievements might have seemed to signal better days ahead for the comic book industry, the seemingly inevitable boom-and-bust mentality continued. Although the Marvel cartoons were popular, sales nosedived in 1967 when the televised *Batman* TV show sputtered and limped through a final year. The program's demise more or less pulled the entire comic book industry down in its wake. DC remained on top, but total circulation across the industry decreased. *Spider-Man* was Marvel's highest-selling comic, but only placed fourteenth on the year-end list of top sellers.[15] Overall, Marvel did better than most of its competitors. Surprisingly, its books basically stayed even with the previous year's sales or showed slim increases. In a down year for the industry, the fact that Marvel circulation remained consistent revealed how hipness and good marketing could overcome market forces.

★   ★   ★

The many changes Stan faced in his professional life were mirrored in his life at home. He and Joan rented their teenage daughter J. C. an apartment in the city so she could study acting. They enjoyed reacquainting themselves with New York on visits and thought they should get a place there too. Stan and Joan thought the house in Hewlett Harbor seemed too big for just two people. Lee convinced the production company that bought the Spider-Man animation rights to rent him an apartment in the city so he could serve as a consultant on the series.

After a yearlong tryout, the couple were convinced they should live there full time. They moved into an apartment at Sixtieth Street, where they stayed during the week. Then, shortly thereafter, they sold the house and bought an apartment on Sixty-Third with a large terrace, which had been Joanie's primary prerequisite. After about two decades of suburban life, Lee and Joanie found themselves once again in the heart of the Big Apple.[16]

Moving into the city was a minor decision in comparison to the challenges Stan had with other family members. His popularity continued to grow among college students, both as a speaker and as de facto leader of the one hundred or so campus chapters of the Merry Marvel Marching Society fan club. The spotlight, however, caused tension with Martin Goodman. "I began to think he almost resented the success of our comics line," Lee remembered. "I felt it wouldn't displease him to see sales slip and have my confidence taken down a peg." After the many decades of working together, Stan felt that Martin viewed him as a competitor, just as much as the fledgling publishers and DC.[17] The situation became a double-edged sword: Lee was too valuable and popular for Goodman to fire, but his fame caused resentments between them. It didn't really matter if Stan was toned down or thoughtful in the many newspaper and magazine articles or interviews on the radio, his sound bites fueled the public's fascination. Goodman, regardless of how he viewed himself in light of Marvel's success, stayed out of the spotlight and rarely spoke publicly. Success bred contempt. Stan clearly enjoyed his expanded role (quickly becoming the face of the comic book industry) and it benefited Marvel, but any rise in notoriety is going to cause resentments and hurt feelings.

The national spotlight increased in the 1960s as more people grew aware (or curious) about what was happening at Marvel. One of Stan's highest-profile appearances took place on the popular *Dick Cavett Show*. Realizing that many nonreaders were tuned in—and facing a doubting Cavett, who seemed less than enthusiastic about the idea that comic books were important—Lee contextualized comics for the host, explaining that comics had become a significant part of "the age of the offbeat." In this era, Marvel superheroes specifically represented the decade (perhaps despite their powers and seeming invincibility) because they had human feelings and problems even as they were saving the world from all-powerful aliens, supervillains, and other crises. Lee told Cavett—at the time one of the nation's great promoters of both high- and lowbrow culture—that within Marvel fandom, "Our most popular heroes are the most wackiest." He singled out Hulk ("a green-skinned monster") and Spider-Man as representative of the quirky era.[18]

While Cavett and his comedian sidekick Pat McCormick poked fun at Lee and comics in general, the Marvel chief kept his cool. He discussed the heroes in relation to the era, rationalizing Spider-Man's popularity based on his status as an "anti-hero hero" who "gets sinus attacks, he gets acne, and allergy attacks while he's fighting." Prior to a commercial break, McCormick fired the kind of zinger that Stan had been fighting against his entire career. The jokester snickered, "One thing I like about those comic books is that they're easy to turn while you're sucking your thumb with the other hand."[19]

A comedian like McCormick might have been able to play the dumbed-down nature of comic books for gags on television, but Lee stood at the center of a new comic book universe—one that he cocreated with Kirby, Ditko, Romita, Shores, and the countless others whom it took to produce comic books. When Jenette Kahn, later the head of rival DC, was asked what she considered the "most significant event" in the post-1950 comic book world, she pointed to Lee, explaining:

> Comic book characters pick up the unconscious trends of the time and become the spokesmen for those trends. That's why people can identify so fully that the characters can become part of the mythology. Stan Lee's characters did that in the sixties. He picked up on anti-Establishment feelings, on alienation and self-depreciation. . . . Stan came in with characters with bad breath and acne, punkier, younger, when young people needed symbols to replace many of the things they were rejecting.[20]

Not a bad tribute from Marvel's primary competitor and rival or considering the lowbrow roots the industry fought to overcome. In a flurry of creativity over a few short years, Lee upended American popular culture and forever changed the way people looked at heroes.

While Lee fixated on art, word balloons, continuing story lines, and the countless other responsibilities he faced, Goodman searched for an exit strategy. By the late 1960s, large corporations had started to gobble each other up in a series of mergers and acquisitions. For Goodman, who had built Marvel from scratch, the wholesale corporate merger-mania provided a long-awaited opportunity to cash out. Martin could finally turn over the business to his son Chip, who had been apprenticing under his father's tutelage. Selling Marvel meant that he could walk away from the constant upheaval in magazine and comic book publishing.

At the midpoint of 1968, a budding corporate mogul and lawyer named Martin Ackerman approached Goodman about selling his entire company—both the men's magazines and the comic book division. Ackerman ran a handful of photo stores, pharmacies, and other concerns under the banner Perfect Film & Chemical Corporation. He fancied himself a major business figure, chomping away on cigars and pushing around staff and underlings, despite his diminutive stature.

In a recent deal, Ackerman had extended a $5 million loan to Curtis Publishing, under the stipulation that he serve as president. What Ackerman really wanted out of the transaction was to control the distribution firm Curtis Circulation. Buying Goodman's Magazine Management collection of periodicals and comic books would ensure Ackerman that he had the content required to distribute via Curtis, a kind of double-dipping that gave him more revenue and power within the larger publishing industry. Ackerman wanted to be known as a legendary business leader, and he viewed Marvel as an essential building block and catalyst to his ultimate aspiration.

Goodman, though wracked with internal strife over the idea of selling, ultimately demanded a cash deal to overcome his cold feet. He eventually sold the entire business to Ackerman for about $15 million. When Goodman made the sale, however, he pulled Stan aside and promised his longtime chief "warrants," which he said were like stock options. Not only would Goodman get rich, but he explained that Lee would too. "My pot of gold had arrived," Lee thought, "and I didn't even have to ask!"[21] As the deal got closer to fruition, however, Goodman not only didn't give Lee options; he never mentioned warrants again. Instead, Martin signed a deal to remain as publisher of Magazine Management, while his son Chip would serve as editorial director with the assumption he would eventually replace his father.

Ackerman and his underlings, according to Lee, "told Martin they wouldn't buy the company unless I signed a contract to stay on."[22] Ackerman saw Lee as the essential element in the purchase, but Stan didn't press Goodman for a big raise or other long-term financial gains because he trusted his longtime boss to take care of him. The three-year deal Ackerman eventually inked bumped up Lee's salary, but Stan started having lingering doubts about Goodman's backslapping and assurances.

The sale to Perfect Film called for a celebration, but Stan joined many other Marvel employees who believed they should have profited from the transaction. Goodman had a party at his home the night the deal went through. He wanted to celebrate and his wife, Jean (Stan's cousin in-law), invited Joan, who was one of her close friends. At the party, Martin pulled Stan aside, promising: "I'll see to it that you and Joanie will never have to want for anything as long as you live"[23]—another promise left unfulfilled.

Ackerman celebrated too. He bought a $1.5 million private jet and a snazzy Park Avenue apartment to conduct business. Lee continued to worry about what might have been if Goodman had fulfilled his promises. Yet he didn't press or threaten to leave Marvel, potentially at a time when he could have demanded a hefty fortune to not go running to DC.

Although Ackerman's Curtis Circulation took over Marvel's distribution, erasing the disastrous deal Goodman had been forced to sign ten years earlier, the entire industry reset somewhat as sales flattened. In response, Goodman took a heavy-handed approach with Marvel, threatening layoffs and canceling titles outright, including Lee and Ditko's beloved *Doctor Strange*. The publisher even demanded that comics drop a page (from twenty to nineteen) in an effort to save money. All the interference boiled Lee's blood and again got him thinking about quitting the business. Chip Goodman also took the insane step of shutting down the Merry Marvel Marching Society fan club, which Lee felt energized the company's most loyal readers.[24]

Once again, Lee felt trapped. He did everything in his power to build Marvel into the biggest comic book publisher in the industry, yet the sales slump and Martin's reneging on his pledge put him right back in a vulnerable position. Goodman had not come through on his promises and, as a matter of fact, began hinting at another round of mass layoffs, which Lee would have had to orchestrate. Stan yearned for a way out but couldn't figure which way to turn. "It's time I started thinking of other things," he said, considering a range of options, from writing a play or film treatment to poetry.[25] The popularity of science fiction made Hollywood seem the most logical avenue for someone with Stan's innate storytelling skills. Secretly, he dreamed of taking Kirby and artist John Buscema to Los Angeles with him where they could work on set designs or storyboards while he crafted scripts.

While Lee considered his options, the company's new owner felt its first tremors. Perfect's board of directors ousted Ackerman. The combination of pressure from running Curtis and his flamboyant, decadent spending habits were too much for the company to bear. They replaced Ackerman with Sheldon Feinberg, another aggressive young executive with a law background.

Feinberg wanted a fresh start and to distance himself from Ackerman. He led the charge to change the company's name to Cadence Industries. Next, he instituted a tightfisted campaign to reduce the company's enormous debt. No longer the captain of the ship, Goodman fell in line. He ordered Lee to publish reprints of certain comic lines so he didn't have to pay freelancers for creating new pages while Marvel attempted to weather the bleak sales outlook. Inching ever closer to the end of the decade, Feinberg and his young, bellicose team had quite a task ahead. Lee tried to keep the Marvel staffers and freelance team in high spirits, but the business side of the corporation controlled decision making.

The early 1960s hinged on creating new characters and establishing the Marvel universe as readers took notice of the revolution occurring in the industry at the hands of the perennial second-tier company. In the latter part of the decade, Lee and his crew shifted their emphasis to solidifying Marvel's standing, as well as deepening and broadening the story lines. Lee also gave some heroes their own solo titles, including Captain America, Hulk, and Iron Man.

While many publishers watched sales drop, Marvel's stayed level during the downturn. When it upped monthly production, the additional revenue staved off mass layoffs, thus keeping Lee from having to eliminate coworkers and staff members that he considered almost as close as family. While the industry reeled, at least the good cheer and hipness factor remained with Marvel. DC went through tougher times. The company was sold to Kinney National, yet another corporate conglomerate. Adding to its challenges, DC still couldn't figure out how to best its smaller competitor.

As 1968 unfolded, Lee and Marvel would get increasingly caught up in world events. No one could ignore Vietnam, campus unrest, civil rights protests, or the growing women's rights campaigns. On the *Dick Cavett Show*, Lee discussed an earlier *Thor* issue that had the Norse god criticizing college students who drop out rather than "plunge in." At the time of the interview, however, the significance of the protests had changed, as had the world in general. Lee could no longer use a superhero story to write "a good little sermon" in response. "Youth today," he told Cavett, "seem to be so much more activist, which I think is a very healthy thing."[26]

In 1968, the comic book business stood almost unrecognizable compared to the start of the decade, when *The Fantastic Four* launched a series of new villains, heroes, and monsters. All the new solo titles necessitated an increased universe of intricately woven plots and new characters to fill the superhero books. Lee feared that Cadence executives could possibly close down Marvel at any moment, yet he soldiered on, hoping that the superhero universe he created would endure the bumps and blips of the chaotic era.

Just forty-six years old, Stan trafficked in a business centered on youth culture and the whims of consumers drawn to new and exciting mediums, like television and film. He could draw hundreds of college students to a question-and-answer lecture, but inside he couldn't overcome feelings of inadequacy. His and Joan's marriage had grown more loving and resilient, and they moved back into the Big Apple, then the cultural center of the country.

Whether Stan stood on his apartment terrace picturing a wonderful future or felt wracked with doubts, the nation was changing in 1968. The year had begun with the Tet Offensive in Vietnam, included the assassinations of Martin Luther King Jr. and Bobby Kennedy, and ended with the election of Richard Nixon. Marvel, under new ownership but still under Goodman's thumb, had pulled a bit of the cultural zeitgeist from the sky and made superheroes important, yet the company struggled to maintain the momentum it had built.

The only consistency had been Stan Lee. In the future, nothing remained the same.

America's Pop Culture Ambassador

$\mathcal{W}$hat Stan Lee understood better than anyone else associated with Marvel—from his boss Martin Goodman and the Cadence executives overseeing the company to the newest assistant editor or freelance letterer—was that if the company had a spokesperson with stories as large-as-life as the Marvel superheroes, then that person could be almost as significant as the creations. Regardless of who drew, inked, or colored the comics, Lee had been the voice of Spider-Man, Thor, the Fantastic Four, and others. His writing created the sound of Marvel Comics.

When journalists attempted to experience the hubbub firsthand, Lee seized on their interest. Reporters may have expected Stan to be younger, but they recognized the enthusiastic, witty, quote-a-minute Lee had tapped directly into youth culture. When the press looked for a spokesman to contextualize Marvel's rampant success, Lee jumped at the chance. The new role not only played to his ego but also allowed him to try out some of the acting chops that he not-so-secretly harbored.

Stan also grasped the monetary and branding value of serving as the company's primary face. If the role made him essentially indispensable, then that position amounted to job security. He carried a deep aversion for unemployment or even the hint of being underutilized. With his father's humiliation a painful memory, that idea shook Lee to the core.

In addition, the spokesperson role ensured that Marvel remained in the public eye. Stan did not have to be a supergenius like Reed Richards to realize that the superhero craze would lead to an increased number of entertainment options that would build on Marvel's reputation *and* Lee's. The public reaction to the superhero characters he helped create stacked up on his desk in the form of three hundred to four hundred fan letters daily. In some sense, Lee realized, he could become a real-life "Mr. Fantastic" just by capitalizing on his natural strengths and gregarious personality.[1]

Ironically, as Lee's position expanded, he subsequently became further entrenched as a company man. He realized that his fate—as always—remained deeply entwined with Marvel. Although many comic book insiders would accuse Lee of self-aggrandizement for assuming this self-created mantle, he smartly moved in a direction that capitalized on his talents. He was never going to be an inspirational chief executive—he wasn't completely interested in the business aspects—but he could rally crowds and fans. He could just as effectively talk up comics to worried parents or curious journalists.

After spending decades toiling in virtual obscurity and chagrined when people learned of his occupation, his tables turned when Marvel found itself at the center of the cultural zeitgeist. Lee leapt at the prospect of establishing himself as a brand (within and outside Marvel).

Goodman remained the prototype business leader, keen on revenue and profit. He lacked the sense of pure creativity needed to appreciate the work of Lee, Kirby, and the Marvel bullpen, but he built a financial infrastructure that enabled them to flourish. And he continued to serve as a foil to Lee, even as Stan's power increased and Goodman's lessened. Stan may have bristled at the many financial moves, but he understood that Goodman and the Cadence management team played a critical role in the company's success.

The expansion of titles per month meant that Stan had to corral a growing team of staffers and freelancers. Titles had to hit publication deadlines. Missing the mark cost the company money in penalty fees and potential sales. The ironic aspect of Lee's concentration on marketing Marvel was that it took place after so many years. "I had to write just about everything," he recalled. "I was the editor. I was the art director. I was the head writer. So because of that, for better or worse, I had my personality stamped on those comics." It is important to remember that the front-end creation—from writing to artwork and production—was the glitzy outcome that required a great deal of behind-the-scenes effort. "I was designing covers, writing cover blurbs, writing ads, the soapbox column, the Bullpen page," Lee explained.[2]

The persona Lee fashioned—part sarcasm and large dollops of self-deprecation—created a voice that permeated Marvel. The popularity of Spider-Man, Hulk, Iron Man, and the others went beyond mere fandom to a kind of cult status and made Marvel a major cultural influence. Yet, even though it became hip, Marvel still trailed DC Comics in total sales. In 1968, for example, DC Comics published forty-seven titles with sales of approximately seventy-five million, while Marvel had twenty-two titles and fifty million (although in an August 1968 interview, Lee claimed sixty million). Even though Marvel published fewer than half the number of titles that DC did, its sales were at least two-thirds as much, making the company in some way more successful.

In countless speaking engagements and interviews, Lee continued to hone his persona. Simultaneously, he never missed a chance to recognize Marvel fans and his creative team (then numbering around thirty-five staff and freelancers). "Marvel readers must be among the most fanatical in the land," he claimed. "They ask questions, find mistakes, [and] make suggestions."[3] The letters and interaction with fans at comic industry gatherings gave him direct insight into his target demographic, from the obsessed diehards who chided Lee for every *Spider-Man* frame that left out some minor detail to the casual observers attempting to understand how comics got so popular.[4] Stan rarely shied from explaining how innovative or creative Marvel's new work (and by extension his writing) stood in comparison to past characters and publishers, particularly DC, which he constantly chided as a monument to an outdated era.

Lee sincerely believed in the educational and cultural value of comics, so his basic earnestness led to an authenticity that people accepted, particularly when delivered in the corny, self-deprecating style that he perfected. He grasped that fans wanted Marvel books to engage with real-life socioeconomic and political topics. Staying flexible and listening to fans, Stan explained: "They want a whole ethos, a philosophy, within the framework of the comic character. They seem desperate for someone to believe in. . . . I don't want to let them down."[5] In the late 1960s, Lee's willingness to have Spider-Man, Thor, and others address pertinent issues helped legitimize comic books for wider audiences.

Although Lee could be criticized for not taking a more progressive tone, given that he had the youth market at his feet, he often dropped his self-deprecating mask and spoke to readers about serious issues. In late 1968, for example, he used a "Stan's Soapbox" column to speak out against bigotry and racism, which he labeled the "deadliest social ills plaguing the world today." The kind of hatred spread during that era prompted Lee to declare that it was "totally irrational, patently insane to condemn an entire race—to despise an entire nation—to vilify an entire religion." Instead, he urged Marvelites to be tolerant.[6]

Similar thinking led Marvel to create several African American characters, including Robbie Robertson, a city editor at the *Daily Bugle* in Spider-Man. More importantly, he and Kirby cocreated Black Panther, the superhero guise of T'Challa, the prince of a mythical African country. Marvel also introduced the Falcon, another black superhero but this time an American. After debating about what to do with the Black Panther, Lee confessed to hoping that the fan mail would provide him with insight about how to proceed. In 1970, Lee claimed that he wanted to offer black heroes earlier, but "the powers-that-be" were "very cautious" and would not allow it.[7] Whether this finger wagging was aimed directly at Goodman or Cadence, Lee did not feel that he had to hold back.

In March 1970, Lee again turned to the Soapbox to lay out Marvel's policy on "moralizing." While some readers simply wanted escapism, Lee countered: "I can't see it that way." He compared a story without a message to a person without a soul. Stan explained that his visits to colleges led to "as much discussion of war and peace, civil rights, and the so-called youth rebellion as there is of our Marvel mags." All these pieces, Lee said, shape our lives. No one should run from them or think that reading comic books might insulate someone from important societal matters.[8]

★   ★   ★

Despite the attention and outpouring of fan affection bordering on cult-like devotion, Lee couldn't shake feelings of inadequacy. He continued to receive off-putting reactions from adults who worked in mainstream jobs. As a result, Stan still searched for legitimacy. No accolades seemed enough to erase those initial negative perceptions of being "just a comic book writer."

Often, when Lee faced challenges, his answer was Spider-Man. From a literary standpoint, the character tapped into 1960s existentialism—an average person who fell victim to an accident, thus transforming his life. The radio-active spider that injected its venom directly into Peter Parker's bloodstream enabled the boy to become a superhero, but the venom did not cast aside Peter's insecurities, anxieties, or basic humanity. As a matter of fact, a moment of indecision and exaggerated hubris led to the death of his beloved Uncle Ben, leaving the boy reeling. The dichotomy between arrogance and humility made the character compelling.

As a symbol of the 1960s and its collective unrest, which resulted in a kind of split personality between protest and conservatism, Spider-Man was another iteration of the figures populating books, film, and celebrity tabloids. Peter Parker occupies the same city that drove young Holden Caulfield to the brink in J. D. Salinger's *The Catcher in the Rye* (1951). Similar to Caulfield, Parker questions his place in the world. While Lee knew the character reso-nated with younger audiences, he believed that more mature readers would connect with the character as well. Stan just needed to get the superhero in front of a larger audience. The growing college-aged population gobbled up *Catcher*, just as it devoured Marvel comics.

In July 1968, in hopes of thwarting some of the criticisms he faced about being in an inferior industry, Lee launched *The Spectacular Spider-Man*, which was not only magazine-sized but black and white, like the popular under-ground comics. More than fifty pages, the magazine cost thirty-five cents, nearly triple the newsstand price of regular comic books (twelve cents).

The first issue featured a rewritten and redrawn origin story and a Lee original: "Lo, This Monster." The covers were distinctive as well. Harry Rosenbaum, an artist who did cover art for men's adventure magazines, painted an image of the hero in acrylic paint, making it deeply textured. The second issue presented a striking cover by artist John Romita that showed the Green Goblin zapping Spidey with a colorful yellow burst. The energy of the Romita cover exploded from the page, quickly becoming a fan favorite.

In a Soapbox update, Stan called the magazine "a real, glitzy, status-drenched, slick-paper publication" that readers could find "amongst the so-called 'better' magazines at your newsstand." Lee declared it "possibly Marvel's finest achievement to date," as well as a "Marvel milestone" that would go down in comic book history. The editor-in-chief saw the magazine as a chance to bridge to adult readers (featuring more mature themes/topics).

What Lee didn't anticipate is that the new adult-oriented comic seemed to occupy a no-man's land between youngsters and older readers. No amount of bluster could save it from bombing. For average fans, *The Spectacular Spider-Man* cost too much. The foray into black and white did not help either. The second issue went back to interior color, but it was too late. That second issue with the beautiful cover would be its last, though Marvel rehashed the Lee story later in 1973 in *The Amazing Spider-Man #116–118*, with revisions by writer Gerry Conway. Another story from the second issue featuring the Green Goblin would later be repurposed (as Marvel so frequently did) in *The Amazing Spider-Man Annual #9* (1973).

Although the failure delivered a blow to Lee's notions of crossing into mainstream success, the magazine didn't diminish Spider-Man's overall popularity. Nonetheless, Lee still reeled with frustrations. Since the late 1940s, he had attempted to gain legitimacy by self-publishing material for older readers or moonlighting for Goodman's adult-oriented magazines. On the outside, Lee seemed upbeat and passionate about comics and superheroes, but he had internalized the negativity, hiding deep fears about working in an industry that others deemed distasteful.

In early 1970, Kirby's contract expired around the time Goodman sold the company to Perfect Film. They had little interest in re-signing Jack for the big money he anticipated. Moreover, Goodman didn't support him. Kirby correctly gauged that it was his turn to get paid for all that he had done to build Marvel, but according to Mark Evanier, no one would talk to him or his lawyer about a new contract.[9] Eventually, Jack turned to Lee for help, incorrectly assuming that the editor had that power. Though Kirby thought Stan sandbagged him, there is no evidence that he could have swayed Goodman or the management team.

The contract impasse drove another wedge between Stan and Jack, one that, in hindsight, seemed based on misjudgment rather than malice. The irony of the relationship between Kirby and Lee is that the two are tied together forever in comic book lore, yet their complexities turned the relationship indifferent, begrudgingly cordial, sour, and even hostile.

Jack seemed to care less about the fame that came with creating successful superheroes and comic books—he was a craftsman. His desire centered on earning a living and getting treated fairly—receiving an equitable share of the money others were making off his art, ideas, and reputation. With Kirby, the feeling emerges that no matter how financially sound he might have been, the haunting recollections of his youth in the Lower East Side slums would never be far from his mind. "All of Kirby's work in the '60s was for Marvel, and he was always terrified that he would stop getting assignments," Joe Simon explained. "It was a big deal for him."[10]

Both Kirby and Simon, like Lee, had lived through the hardscrabble Great Depression, which fundamentally colored their views of work and money. According to Simon, Kirby put a lot of pressure on himself to provide for his family at least in part because his own parents had been poor. "He had to bring the money home for Roz, put food on the table for the kids."[11] Kirby's demons regarding money hovered ominously over his worldview. This kind of intimate relationship with poverty never leaves a person. Yet his $35,000 freelance salary in 1970 (about $220,000 in current buying power) allowed him to make a decent living, but one could certainly argue that he should have been making multiples more, perhaps millions.

Despite their shared history of growing up poor, for Lee, recognition was a far greater desire than the financial safety Kirby sought. Stan drew from lessons bestowed on him as a child—a mother that demanded perfection and success and the toll financial hardship had on his family. Adulation was the check Lee needed to cash.

Though forever linked as a creative duo, Stan and Jack's complex relationship suffered from different desires—one wishing for fame, the other for financial security. Thus, Kirby's frustration with Goodman's penny-pinching and reneged promises, as well as lingering exasperation with Lee, led him to reject a new contract with Marvel in 1970. Instead he boarded DC, where Carmine Infantino ran the editorial ship. Kirby was given free rein to develop a new superhero universe dubbed "The Fourth World." At DC, the artist/writer created three new titles that enabled him to tackle the biblical, existential, and science fiction machine-driven questions that were at the center of his mythical worldview.

★   ★   ★

Comic books became big business and successful across other mediums, demonstrating how central superhero narratives were in contemporary American culture. Envious of the way Superman and Batman had moved from radio to film and television, Marvel made similar plans. Historically, the emphasis had been on creating demand for comic books first. In the new era, publishing executives realized television and film would drive licensing.

For Lee and the corporate honchos in New York, the ultimate dream centered on a series of Marvel movies and television shows. Increasing audience size would establish the characters for successive generations. Wider exposure would lead to greater demand, thereby generating a catalog of profitable licensing deals.

The early *Marvel Super Heroes* animated program (produced by Grantray-Lawrence) proved that even a crudely done show would find an audience. Logic dictated, based on the ever-growing popularity of Spider-Man, that the webslinger would be next. In late 1967 and 1968, Grantray-Lawrence led production efforts, but the struggling studio went into bankruptcy. When famed animator Ralph Bakshi took over, the Spider-Man series aired on ABC and proved a hit, running until 1970.

Animation juggernaut Hanna-Barbera Productions created a Fantastic Four show for ABC (airing 1967–1970). The new program ran alongside *Spider-Man*, giving audiences an extended dose of superhero stories. Lee and Kirby's original comic books were truncated to fit into thirty-minute time slots and watered down so children could easily follow along. Considered one of the first Saturday morning educational cartoons, each episode had a segment dedicated to Mister Fantastic explaining a scientific term or concept.

Producers downplayed Kirby's ominous depiction of Doctor Doom and made Galactus less imposing, but these stylistic changes were offset to a degree by the enthusiasm of the voice actors, including film and television star Gerald Mohr voicing Reed Richards. This formula—making some characters more generic and operating within the technology boundaries (in this case, clunky animation)—seemed to hinder how production companies brought Marvel to the screen. Publicly, Lee supported the show but had little to do with it otherwise. The lack of control irritated him. He believed that if Marvel created its own programming, like Disney, its superheroes would rival Walt's famous mouse and princesses. The urge to start a production company began to gnaw at Lee.

In 1971, a *New York Times* reporter estimated that about three hundred million comic books were published annually.[12] Considering even a conservative pass-through rate equating to four others reading each comic sold, that means around 1.2 billion comic books were read at a time when the total world population stood at 3.7 billion. Despite lingering questions about their negative consequences on younger readers, comic books were a central component of mainstream culture with Lee as their pivotal figure. In the eyes of many, the name "Stan Lee" was synonymous with comics, a kind of Johnny Appleseed that toured the nation spreading joy and expounding on the importance of comic books.

In May of that year, Lee showed how comic books could be used for good in *The Amazing Spider-Man #96*. Spidey saves a young black kid who mistakenly jumps off a rooftop, as the superhero explains, "The poor guy's stoned right out of his mind." After the rescue, other characters exchange words about drug use and Spider-Man thinks: "My life as Spider-Man is probably as dangerous as any—but I'd rather face a hundred super-villains than toss it away by getting hooked on hard drugs." Peter Parker's African American friend Randy later gets into a heated exchange with Norman Osborn, explaining that blacks hate drugs the most because young people "got no hope," which makes them "easier pickin's for the pushers."

Casual readers may have regarded the anti-drug message as yet another nod to realism, but most probably didn't know Stan had received a letter asking for his help from an official at the National Institute of Mental Health, a division of the Department of Health, Education, and Welfare. The executive implored Lee to use Spidey's popularity to fight drug abuse in comic book form. Government officials believed the character's esteem among high school and college students would help them get factual information to this key demographic.

Although Lee realized that mentioning drug use would be a violation of the Comics Code, he decided to fulfill the request. Understanding the broader implications, he explained: "We can't keep our heads in the sand. . . . If this story would help one kid anywhere in the world not to try drugs or to lay off drugs one day earlier, then it's worth it rather than waiting for the code authority to give permission."[13]

Most comic book publishers and editors set internal rules about dealing with the Comics Code. Despite regulations about sex and the depiction of government officials in a bad light, the Code did not include drug abuse. Publishers could not feature werewolves or vampires, but drugs were not explicitly outlawed.

The Amazing Spider-Man #96 did not bear the Comic Code seal of approval. Stan continued the drug plot for the next two issues, revealing that Harry Osborn had a pill addiction. Parker chalks Harry's habit up to him being "so weak." Later, the younger Osborn obtains pills from a dealer (resembling a blond version of Stan Lee), who promises the pills are "just what the doctor ordered." Back at the apartment he shares with Parker, Osborn passes out after taking a handful of pills. When Peter finds him, they are interrupted by the Green Goblin, who wants to kill Spider-Man. After battling the villain above the New York high rises and apartment buildings, Spidey eventually rodeos the Goblin into seeing his hospitalized son. The trauma causes Norman to black out, which ends his villainous ways.

While government officials were happy to have Spider-Man and Lee on their side, not everyone agreed. John Goldwater, the publisher of Archie Comics and founding president of the Comics Magazine Association in 1954, publicly announced disapproval, including declaring topical use of drugs or drug abuse in comic books "still taboo."[14] Yet the far-reaching positive publicity Marvel received handcuffed Goldwater and the CMA. The organization issued no sanctions against Marvel or Lee.

In addition to bringing the Comics Code into modern times, Stan's decision to publish the *Spider-Man* issues put Marvel out ahead of DC, which had been rumored to be working on its own issues based on the same topic. Carmine Infantino, the editorial director at DC, also railed against Marvel, implying that the move should be considered potentially harmful, particularly to children.[15]

Rejecting the code enabled Lee and Marvel to push harder on other social issues and allowed them to take a stab at appealing to more college-aged readers. One method for proving the relevancy of comics focused on introducing nonwhite and ethnically diverse superheroes. In June 1972, Marvel launched *Hero for Hire*, featuring Luke Cage, a black superhero that fought crime in Harlem. Two years later, Cage became Power Man, successfully teaming up with white martial arts legend Iron Fist.

Following these pioneering efforts and after the company introduced Black Panther, using the character in a series of titles, Marvel published *Red Wolf* (1972–1973), a Native American superhero. Shortly after, when the television show *Kung Fu* (starring David Carradine) hit the air in 1972, Marvel picked up on the martial arts wave (which included the work of Bruce Lee and others using karate). The company developed *Master of Kung Fu*, featuring Asian superhero Shang-Chi, who first appeared in *Special Marvel Edition #15* (December 1973). By April 1974, the title changed to *The Hands of Shang-Chi: Master of Kung Fu* and began a long, popular run, eventually appearing in crossovers with Marvel's top superheroes.

Lee always harbored ambitions to be more than "just" a comic book writer and editor. When he was a boy, his mother showered him with praise and joked almost daily that Hollywood talent scouts would soon take him from her. He acted out scripts for artists and other writers and enjoyed the constant bustle of hustling from campus to campus as a one-man Marvel marketing machine. Most of these efforts paid dividends in terms of growing fan loyalty or spreading the comic book gospel. Sometimes, however, Lee's willingness to take chances backfired.

In early December 1971, a distinctive ad ran in the hip NYC paper *The Village Voice* announcing "Stan Lee at Carnegie Hall!" in January. For $3.50 in advance or $4.50 at the door, fans could attend the show, which promised "All Live! Music! Magic! and Myth!" The advertisement didn't feature many details, but Thor, Spider-Man, and Hulk were crammed into the image, with Spidey (in characteristically Lee style) promising: "An erudite evening of cataclysmic culture with your friendly neighborhood bullpen gang."[16] Later, the official name of the event changed to "A Marvelous Evening with Stan Lee."

Whether the evening was "marvelous" or not most likely depended on the viewer's feelings about Marvel and its band of superheroes. Most adults, particularly those reviewing the shindig for metropolitan newspapers, found the evening anything but amazing, likening it to an "employer at his own Christmas party" and "a company revue." Lee served as host and ringleader, which is an apt description, since the night devolved into a chaotic mess. There were second-rate music acts, some vague discussions of comic book arts with Romita and Buscema, and an appearance by new journalism star Tom Wolfe, who completed his white suit ensemble with an Uncle Sam top hat. Other oddities included the world's tallest man, nine-foot-eight-inch Eddie Carmel, reading a poem about the Hulk and Geoff Crozier, an Australian illusionist, performing a strange magic act.[17] The highlight for Lee was reading parts of the poem "God Woke" from the stage with his wife, Joanie, and daughter, J. C. Fans really didn't know what to make of the show and made paper airplanes to lob at the stage in mockery and frustration.

★   ★   ★

Continually trying to establish Marvel as different, Lee started calling the company the "House of Ideas," which stuck with journalists and became part of the company's cachet. If a downside existed in the surge of Marvel comics into the public consciousness, it is that Lee and his bullpen teammates had to balance between entertainment, social issues, and profitability. Stan valued the joy derived from reading comics, but he wanted them to be useful: "Hopefully I can make them enjoyable and also beneficial. . . . This is a difficult trick, but I try within the limits of my own talent."[18] Lee wanted to have it both ways— for people to read the books as entertainment but also take them seriously.

At the same time, Marvel had to sell comics, which meant that little kids and young teenagers drove a sizable chunk of the market. In 1970, Lee estimated that 60 percent of Marvel's readers were under sixteen years old. The remaining adult readership was enormous given historical numbers but kept Lee focused on the larger demographic. "We're still a business," he told an interviewer. "It doesn't do us any good to put out stuff we like if the books don't sell. . . . I would gain nothing by not doing things to reach the kids, because I would lose my job and we'd go out of business."[19]

The industry moved so quickly that Lee and his creative teams constantly fought to get issues out on time. The number of titles Marvel put out meant that everyone had to be constantly producing. So when Lee was in the office or working from home, he committed to getting content out. Roy Thomas recalls, "Stan and I were editing everything, and the writers were editing what they did, and we had a few assistant editors that didn't really have any authority. . . . That was about it."[20] However, that chaotic atmosphere made it rife for animosities to form or fester. Lee needed content out the door, and Goodman tried to maintain control over cover artwork and other little details that inevitably slowed down the process.

"Stan and Goodman were increasingly on different wavelengths as the time came near the end of their relationship," Thomas explained. "Goodman and his son, Chip, were still making those decisions at that time." According to the editor, "Chip, in that last year or less before Stan took over, was the official publisher as Martin withdrew from the business more. I don't know if Goodman was even in the office then, because I never saw him very much anyway. His office was way at the other end of the hall."[21]

In 1972, Goodman finally made good on his wish to retire, four long years after Cadence took over. He expected that his son Chip would be named the new publisher. Instead, shortly thereafter the new owners showed his son the door—so much for handshake agreements and family ties. Cadence CEO Sheldon Feinberg named Stan Marvel's publisher and president.

The new post meant that Lee would have to step down as editorial director. After some internal wrangling and indecision regarding who would replace him, Lee handed over the duties to Roy Thomas. "Now I'll be able to do things the way I want them," Lee thought, but he was wrong. Instead, he attended a dizzying succession of meetings and strategy sessions to discuss the financial status of all the company's publications, including the men's magazines. "I suddenly realized that I am doing something that millions of people can do better than I can do. The thing I enjoy doing—the creative stuff—I'm not doing anymore." This realization led Lee to give up the president position to concentrate on the publisher's duties.[22]

In the meantime, Goodman didn't stay retired for long. Angered by his son's termination, Goodman retaliated by founding Atlas Comics. He put Chip in charge and began an aggressive poaching program, even hiring away Lee's younger brother, Larry, to serve as editor. Many other Marvel freelancers and artists also left because Goodman paid more. The desertion grew so prevalent that Lee had to issue a memo reminding staffers and freelancers of

Marvel's commitment to them. Although a negative blip for Lee, the industry had changed, so Goodman's maneuverings were outdated. Atlas soon folded.

There were additional growing pains for Lee as publisher and Thomas as editor. Lee had a looser vibe with people but also was a legendary figure. "He sent them off feeling very enthused about doing something new," says writer Mark Evanier, who worked with both Lee and Kirby. "They didn't operate for him out of fear, as they did for some editors."[23] Thomas inherited a staff loyal to Lee, but they still had to churn out some forty titles a month. The production schedule remained king. "I knew I didn't have the power Stan had had as editor-in-chief, because he was right there, and I wasn't looking for that," Thomas recalled. "I wasn't threatened by anybody, and who's going to have a better rapport with Stan than I did? It was very good, most of the time, so I didn't feel that insecure."[24]

Thomas's ascension and Lee's pull toward management did shift the editorial direction, if for no other reason than that Stan wouldn't be writing full time any longer. "It was time to kind of branch out a little bit," Thomas explained. "We wanted to keep some of that Marvel magic, and at the same time, there had to be room for other art styles and other writing styles."[25] The most overt change came when Lee turned in the copy for *The Amazing Spider-Man #110*. The late 1971 issue was the last Lee wrote for the character. Writer Gerry Conway succeeded Lee, and the next books in the series would be cocreated by Conway and star artist John Romita.

While many adults looked down on Lee for writing comic books, especially early in his career, he developed a masterful style that rivals or mirrors those of contemporary novelists. Lee explained:

> Every character I write is really me, in some way or other. Even the villains. Now I'm not implying that I'm in any way a villainous person. Oh, perish forbid! But how can anyone write a believable villain without thinking, "How would I act if he (or she) were me? What would I do if I were trying to conquer the world, or jaywalk across the street? . . . What would I say if I were the one threatening Spider-Man? See what I mean? No other way to do it."[26]

Lee's distinctive voice captured the essence of his chosen medium.

Lee also understood that the meaning of success in contemporary pop culture necessitated that he embrace the burgeoning celebrity culture. If a generation of teen and college-aged readers hoped to shape him into their leader, Lee would gladly accept the mantle, becoming their gonzo king. Fashioning this image in a lecture circuit that took him around the nation, as well as within the pages of Marvel's books, Lee created a persona larger than his publisher or employer. As a result, he transformed the comic book industry.

Marvel's Multitude of Maladies

*A*lthough it might have been difficult to put downbeat words in the mouth of the company's most important promoter, the 1970s were troubling times for Lee and the company. Everyone at Marvel—including Lee, the creative teams responsible for putting out the comics, the accountants struggling to make sense of internal spending, and corporate managers determined to rein in the comics division—seemed at war with one another, desperate to counteract sagging sales.

Mirroring the national political and cultural scene, the comic book industry faced years of uncertainty, slippery footing, and ultimately an epic battle for survival. Marvel's per-comic sales plummeted, so the company attempted to offset the decrease by publishing more titles. For example, there were ten comics with "Marvel" in the title (ranging from *Mighty Marvel Western* and *Marvel Triple Action* to *Special Marvel Edition*).[1]

By January 1973, Lee oversaw annual production of some sixty-nine titles, including twenty-eight superhero books, sixteen mystery/monsters, and ten Westerns. Total sales rose, but Marvel published so many comics that it concealed internal weaknesses and industry stagnation.[2] Flooding the market had long been a Goodman trick, enhancing the overall financial picture but simultaneously increasing pressure on the creative teams.

Yet, in front of a microphone or with a reporter nearby, Lee remained positive, trumpeting Marvel's successes. Reading the Stan's Soapbox essays, no one would have guessed at the troubles. After the company replaced DC at the top, Marvel struggled to find its next objective. For some organizations, that drive to the top defines their culture. Marvel had to find a new path.

Amid the chaotic early 1970s, Stan's transition from writer, art director, and editorial lead to publisher proved jarring. In the office, he shifted from creative force to company man, a kind of conduit between the intransigent figures running the corporation at the top of the executive food chain and the chaos of the creative bullpen filled with artists and writers who—like the 1970s as a decade—wanted to buck the system.

Lee struggled to find his place in the unfamiliar corporate system, never fully understanding his fellow "suits" but also constantly worrying about the artists and writers who thumbed their noses at conformity and economic realities. He was the boss, creating an approval process for cover art and copy, while also balancing story lines and juggling workloads.[3] The operation grew too large for one person to manage everything, but the publisher role demanded his attention across business and creative functions.

Unlike his friends and protégés (many younger writers and artists drew inspiration from his work), Lee knew the intricacies of company finances. "What I do mainly is worry about the product we are turning out," Stan explained. "I'm really like an over-all executive editor."[4] Stan worked with Cadence execs on approvals for new magazines and comics, each decision having significant financial consequences since profit margins were so thin.

Even into the 1970s, Lee and other industry insiders expected the superhero craze to eventually fizzle. If Marvel faltered, the best-case scenario for Lee would send him back to his editor's desk, writing multiple books for whatever the next fad might be, again relying on freelance artists to keep the company afloat. Fear drove him to keep a relentless pace. At any given moment, Stan could be overseeing strategic editorial decisions, managing the expectations and meddling of the corporate execs, launching new magazines, or flying from college campus to campus to fulfill his marketing and lecturing roles.

★   ★   ★

Demographics worked against Marvel. Superhero popularity skyrocketed, yet sales slumped. Readers skewed younger, buying titles like *Archie Comics*, the best-selling comic of 1970 at 515,000 sold per issue versus *The Amazing Spider-Man* at about 373,000.[5] At the end of 1971, the official Audit Bureau of Circulation (ABC) stats revealed that monthly paid circulation had dropped over the preceding three years. Marvel sold about 96 million comic books in 1968, but the figure fell to 91.8 million in 1971, despite more total books on sale.[6] Over the following year and a half, the number would plummet to just over 5.8 million per month or just under 70 million annually for 1972 and 1973. In comparison, DC dipped from about 6.3 million per month in 1968 to just 4.7 million five years later.[7]

Desperate, the comic book division again pushed different fads. Marvel rushed headlong into fantasy and horror, publishing *The Tomb of Dracula*, *The*

Monster of Frankenstein, and *Man-Thing*, among others. Stan urged fans to accept the new direction in Soapbox columns, calling the new *Monster Madness* title "the most frantic, far-out, fabulously frenzied monster mag you've ever goose-pimpled over!" He implored readers to obey the first Marvel Commandment in his faux biblical exhortation: "Thou shall not miss it!"[8]

The move into horror came after the Comics Code adapted to shifting cultural norms initiated by Lee's efforts to publish the Spider-Man issue tackling drug use. In 1972, Code regulators officially eliminated restrictions prohibiting horror comics, particularly those featuring werewolves and vampires.

Cadence executives did not really understand the comic book division, so they had difficulty comprehending fluctuating sales numbers or stemming the decline. Historically, comics garnered a high pass-through rate, which meant that for every comic purchased, about three to five additional people read it—a large number of people with no reason to purchase a copy.

Yet no one expected the numbers in 1971 to set a trend. Sales told a different story: Marvel would not reach 1971's monthly circulation (7.4 million copies) threshold again until 1987. Cadence reacted by tightening editorial control but giving Roy Thomas the chance to move in new directions. For example, in 1970 he convinced Stan to support the sword-wielding *Conan the Barbarian* series, and it became a hit.

In late 1972, Lee's role took on a strategic component when he became publisher of Marvel Comics. "I was deciding what books we would publish and what to concentrate on," Stan explained. "I worked with the editor and oversaw most of what we did."[9] With Thomas as new editor-in-chief, they charted a fresh course but had to do so during a period of weak sales. Roy attempted to move comics into new genres less reliant on traditional superheroes, including books featuring Man-Thing, Ghost Rider, and Dracula. The 1970s seemed a topsy-turvy mix of innovative new characters trying to survive in a down market, while Lee mixed his publisher duties with promotions and marketing. Stan's personal celebrity skyrocketed, but decreasing sales rocked Cadence.

Merchandising and licensing had been an afterthought during the Goodman era. That changed with Cadence but caused schisms between the leadership and the creative staff. Critics of Cadence argued that the company wanted to turn Marvel into a marketing machine, essentially ignoring superheroes and comic books unless they had licensing potential. But licensing did provide some financial relief. In 1973 and 1974, the push resulted in deals with toy companies and publishers, including Columbia Records, Hostess, Mattel, and others.[10] The merchandising deals grew important as circulation waned.

While editor, Lee had been somewhat distanced from licensing, often bemused when he saw a new Spider-Man or Hulk tchotchke. As publisher, though, Lee served as conduit between Marvel and potential advertisers, particularly with young salesmen who grew up reading his comics. Lee's celebrity made him an attraction at trade shows and other venues where Cadence leaders hobnobbed with corporate execs. Thus, Lee's importance actually increased as circulation plummeted. Even meager advertising and licensing money meant something when comic books were priced at twenty cents a copy.

Despite the downturn, the public Lee—the face of Marvel—remained as joyful as ever. Legions of fans flocked to see him as he spread the gospel of comic books. In mid-1975, the *Chicago Tribune* dubbed Stan "the creator of a modern mythology" and, more blatantly, "the Homer of pop culture" (a moniker originally used by Princeton students in 1966)[11]—heady stuff for a guy frequently self-conscious about his profession.

Stan increased his lectures, averaging one per week, and went on trips to Europe, Canada, and Latin America.[12] In the first two months of 1975, for example, Lee spoke at seven colleges, from Sir George Williams College in Montreal to Augustana College in Rock Island, Illinois. During that stretch, he also did numerous radio shows, interviewed with print journalists, appeared on a Canadian television show, and served as featured speaker at Creation Con in New York City.[13] As Lee's celebrity ballooned, his appearance schedule had to be booked a year in advance.

Attempting to fill Stan's shoes as editor-in-chief turned into a nightmare. As sales bottomed out, Cadence managers increasingly meddled. The friction proved too much for a series of editors that began with Thomas (who left in 1974, contending that he would rather write than worry about climbing corporate ladders and managing staffers) and ended with the promotion of Jim Shooter in 1978.

The revolving door shook up the creative staff and spooked freelancers. For example, when Archie Goodwin took over in 1976, he had broad authority since many people considered him one of the best writers in the business. Yet Goodwin only lasted until late 1977. The strain of Cadence president Jim Galton's cutbacks simply took the joy out of the work.

Yet while both Thomas and Goodwin bristled at the business and strategy aspects of the job, both played an instrumental role in reversing plummeting sales. Before Thomas left, he met with a little-known filmmaker named George Lucas—about to debut a science fiction movie called *Star Wars*. Thomas urged Lee to okay a comic book version, but Stan was lukewarm about the film and denied the request. Thomas, however, continued to pester Lee, finally telling him that Alec Guinness was one of the film's stars. The esteemed actor's role changed Lee's mind.[14] With Stan's approval, Roy worked out a deal with Lucas. The director cut a sweetheart deal with Marvel because he wanted to use the comic book as a lead-in to the film.[15]

When *Star Wars* eventually took the world by storm, Marvel basked in the demand. The six-issue adaptation, written by Thomas (even though Goodwin was then editor), sold more than one million copies per issue—the first comic to hit that figure in decades. When *Star Wars* became a monthly title, Goodwin took over, gladly vacating the editor's chair.[16] Some insiders, particularly Jim Shooter, felt that the *Star Wars* adaptation saved Marvel from certain bankruptcy.

★   ★   ★

Although Lee relinquished his editorial duties, he never really stopped producing. He couldn't help coming up with new ideas, carrying tiny two-by-three-inch spiral notepads that fit in his front shirt pocket. Stan jotted down thoughts in his scratchy, left-handed scrawl. He also kept a tape recorder bedside for middle-of-the-night inspiration.

As publisher, Stan exerted additional control over publications other than comic books. Whether it was his own feelings of inadequacy or the fear that the superhero craze might end, Lee poured great effort into the magazines. He had always believed working on magazines was a step or two above comic books.

Looking at magazines, it seemed Lee had a difficult time coping with the success and influence of *Mad*. Perhaps he envied publisher William Gaines's ability to get out of comics after the Wertham mess or maybe it was that he knew and worked with so many of the writers and artists that gave *Mad* its unique voice, such as Al Jaffee, Wally Wood, and others. Stan attempted to duplicate the zany humor and satirical wit in *Crazy* (October 1973), basically using the staff that produced Marvel comics. Although it seemed new, *Crazy* had been one of Goodman's attempts to mimic *Mad* in the early 1950s—a venture that failed.

Crazy featured the "Stan Lee presents" banner. Marv Wolfman, who wrote *The Tomb of Dracula* comic and later created African American vampire hunter Blade, edited the magazine. Thomas served as executive editor. *Crazy* featured a mix of black-and-white illustrations and photographs, the latter captioned with puns and quips. Like *Mad*, the magazine took on popular culture topics, parodying films and fads, like the James Bond thriller *Live and Let Die*, which they changed to *Live and Let Spy*, featuring Agent 07-11 and drawings of scantily clad females. In addition to overseeing the magazine, Lee contributed, often adding one-liners to campy photos, like on the campus streaking craze. A photo of two officers carrying a naked man by the shoulders and feet: "Wait'll they find out I'm the Dean!"[17] The magazine also lampooned current events—taking swipes at race relations, President Richard M. Nixon, and even Marvel, including a recurring feature on the challenges of Teen Hulk.

Growing up, Lee loved newspaper comic strips. His contemporary, *Peanuts* creator Charles Schulz, had inspired a generation of artists to establish their own comic strip franchises. Over the years, Stan created heartwarming strips like *Mrs. Lyon's Cubs* and *Willy Lumpkin*, but they never caught on as he hoped. In October 1976, Lee teamed up with freelance artist Frank Springer to create *The Virtue of Vera Valiant*, a campy strip that satirized TV soap operas. The title character earned her moniker because of her role in an odd love triangle—head over heels for a man whose wife fell asleep on their honeymoon and never woke up.

After time in the Army during World War II and getting an art school education, Springer launched a career in comics but did not start with Marvel until the mid-1960s. Soon, though, like many of Lee's favored freelancers, the artist worked on several different characters, honing each style under Lee's guidance. Eventually, Springer took over *Spider-Man*, drawing the book from the mid-1970s into the 1980s. When he worked with Lee in the mid-1960s, Springer remembered Stan's unwavering influence: "At that time, Stan Lee was the guy you talked to about whether you did this book or not and how you did it and whether you did the next one."[18]

Vera Valiant featured Lee's madcap sass and dry wit. The strip opened on a macabre note, when Vera's brother Herbert botches a suicide attempt. Vera learns that he is flunking out of correspondence school and is distraught. When she turns to Winthrop, the dashing CPA, for comfort, she exclaims, "What will become of Herbert . . . if he's expelled from correspondence school?" Winthrop deadpans: "We won't let that happen! The world needs podiatrists!" Later, when the accountant confronts the deadbeat sibling, he explains, "She's always dreamed of a podiatrist in the family!"[19] In three panels per day and eight on Sundays, Lee and Springer presented a zany adventure featuring podiatry, space alien real estate agents, and a wife suffering from "sleeping disease" for fourteen years.

Much closer to his heart, Lee debuted a syndicated *Spider-Man* comic strip in 1977. *Spider-Man* sold millions of comic books a year, giving Marvel and Lee a great deal of cachet with newspaper editors. Initially appearing in about one hundred newspapers nationwide, the *Spider-Man* strip—penned by Lee and drawn by John Romita—gave newspapers a shot at attracting a younger readership. By mid-1978, about four hundred newspapers ran the strip, which gave Lee entrée to a new demographic of adult readers.

Stan had some difficulty adjusting to the constraints of a daily strip. How could a writer used to filling page after page boil a plot to three frames? According to Lee, the first box had to recap, the next box moved the story ahead, while the last ended with a cliffhanger.[20] Steadily, he adapted to the minimalist style, growing to love the daily cartoon. The work gave him interaction with readers who wrote detailed letters about plot points, character motivations, and other topics. He enjoyed the interaction: "At least I know someone's out there—someone's really reading the stuff!"[21]

Spider-Man's popularity led the Tribune syndicate to launch a full frontal assault—in response asking DC to create a Justice League of America strip, dubbed *The World's Greatest Superheroes*. Veteran *Superman* writer Martin Pasko served as writer. George Tuska, who had previously been the writer/artist on the *Buck Rogers* strip over its last decade (1959–1967), as well as drawing *Iron Man* and *The Hulk* for Marvel, penciled, and Julius Schwartz edited. Initially the strip centered on the adventures of all the JLA heroes, including Wonder Woman, Batman, and the Flash, but eventually focused primarily on Superman. The competing cartoon strip also found its way into newspapers nationwide.[22]

Discussing his creative process for Spidey, Stan explained: "I first try to come up with a unique human interest angle, or a compelling sub-plot, some problem for Peter that seems virtually unsolvable. And one of the best ways to do that is to say 'What If?'"[23] Lee liked to load in complicated plots and obstacles, creating momentum toward a conclusion: "The formula for the Spidey strip should be to treat it almost like a soap opera."[24] Lee faced an inherent challenge: entice younger readers to daily comic strips, while simultaneously keeping older readers engaged.

Publishing books was in Cadence's wheelhouse. Stan had long hoped to pen a novel and dabbled in self-publishing, so the idea of a series of Marvel books (really more like edited collections with brief new introductory essays) appealed to his vanity and ever-pressing time constraints. The venerable New York publisher Simon and Schuster brought out a series titled Marvel Fireside Books, written or edited by Lee and comprising short essays and reprints of superhero and villain origin stories. Between 1974 and the end of 1979, some eleven Fireside Books were published, ranging from the launch of *Origins of Marvel Comics* (September 1974) to *Marvel's Greatest Superhero Battles* (November 1978).

Readers delighted in the Fireside series, granting them a relatively inexpensive and convenient method for digging into the birth of the Marvel universe (*Origins* cost $11.95 in cloth, while a book on Silver Surfer ran $7.95). Until that time, they had to rely on reprint issues or tracking down old issues. According to a Marvel internal document from May 1978, the series sold well, listing the following sales figures: *Origins* (160,000 sold), *Son of Origins of Marvel Comics* (100,000), *Bring on the Bad Guys: Origins of Marvel Comics Villains* (70,000), and 1978's *How to Draw Comics the Marvel Way*, coauthored with artist John Buscema (20,000 hardcover alone).[25] Lee worked on these titles in the evenings, after he finished the *Spider-Man* and *Vera Valiant* newspaper work and other writing commitments.[26]

In 1977, Lee edited one of the titles in the Fireside series, *The Superhero Women*, a book of essays and reprints featuring female heroines and villains, including Wasp, Red Sonja, and Medusa. Lee explained that Marvel never had a policy of creating books for male versus female readers and instead crafted stories "savored by anyone who loves fantasy and adventure."[27] Yet, over the years, Stan had attempted to build readership for female superheroes, scrutinizing subsequent sales figures. His interest seemed to go beyond circulation numbers to a genuine concern for attracting female readers.

Although not considered revolutionary when it came to writing and publishing books for female readers, Lee had great success writing *Millie the Model* and its many offshoots, as well as other titles aimed at girls and young women. He and Kirby had made the Fantastic Four's Susan Storm an interesting character with real power, not just a weak sidekick or stereotypical girlfriend figure (despite some cringe-worthy dialogue in the initial issues). Still, female superheroes were not always progressive. Wasp, for example, spent a great deal of time in early *Avengers* comics gushing over the dreamy Thor and basically flirting with all the male stars, despite her seemingly serious relationship with Henry Pym.

Lee's response to criticisms about Marvel not publishing enough heroines was tied to sales figures. Circulation numbers held final authority. Books that didn't sell could not take up a valuable spot on the limited roster.

The Fireside books were one aspect of the Cadence strategy, but the company also pursued another book lineup designed to entice younger readers, such as *The Mighty Marvel Superheroes Fun Book* (1976) and *Marvel Mazes to Drive You Mad* (1978). Also included were a series of coloring books, activity pads, and even a Marvel cookbook, along with calendars that booksellers could use to entice readers. Marvel even constructed special sales racks designed specifically for its books and collections. The 1977 display featured a three-sided color riser card designed by Lee. The launch of the Spider-Man and Hulk books were timed to the release of the live-action television series featuring the Marvel heroes.[28]

Lee's writing schedule while publisher juggled the Fireside books, approving merchandise and advertising copy, and the comic books themselves. In addition, he wrote a "Publisher's Perspective" column each month for Cadence's *Celebrity* magazine and continued to author Soapbox essays. As outside production companies worked on the live-action adaptations, Lee also contributed as "consulting editor or associate producer," mainly to "read all those scripts and give opinions."[29]

Other projects were outside the Marvel universe. In 1979, *Stan Lee Presents The Best of the Worst* came out. An odd conglomeration of illustrations, pithy facts, and Lee's irreverent humor, *Best of the Worst* drew from Stan's earlier work on Goodman's humor magazines. In *Best of the Worst*, for example, Lee identified Australian William Gold as "The Worst Writer"; Gold wrote fifteen books over eighteen years but only sold one article to a Canberra newspaper, earning a whopping fifty cents. Lee's primary contribution was a sentence after the narrative, joking: "Probably after lengthy negotiations."[30]

Although relinquishing the editor-in-chief position, Stan still spread himself thin. Yet, from another perspective, he enjoyed the freedom. Like other celebrities, Lee had to maximize his efforts at monetizing his fame. He explained: "People feel comic books make millions and millions of dollars, but there are many years when the companies have literally lost money. . . . It's not a case of everybody's pocketing millions and just trampling on the poor artists and writers."[31] Given the freedom to take on additional work outside Marvel, Stan jumped at the chance.

★ ★ ★

The animation work that kicked off in the late 1960s and came together in the early 1970s continued throughout the decade. In 1978, *The New Fantastic Four* appeared. Both Lee and Thomas wrote scripts. However, the show served a more dubious role as well—the final nail in the coffin of the Lee-Kirby relationship and the King's days at Marvel. Although Lee had been able to lure Kirby back to Marvel in 1975, the artist had an uneasy relationship with management and still held a grudge against Stan for numerous slights (some real and many imagined). According to Kirby biographer Mark Evanier, "He was sick of the business" and wanted out, if only he could think of a different way to earn a living.[32]

Perhaps the magic had ended for Stan and Jack or maybe the King couldn't stomach any additional snubs. His final stint at Marvel seemed doomed from the start. He decided against renewing his contract, which would have limited his rights of ownership to past work under copyright and failed to address other issues he had with management. Instead, in 1978, he accepted an offer to be an artist for the *Fantastic Four* series. First with Hanna-Barbera, then with the DePatie-Freleng studio, which ultimately made the FF show, Kirby found deeply respectful colleagues, bosses that cared for him, and enough money to get him out of comics.

Jack and Stan had a notoriously rocky relationship, but their combined successes enabled them to cover over the animosity with a patchwork of excuses. Once the final schism occurred, though, they would never fully mend the break. They ignored the issues that caused the fallout, getting along well enough on the FF animated series that they actually teamed up on *Silver Surfer*, a graphic novel version released in 1978.

Kirby spent his later years blaming Stan for the problems he had with Marvel executives and others, just as he had insinuated that Lee squealed on him and Simon when they were moonlighting for DC in 1941. It is not difficult to imagine Kirby nursing that wound for more than thirty years. Though loving and kind to those around him, his fans, and his family, the King had a long memory when it came to perceived professional slights. The feeling of being a permanent outsider was always front and center—believing his art was underappreciated—even as he was universally acknowledged as the comic book world's greatest artist.

Certainly Kirby could be cantankerous, but he had another side rarely highlighted: quarrels with artistic partners and subsequent feuds or mini-feuds. Of course, Jack and Stan had both devotees and critics over their long careers. Some insiders with little or no skin in Kirby's long-term reputation, however, have weighed in on the topic. George Kashdan, a longtime DC writer and editor, explained, "Kirby always had fallouts with friends." He remembered, "Once, we were having lunch together, and he talked about his falling out with Joe Simon."[33] Kirby and Simon were polite in later years but disagreed about Captain America's origin and who deserved more credit. Later, Jack unleashed on Stan, essentially attempting to diminish or eliminate him completely from the creative process. In other instances, Kirby gave himself sole credit for the *entire* Marvel universe.

Kirby's Hollywood efforts seemed rejuvenating. He worked with young, admiring artists and received a salary and benefits commensurate with his status as the industry's titan. Jack later hooked up with Ruby-Spears Productions, enabling him to work on the animated *Thundarr the Barbarian* (1980–1981). They loved his work and gave him the producer title, which he cherished.[34]

Where Marvel could have used more Lee-Kirby magic was in live-action programming. Reporters salivated in 1975 when Lee announced a *Spider-Man* movie was eminent, though one wire service didn't take comic books or Lee all that seriously, calling him "the man behind Spidey and a horde of other weirdos found in Marvel Comics." Later, the writer dubbed comics "flaky" and filled with "kinky dialogue." Lee, always working to expand the idea that comic books crossed age boundaries, told the reporter: "The books combine humor for college kids with action and adventure for the little ones." Despite the publicity and media response, however, the proposed *Spider-Man* flick never materialized.[35]

In 1977, when *Spider-Man* debuted as a live-action television series, Lee was horrified. "It was so juvenile. Spider-Man had no personality and no humor," Stan explained. "It was one-dimensional." Film technology didn't yet exist to make superheroes larger-than-life. No matter the character, they just seemed like an actor in tights. Lee found the adaptations bland—far less sophisticated than the comics themselves.[36]

Live-action *Spider-Man* worked well, though, in "Spidey Super Stories" on the PBS children's television program *The Electric Company*. Designed to help kids learn to read (dancer Danny Seagren donned the iconic costume), the short skits first aired in the 1974–1975 season, making the program a "must-see" for youngsters who couldn't get enough of the superhero. The writing mimicked Lee's style, but Spider-Man never actually spoke. His speech appeared in word balloons, getting children to practice reading as they watched the text.

Most stories on *The Electric Company* were silly romps. The show's mainstay actors (such as Morgan Freeman and Luis Avalos) played a variety of odd villains and supporting characters, as well as narrating the action. Running about a dozen skits each season for three years, a typical encounter has Spidey battling the Birthday Bandit. The villain speaks in a rhyming, singsong voice ("that foe of fun and festivity"), wearing a playfully colored suit adorned with a cummerbund and top hat, but also steals from children's birthday parties. After a cake-smashing episode and some fisticuffs that gets cake smeared on Spider-Man's costume, the hero fights off the villain, eventually snaring the bandit in a web and thus saving the day. Keeping with the Lee playfulness, the final panel is a drawing of Spidey at a laundromat covered with a blanket while sitting in a chair, waiting for his costume to wash. The skit theme song ends with a brassy horn section. The singer wails: "Nobody knows who you are . . ."

★   ★   ★

As 1979 drew to a close, Marvel had its internal woes splashed publicly in the pages of the *New York Times*. Utilizing anonymous interviews and insider perspectives, writer N. R. Kleinfield revealed the comic book division as a dysfunctional outfit that pitted editors against writers and artists against management. The days of Lee's Merry Marvel Bullpen and the singsong nicknames seemed like a distant past.

Editor Jim Shooter was the target, labeled "power-thirsty." Shooter, who began his comic book career with DC at the precocious age of thirteen, was either loved or hated by Marvel staffers. His critics accused the imposing writer/editor of having an ego larger than his six-foot-eight-inch frame. A group of Marvel employees were jealous, feeling someone with more seniority should have become editor.

Other unnamed company executives were considered "more interested in coining money from licensing deals than they are in the superheroes." Thomas sided with the creative teams, calling Marvel both "callous" and "inhuman."[37] The article also revealed deep mistrust between the comic book editorial team and management. The creatives wanted to focus on craft, while corporate leaders demanded profits. The age-old battle between inspiration and capitalism roared on.

Lee was lauded in the article but also came under some fire. Kleinfield called Stan a "creative genius" made famous by "inventing heroes" with realistic lives. But an anonymous writer painted a portrait of sour grapes at Marvel HQ, chiding Lee because he "wants to be like Walt Disney" and viewed comic books as "sort of beneath him."[38] The article was a harbinger of general softness in a comic book market squeezed by television and a smaller buying pool. Baby boomers were aging out of the medium. Other longtime fans thought that the comics simply weren't as good as they had been in previous years.

In response, DC Comics and Marvel both cut monthly titles (Marvel from more than forty down to thirty-two). The move made sense from a business perspective, since the companies made more money via licensing deals than comics. But Stan understood the new in-house licensing division ruffled feathers. "It used to be that the only artists in the place were drawing the strips," he explained. "Now we have artists who have to draw box tops."[39] The nightmare scenario for comic book purists had come true—Spider-Man lunchboxes, action figures, and bath towels grew more essential to Marvel than the comic books that ran the superhero stories.

The entire industry seemed less stable. Prior to the cutbacks, the market leaders published dozens of new titles, attempting to grow revenue. In 1979, Marvel's operating income was a measly $1.5 million after sales that exceeded $23 million.[40] Given this tight financial pinch, Lee's Hollywood dealmaking held endless potential but was also an enormous question mark: *if* Marvel could deliver a hit or expand licensing. The traditional notion that comic books drove merchandising was flipped on its head. Clearly, the big two of Marvel and DC were licensing agencies first because that drove revenue.

Depending on one's perspective, the end of the 1970s could be viewed as a complete downer or a new era for Stan. On one hand, as Marvel publisher, he earned over $150,000 a year and created steady additional income from college lectures and television projects. Fans mobbed Stan at comic book conventions. He received thunderous applause from college audiences, students packing tightly around him, just to inch a little closer to the man who created their heroes. In their minds, Lee fundamentally created the central narrative of their young lives. These were heady experiences for a person who had toiled in comics for decades without much adulation or even respect.

Despite his personal success, though, Stan still chafed at the notion he was stuck in comics. He really wanted to make a splash in Hollywood. Lee explained to a reporter: "I would have liked to make movies, to be a director or a screenwriter, to have a job like Norm Lear or Freddie Silverman. I'd like to be doing what I'm doing here, but in a bigger arena."[41] Although a celebrity and out-and-out hero to fans globally, Stan couldn't shake the notion that he could be doing more.

As Lee searched for additional outlets for his superheroes, the effort increasingly brought him to Hollywood, the great American dream factory. As he envisioned the next phase of his career, he looked west to California's golden shores.

· *12* ·

Hollywood

*W*hether the Lone Ranger cry of "Hi-Yo, Silver! Away!" or the sound of air rushing by as Superman flew through the skies, the early history of television is entwined with superheroes. While comics could take readers inside the mind in ways that film couldn't, something about actually seeing the live-action hero gave fans a different thrill.

The popularity of televised superheroes often caused boom and bust cycles in comics that usually had little to do with quality. The volatility would drive most people batty. Both the *Superman* and *Batman* television shows caused sales to surge in the 1950s and late 1960s. Looking at the television landscape, Marvel executives wondered why they couldn't replicate these successes in the 1970s, particularly given Marvel's standing as industry leader.

Jim Galton planned to capitalize on Marvel's victory by establishing a stronger Hollywood foothold. He also hoped to use television as proof for film studios that superheroes could carry movies. These moves would potentially drive large profits and offset the cyclical nature of print.

Searching for new ways to attract audiences, Stan did what others had done for a century: look to the golden shores of California. In his late fifties, Lee hoped to reinvigorate his career, as he had a decade earlier when he launched the college lecture tours. Galton and Lee put together various strategies, including the notion that Marvel buy a Hollywood production studio outright. When television networks showed interest in Marvel's superheroes in animation and live-action programming, Galton sent Stan to Los Angeles to plot the course.

Lee was in an odd position in Hollywood. He was already a big name, which made it difficult (if not impossible) for him to learn the business from the ground up. Lee had the mighty Marvel content, which opened doors but

147

simultaneously raised expectations on the part of his bosses that the path to success would be smooth. Lee was also used to calling the shots, but Hollywood simply didn't work that way. Stan had to attempt to win over skeptical television executives.

Yet the winds of change seemed to help. In addition to Marvel's ascension to the top of the comic book world and Lee's pervasive influence on popular culture, science fiction and fantasy films and television shows were wildly popular. On the small screen, *The Six Million Dollar Man* (1974–1978) proved that audiences would respond to a superhero-like lead. Steve Austin (actor Lee Majors) developed into a pop culture phenomenon, spawning comic books (featuring artwork by Lee's friends Howard Chaykin and Neal Adams), albums, and action figures. The spinoff *The Bionic Woman* (1976–1978) , featuring Jaime Sommers (actress Lindsay Wagner), expanded the cyborg adventures. Her popularity also meant a merchandise line, ranging from action figures and a board game to lunchboxes (a must-have item for elementary school kids).

The late 1960s had paved the way for superhero and science fiction narratives. In 1968, for example, the films *2001: A Space Odyssey* and *Planet of the Apes* thrilled audiences, generating strong box office returns. These films reinforced a new style of storytelling. Later, a film like *Logan's Run* (1976) demonstrated how science fiction could be enhanced by technology and special effects. In 1977, George Lucas's *Star Wars* showed the world the genre's vitality. After all, didn't Luke Skywalker seem like a futuristic version of Spider-Man, an outsider who must deal with possessing extraordinary powers? And Darth Vader's similarities to Dr. Doom were clear.

A year later, the mighty *Superman* (actor Christopher Reeve) flew into theaters, touting the use of special effects to blow the audience's mind. These films proved that technology improvements could power plots and characters. Special effects were finally catching up with the imaginations of writers and artists, opening doors for science fiction and fantasy on large and small screens. The time was ripe for comic book characters to make the transition.

Lee crisscrossed the nation, attempting to keep his fingers on the comic book division while increasingly focused on Hollywood. Los Angeles was "Nirvana," a celestial utopia enabling him to launch a new path without discarding his accomplishments.[1] The trepidation of leaving New York City got swept away in the excitement about the work and sheer magnificence of the West Coast—warm breezes blowing off the Pacific Ocean and hidden hillside enclaves deep in thick woods.

★   ★   ★

The transition from print to television seemed natural in a world increasingly dominated by images and movement. Lee called the Marvel style "a very cinematic approach" marrying dialogue and art.[2] A quick flurry of activity in Los Angeles that resulted in deals with several networks and production companies gave Marvel a lift. However, some of the resulting television shows were weak or didn't catch on with viewers. Hollywood studio executives underestimated the importance of Lee's style and voice in making Marvel superheroes iconic. Honestly, they felt that they could get it right themselves, since they were the experts, or could at least duplicate what they viewed as pithy banter and human pathos. For movie and television leaders, Marvel characters were "properties" or simply sellable content. The soul of the superheroes and what turned fans into rabid consumers of Marvel content often died in the translation.

On the surface, many of Lee's characters seemed a natural fit for live-action television. However, one of the least likely—the green-skinned, raging behemoth Hulk—made it to the screen. Former Mr. Universe Lou Ferrigno, a six-foot-five-inch, 285-pound mass of ripping muscles, played the lead, while veteran television actor Bill Bixby was the mild-mannered alter ego, physician/scientist David Banner (series writers changed his first name from Lee's original "Bruce"). Critics boiled the show's popularity down to a mix of women gawking at Ferrigno and the dramatic sensibilities aimed at adults, rather than the teen audience. Producer Ken Johnson explained the tone, "We've tried to make it an adult show that kids are allowed to watch." The writers purposely played down the "camp" elements, instead keeping the show "as straight and honest as possible."[3] Lee appreciated the adaptation, honing in on the acting and story changes that allowed the superhero to appeal to older audiences.

Some commentators speculated that adult viewers took pleasure in seeing a character go into a rage when angered. Lee identified with the cathartic impulse: "We'd all like to 'Hulk out' sometimes. Nobody pushed the Hulk around, and people can identify with that."[4] The show was a surprise hit in the United States but even bigger in the United Kingdom (reaching number one). In the 1970s, perhaps the British had a stronger desire to "Hulk out" than Americans. Ultimately, it would be Marvel's most successful live-action property for several decades.

CBS also brought Spider-Man, Doctor Strange (changed to "Dr. Strange"), and Captain America to the small screen. *The Amazing Spider-Man* starred Nicholas Hammond as Peter Parker and ran off and on for two seasons. *Dr. Strange*, featuring Peter Hooten, debuted as a television film/pilot in September 1978, while *Captain America* also came out as a TV film, starring Reb Brown.

Spider-Man had the greatest success in terms of viewers. Demonstrating how pervasive Spidey was in popular culture, the pilot earned a 30 share, the network's highest rating for 1978. CBS execs worried, though, that the movie did not do well enough in the critical eighteen- to forty-nine-year-old demographic. They hedged their bet, only picking up a five-episode run (April and May 1978). The series debut also did well; it was the network's top program for the week and placed in the top ten overall. Although *Spider-Man* eventually placed in the top twenty for the season, network officials deemed it a failure because it didn't attract an older audience.

While young fans (including this author) tuned in, Stan hated it, saying the show "looked silly . . . juvenile, comic-booky." He also had run-ins with producer Daniel R. Goodman, urging that the series should be aimed at adults. "Spider-Man was a TV series for a while, and it was terrible. Just dreadful. It had no personality. No humor. None of the ingredients it should have had."[5] In a bind, CBS ordered seven new episodes but aired them in mishmash fashion, usually up against ratings juggernauts on competing networks. New producer Lionel Siegel took control, downplaying Spidey's superpowers and adding a love interest. Despite solid ratings, CBS axed the show, fearing audiences might typecast the network since it had multiple superhero programs.

While Stan really hated the *Spider-Man* series, he barely contained himself regarding the *Captain America* movie, declaring it an "abomination."[6] Each show that aired deviated from the overriding concept that Lee and his cocreators established when they constructed the Marvel universe. Shuttling between the coasts, Stan shuddered at the way Hollywood fiddled with the superheroes. Many West Coast execs held the same elitist notions that he had encountered most of his career—superheroes were for kids and adults wouldn't respond without heavy doses of romantic intrigue added. The countless issues sold over the previous two decades and the billions of times Marvel comic books had been read and passed around by a generation and a half of readers could not convince Hollywood that superheroes would succeed. The studio heads and creative teams wanted to meet Stan, but few actually wanted to make deals.

The Soapbox columns and college lectures continued to promote Marvel, but Stan's over-the-top approach didn't translate well in Los Angeles. He habitually announced deals and hyped the production work, which did drive anticipation but certainly backfired when projects got mired in preproduction or fizzled completely. This was a different world for Stan. He answered to many people and had to fight to establish himself as an independent entity apart from his famous characters. All the while, he had to separate the genuine meetings from the ones that took place simply because a director or producer who had grown up reading Marvel books wanted to meet a childhood hero.

Marvel's West Coast operation gradually landed some deals. They worked with NBC to bring the Silver Surfer graphic novel Stan and Jack did to television. Then ABC made noise about developing a Spider-Woman show. Universal also optioned twelve characters, including Thor, Daredevil, and Doctor Strange. But as the announcements piled up, they also served as a kind of ball and chain. Deal after deal fell through. Stan was deflated: "We've been working with other production companies, and I have to go along with what they want to do. It's just taking forever to come up with a story that everyone agrees on."[7]

Lee's perpetual challenge: he could not close the type of deal that would make him and Marvel major players in Hollywood. Stan always drew media attention, followed by a plethora of potential projects, but few were green lit. Even worse, some that were bombed because the script had problems, the production company did not grasp the appeal, or the technology did not exist to make the hero seem heroic or powerful enough. "There is no way of ever predicting which the networks will buy and which they won't," Lee lamented.[8]

The never-ending meetings also hampered Lee's time. "Out here, you get an idea for a movie and years later, you're still trying to get it on the screen," he explained. "Here, it is much more big business. There are contracts and negotiations and turnarounds. I find that a little frustrating, because I like to move fast and write fast."[9] Movie studios and publishing companies approached him about writing scripts and novels, he claimed, but he couldn't find the "few months off" necessary to take the gigs. Life in LA seemed a kind of vicious cycle of meetings, negotiations, deals, and waiting around. Stan spent more time talking about creativity than producing anything creative.

★　★　★

Despite general frustrations with Hollywood, Stan did want to physically move with Joan to LA. In 1978, the Warner Bros. *Superman* film thrilled audiences, boosted when influential critic Roger Ebert gave the movie a strong review. *Superman* earned $300 million in its initial release. The hit movie, combined with the popularity of *The Incredible Hulk*, made the time ripe for additional superhero programming. Stan convinced the corporate hierarchy to establish an office on the West Coast.

In a May 1979 letter to his friend and eminent French New Wave filmmaker Alain Resnais, Lee wrote about his "love" for Los Angeles and hope he might "be able to infiltrate into the TV and movie business." Stan acknowledged an imminent deal with Lee Kramer, a producer and the manager/

boyfriend of popular singer and actress Olivia Newton-John, to make a big-budget Silver Surfer movie.[10]

Stan spent most of the year in Hollywood, dreaming of the permanent move. "The fact was that I had fallen in love with L.A. during my many trips," he explained.[11] But Lee hadn't fully convinced Joanie. Later, she warmed to the idea, chiefly after their apartment in New York was robbed. All of her jewelry and other valuables were stolen. Lee called it "the most depressing and distressing thing imaginable." They viewed Hollywood as a fresh start. Stan attempted a brave face, joking in the letter to Alain and his wife, Flo: "Lock up your jewelry!"[12]

By July 1979, Lee's plans to go west picked up steam. Attempting to adapt the Marvel Method to movies, he dictated the plot for a film into a tape machine about a witch that only killed bad guys, called *The Night of the Witch*. Independent filmmaker Lloyd Kaufman (who would later score big with the cult film *The Toxic Avenger*) transcribed the tapes, working the material into a full script. Kaufman had met Lee earlier while a Marvel-obsessed student at Yale University. The young man later cofounded Troma Entertainment, a low-budget studio that mixed comedy, screwball antics, and horror into reasonably successful midnight movies. *The Night of the Witch* got picked up for a meager $500 but never went into development.[13] Later, they put together another Lee idea, *The Man Who Talked to God*, and pitched it to Resnais, but the director did not option the treatment.

Despite his legendary status as cocreator of iconic superheroes, Lee was actually just a fledgling scriptwriter. He didn't have time to write full scripts himself, which put him at the mercy of other writers who crafted treatments based on his ideas. In the early 1970s, he had teamed with Resnais to option a couple of scripts, but in the intervening years, none of the project were made. The collaborative process fit his frenetic style, but what emerged did not capture Lee's Marvel-like voice. It seemed as if Stan were overly committed to the Marvel Method. He couldn't find partners to fulfill his vision the way he had with Kirby and Ditko.

When Lee finally convinced his Cadence bosses that he needed to be in California full time, he opened a little shop in the San Fernando Valley. Marvel Productions was in a little flat building at 4610 Van Nuys Boulevard in Sherman Oaks. Lee described it as a "mini-Pentagon built around a lush garden atrium."[14] In true Marvel spirit, Stan established an aggressive pace, attempting to live up to the "Excelsior" sign hanging on the office door. A lifelong New Yorker, Lee relished the LA sunshine, frequently venturing into the atrium to work—quite a difference from often cold, gray New York City.

A handful of executives with experience in television and film joined Lee. David H. DePatie, an animation veteran who had worked on Dr. Seuss specials and won an Academy Award for a Pink Panther short, served as president of Marvel Productions. DePatie brought along Lee Gunther as vice president of production. When Marvel announced the studio's formation, it noted the group had already started several animated and live-action projects, including commercials for Oscar Mayer and Owens-Corning.[15]

Stan yearned to land a blockbuster film deal, but his primary task centered on expanding the Marvel universe and following up on opportunities, like commercials and new licensing agreements. Under Cadence's new management structure, Lee added the formal title of "vice president, creative affairs" to his publisher role. The rather nebulous title fit Lee's vague duties.

Galton discussed the interconnectedness, how the studio would "contribute to the success of our licensees, our wholesalers, our advertisers." He recognized that the "future for Marvel has never looked better," particularly given "all the benefits to be reaped from the formation."[16] Lee's marching orders included pursuing numerous projects, while also continuing to champion Marvel in person and in the media.

Lee wasn't scoring the kind of projects he felt Marvel deserved, but others were taking notice. *Time* magazine speculated that Stan was "chiefly responsible" for turning television into "one big electronic comic book." The magazine ventured that CBS had so many comic book shows on air, its name could be changed to "Comic Book Supplier."[17] The hype outpaced the quality, though. The live-action programs—outside of *Hulk*—gave Lee headaches.

Originally Marvel Productions was established to focus on animation, particularly with DePatie at the helm. Saturday morning cartoons seemed to be the best fit. Lee offered "ability, the capability, the know-how and the dependability," while DePatie's credentials helped overcome lingering network hesitation.[18] In the early 1980s, Marvel Productions teamed with other producers, particularly on non-Marvel projects. For example, the popular *Meatballs and Spaghetti* ran in the CBS Saturday morning cartoon block. The show centered on the escapades of a married singing duo that wandered the country in a mobile home. The network also picked up *Dungeons and Dragons*, a Marvel production based on the popular dice role-playing game that swept the nation.[19]

Stan expanded his work as script consultant and narrator on the animated shows *Spider-Man* and *Hulk*. Fans loved hearing Lee's voice, but he found the experience frustrating because he couldn't edit what he said based on timing. Still, he tried to "make the bits of narration sound like my own style."[20]

While the ups and downs of the entertainment industry bedeviled Lee, he found success in merchandising and licensing. While not the most glamorous aspect of his Hollywood years, these deals were essential in amplifying the brand. Creating tie-in opportunities pushed the characters into the consumer psyche, while also giving Stan opportunities to discuss his favorite cause—the benefits of comic books in literacy education.

At corporate speaking events, Lee unleashed demographic information to get companies interested in merchandising deals. He revealed the nation's 225 million comics appealed to young people ranging from six to seventeen years old (about 40 percent girls and 60 percent boys). Lee boasted that 92 percent of the youngsters in this age bracket read comic books and that six in ten were from middle- and upper-income families. While Stan spoke, the company hired actors to dress up as Marvel superheroes to get the audience fired up. Marvel also offered up actors (for a rental fee) in superhero costumes at mall openings, parades, conventions, and state and county fairs.[21]

The attempt to lure female readers led to the introduction of She-Hulk, followed by the Dazzler, and plans for additional superheroines. The first issue of the *Savage She-Hulk #1* (February 1980) sold 250,000 copies. Lee told a reporter, "We've always wanted to do books about females," yet admitted that profits drove editorial decisions, saying, "But for years, we were never able to make any of our female characters sell well."[22] Yet, like other attempts at female superheroes, *She-Hulk* only lasted two years, ending its run in February 1982.

★　★　★

By the mid- to late 1980s, Lee had completely distanced himself from the day-to-day events back in New York, despite several fancy titles, like "vice president of creative affairs for Marvel Productions," that made it seem like he was still in the loop. Actually, Michael Z. Hobson, Cadence vice president in charge of publishing, took over most of Lee's publisher responsibilities. He barely even read the comics: "Sometimes they stack up so high, I only have a chance to flip through them."[23] Instead, Stan worked on scripts and treatments, kept an eye on animated productions, and shepherded prospective deals.

Lee never backed off his role as Marvel's full-time spokesman, though he did up his speaking fee to $3,000 to give colleges *less* incentive to book him.[24] When efforts in Hollywood forced him off the college lecture circuit, he upped attendance at big-ticket events, like comic conventions, as well as on television and radio. The influx of cable television channels and expanding radio industry extended Lee's reach. For talk show hosts and radio deejays, he was a stellar guest. Stan offered great sound bites, as well as tried-and-true, seemingly timeless stories about the superhero origins. He made each host or caller feel as if they were the first to ever ask him which superhero he liked best or if he had a favorite comic book issue.

In a 1984 radio interview, Stan boasted that comics were "far bigger than they've ever been," citing Marvel's role in creating "a fan following for comic books, that never existed twenty or thirty years ago."[25] He also noted the connection between the collecting craze, the rise of independent comic book shops, and the intense fandom Marvel had created.

While Lee entertained fans that called in with questions about changes in Spider-Man's costume and the value of old comics, the episode also revealed why there were angry with him about the superhero origins. In the fast pace of television and radio programming, hosts and interviewers took shortcuts. For example, they might label Stan the "creator of such characters as . . ." without attributing cocreator status or mentioning Kirby or other artists. Interviewers did not understand the context, but should Stan have spoken up to correct the error? At times he did but not consistently. From an interviewee's perspective, correcting an interviewer breaks the flow of the interview, potentially leading to an awkward situation. However, not mentioning the artist/cocreators generated animosity among die-hard fans. Lee constantly balanced an on-air role that mixed spokesperson, provocateur, pitchman, historian, and actor. In doing so, he may have sacrificed truth (or the full truth) for the sake of showmanship and entertainment.

In 1986, Lee wrote a long essay called "Spidey and Me" for an anthology of his *Spider-Man* newspaper strips: *The Best of Spider-Man*. The piece describes the character, revisits the origin story, and serves like a mini-autobiography. Stan admitted his own ideas slipped into the strip: "I feel that it's as difficult for writers to keep their own personal convictions out of what they write as it is for people in general to keep their personal thoughts . . . out of what they say in conversation."[26] Lee explained that each character "is really me. . . . I'm every single one of them . . . [but] Spider-Man is practically my autobiography."[27]

During these years, Stan dedicated three days a week—Saturday, Sunday, and Wednesday—to writing projects, leaving the other days for business meetings and strategy sessions. Just as in New York, he wrote outside, covering his word processor with a cardboard contraption of his own devising, so the glare didn't blind him or melt the various moving parts. Stan still kept up his seven-day-a-week schedule, feeling that the move west "served to keep the creative juices flowing." In an environment where everyone is dedicated to creativity, "I find myself 'thinking story' almost twenty-four hours a day."[28]

In November 1986, Cadence Industries sold Marvel for $46 million to New World Pictures, a film production company and distributor that wanted to pair its TV and film efforts with Marvel characters. Harry Sloan, one of the partners who had purchased New World from director Roger Corman and his brother for $16.5 million three years earlier, told everyone who would listen that he believed the Marvel purchase would turn the company into a "mini-Disney."[29] Marvel employees may have loved hearing this goal, but Disney grew through film and merchandising, not publishing. Becoming "mini-Disney" could be viewed as ominous for comic book staffers.

New World leaders, including chief executive Robert Rehme, welcomed Stan, relocating him to a fancy office at its Westwood headquarters. Several members of the board of directors asked for his autograph for themselves or their children. It seemed Stan finally would get the admiration he earned through his dedication, as well as creative control over television and film.[30] At the same time, though, there were conflicting reports that Rehme didn't really know Marvel from DC or the comic book business in general, confusing the two publishers (and their respective superheroes) when discussing the purchase with New World employees. Supposedly, when Rehme realized that New World bought Spider-Man, not Superman, he yelled: "Holy sh*t. We gotta stop this. Cannon has the Spider-Man movie."[31] Rehme didn't know the characters or read the comic books, but he did push to pursue new ideas.

New World quickly sought to use superheroes in attention-grabbing ways, especially Spider-Man. The webslinger would be turned into a 9,522-cubic-foot helium balloon for Macy's Thanksgiving Day Parade (cost: $300,000). Officials estimated that about eighty million viewers would see the televised parade annually, with two million in person. Next, company marketers decided to bring the character to life in the summer of 1987, having Spidey marry longtime sweetheart Mary Jane Watson at home plate in Shea Stadium before a sellout crowd of fifty-five thousand on hand to watch the world champion New York Mets.[32]

Lee played justice of the peace presiding over the wedding. The event parlayed Stan's celebrity and rewarded him for coming up with the idea in the daily newspaper strip (also replicated in the comic books). New World launched a branding campaign, getting Lee on *Good Morning America* with popular newscasters Maria Shriver and Forrest Sawyer and coverage on *Entertainment Tonight*. Countless newspapers picked up on the buzz. Stan served as the human stand-in for the iconic superhero for the many reporters who wanted to chat about the event.

Despite many public relations successes and Marvel's profitability, its new parent wasn't in a strong position. New World limped on a financial shoestring. The Black Monday stock market collapse in 1987 and the lackluster performance of its big-budget films left New World deep in debt and exceedingly vulnerable in an age of corporate raiders who liked to buy up struggling companies and profit off the juiciest pieces of the carcass. Stan's star fell internally—the precarious financial picture meant the studio couldn't wait on him to sign deals. A New World insider reported: "Stan's not in the loop, because he's not a player; he's not a partner. He wasn't a vote. But he was like a pit bull. He just didn't want to walk away."[33]

Marvel was under the wrong parent company at the wrong time. The full story that later emerged would reveal a series of financial manipulations, leading to New World putting Marvel up for sale. But Stan again had a key role. The buyers demanded he stay on board. Eventually, Ronald O. Perelman, one of the biggest sharks in the capitalist seas, won the bid, putting up $82.5 million via an intricate series of shell corporations under his control.

Celebrating fifty years as a Marvel employee in 1989, Stan once more had a new boss and faced professional chaos. Yet he responded with his emblematic mix of resolve and enthusiasm. His trump card remained—he symbolized the Marvel universe for generations of fans. Lee was Marvel, no matter who actually owned the company, just as he became the father of superheroes to generations of readers and viewers, regardless of how the characters were actually created.

• 13 •

Turmoil

$\mathscr{I}$n 1989, Ronald and Nancy Reagan prepared to return to civilian life after eight long years in the White House. *60 Minutes* reporter Mike Wallace interviewed them just days before they returned to their California ranch. After discussion of Reagan's legacy and their marriage, Wallace turned to an unrelated topic—the president as a "regular" person.

Wallace probed: "You read the comics in the morning?"

The president discussed his morning routine, explaining he first turned to the comics and then read the "serious stuff." Reagan listed *Spider-Man* as his favorite.[1] Although his critics may have joked that *Spider-Man* was as much as Reagan could handle intellectually, Stan felt gratified. The leader of the free world started his day reading his words!

Reagan's admission symbolized how influential the character, Marvel Comics, and Stan had become. When the world found out that the president was a *Spider-Man* fan, Lee had just turned sixty-six years old, but his exuberance matched that of someone half his age.

The tribute from the president was a high point in a rather tumultuous era for Marvel and Lee, facing a roller coaster of highs and lows that would rock the icon and the company he helped immortalize. The challenges, from the public's changing tastes in popular culture to a global financial meltdown, ultimately involved the federal government and an international manhunt. Despite the difficulties, Stan kept fighting, later emerging more popular than even he could have imagined.

At this point, however, his legacy hung in the balance. He would never give up the battle to bolster his position as the godfather of superheroes.

★   ★   ★

In the 1980s, Philadelphia native Ronald O. Perelman was considered a business leader with a Midas touch. In an era accentuated by financial intrigue, leveraged buyouts, and hostile takeovers, Perelman waged corporate warfare in high-stakes chess matches with hundreds of millions of dollars in the balance. When New World put Marvel on the chopping block, Perelman offered $82.5 million through MacAndrews & Forbes, a shell company he owned. While the deal maker was the public face (and investing $10.5 million of his own money), Chase Manhattan Bank secured most of the debt, a typical arrangement in the go-go capitalist takeover era.

Purchasing Marvel—including iconic superhero characters and licensing rights—for less than $100 million seemed like a steal to many observers. "It is a mini-Disney in terms of intellectual property," Perelman explained. "We are now in the business of the creation and marketing of characters."[2]

Marvel's sales in 1990 eclipsed $70 million, with an addition $11 million from licensing, though profits rang in at a relatively meager $5.4 million. That figure, however, was an improvement considering two years before it had been $2.4 million.[3] Some eighty companies licensed Marvel characters. New deals were linked to emerging technology, such as superhero-based video games and television and movie productions distributed via VHS. Perelman's goal was a Marvel initial public offering (IPO), which could generate countless millions.

The mogul hoped to turn Marvel into the next Disney, thus creating a legacy virtually unmatched in the entertainment business. Critics, however, saw the hype as a way to inflate the IPO. Certainly, Perelman's primary interest fixed on making money, not reading *Spider-Man* comic books. In the quest to emulate Disney, the company needed a strong film division, which led to the creation of Marvel Films.

Bill Bevins, Perelman's top manager and former chief financial officer at Turner Broadcasting, was tapped to run Marvel and named Lee as head of Marvel Films. Bevins also tripled Stan's salary. The move obviously pleased Lee, particularly after being marginalized by the Hollywood sharks at New World. In his eyes, Stan believed he had been underpaid over the years, still nursing the wound from Goodman's snub.

The raise caught Lee off guard, causing Stan to wonder if he had misheard his new boss. When he told Joanie that evening, he realized that it was a mistake, and the two tried to figure out what Bevins might have actually muttered. A couple weeks later, however, Joanie checked the mail, finding Stan's paycheck. She ripped it open, saw the amount, and nearly fell over. Indeed, his salary had been tripled. Nothing but kind words emanated from Stan. More importantly, he thought the raise signaled that Bevins wanted to build Marvel into an entity that could compete with any entertainment company in the world.

Lee's future looked bright with the power to oversee Marvel's film and television expansion. He had viewed Marvel as a Disney-like empire long before his new bosses, wondering if Perelman had the cachet to make it work. Stan had never felt comfortable with the staff at New World. Perelman, ever on the prowl, would exact a bit of revenge several months later. He bought New World when the company continued to slip. Now Lee had a larger playground to operate in as he attempted to build Marvel's live-action and animation businesses.

★   ★   ★

Lee's long relationship with Spider-Man never waned. Over the years, whenever Spider-Man would jump back on the pop culture radar, Stan was there with a story or sound bite. Many fans believed Spider-Man had become the most popular superhero in the world, displacing DC's invincible strongman in the red cape and the scowling guy in the black mask.

Proof came in August 1990, when Marvel released Todd McFarlane's *Spider-Man #1*, a stylized reboot, with several colorful covers, almost demanding media attention. The mixture of national exposure and cover variants vaulted it to the best-selling comic in history (2.85 million copies). McFarlane focused on Spider-Man's visual identity: "to break people of reading a comic book the way they've been used to for the last twenty years."[4] In other words, he launched a new conversation around Spider-Man, just as Stan had done at the dawn of the Marvel universe.

Lee hoped that the renewed attention would lead to a Spider-Man film. In the early 1990s, though, other superhero projects were there first. Stan regularly served as a story consultant for Marvel-related media, like the 1990 NBC television film *The Death of the Incredible Hulk* (again starring Ferrigno and Bixby). Although years had passed since the original series aired, the show's popularity increased as fans looked back at it nostalgically. They saw magic in the Bixby/Ferrigno team, particularly the former's tortured, loner persona.[5]

In 1994, Lee edited *The Ultimate Spider-Man*, a collection of short stories by well-known comic book writers and illustrators. Stan's introduction gave hints about the character's birth: "No one at Marvel expected Spidey to become a cultural icon. . . . At that time, he was just one of many, many characters that were being continuously hatched, published, abandoned, and forgotten if they didn't catch on."[6] Rather than disappoint fans and journalists who asked about Spider-Man's origins and expected a triumphant story, Lee admitted he "cooked up" the version after seeing a spider on the window.[7]

Still applying different versions of his own narrative, Lee constantly alternated between downplaying his efforts as cocreator and a more boisterous tone understood (at least partially) as tongue-in-cheek.

This type of lighthearted (yet also personal) banter between Lee and readers had been developed over decades. The consistent patter had a hefty upside: a resultant bond of trust. Whether Lee's story about seeing the spider at his desk on the fourteenth floor of the Empire State Building had even a shimmer of truth or was an utter falsehood, readers lapped it up. They believed in "Stan the Man," regardless of criticism from hardcore fanboys or some comic book historians. The fans came from all over; for example, eminent novelist John Updike instigated a stir when he wrote a letter to the editor of the *Boston Globe* for cancelling the *Spider-Man* newspaper strip (the paper later rescinded). In response, Lee sent Updike a Spidey sweatshirt for his wife and a framed, autographed copy of the strip—another satisfied fan.[8]

The centerpiece of *The Ultimate Spider-Man* was Lee's novella that revised and expanded the character's origin. Uncle Ben and Aunt May are further explored and humanized. Lee's playfulness is on display in the piece—Aunt May whacks a spider while cleaning, exclaiming: "I just can't stand spiders, that's all. Disgusting creatures." She looks at the tiny dead arachnid to make sure it is "good and squished."[9]

Lee's new version revealed how he and later Marvel writers might expand or revise an origin story over time. Stan situated the infamous radioactive spider in Dr. Octopus's lab at Empire State University, infusing the creature with thoughts and feelings. The spider subsequently caused Ock to trigger a nuclear explosion, then delivered the bite that transformed Peter Parker. The accident created Spider-Man and also fused Dr. Octopus's metallic arms. Spider-Man ultimately defeated the villain, but Uncle Ben still dies. Stan even modified the famous ending phrase: "that with great power . . . comes great responsibility."[10]

The Ultimate Spider-Man collection also played a key part in Lee's myth-making. The biography section didn't mention Kirby or Ditko but stressed Stan's role: "Hundreds of legendary characters, such as Spider-Man, the Incredible Hulk, the Fantastic Four, Iron Man, Daredevil, and Dr. Strange, all grew out of his fertile imagination."[11] Certainly, the bio is a form of publicity, but these kinds of winner-take-all statements alienated comic book "true believers" who worshipped at the altar of Ditko and Kirby. From Stan's perspective, he could claim that he didn't write the bio, but as editor, the proverbial buck stopped with him. Still, a careful reader may also notice the book's dedication: "To Steve Ditko, who was there at the beginning."[12]

★   ★   ★

Perelman took Marvel public. As part of the public relations campaign, an actor dressed as Spider-Man appeared on the floor of the New York Stock Exchange, waving and shaking hands with traders. The IPO enabled Perelman to pull money from company coffers as investors purchased shares (totaling $82 million). He poured $50 million back into his parent companies, essentially guaranteeing himself a 500 percent return on his initial investment and a 60 percent stake in Marvel.[13]

Wall Street values momentum. Perelman fed the beast with news of director James Cameron (after the successes of *The Terminator* and *Aliens*) writing and directing a Spider-Man film (launching a friendship with Stan). The stock price more than doubled, trading at $35 per share by the end of 1993 when the company reported revenues of $415 million and earnings at $56 million. On paper, Perelman's stake in Marvel reached $2.7 billion.[14]

Financially, Marvel's future looked promising, but there were looming cracks in the foundation. Perelman gambled in purchasing trading card company Fleer in mid-1992 for $286 million, a shaking moment in professional sports. Then Marvel gave toy maker Toy Biz, which specialized in action figures, a royalty-free license in exchange for a 46 percent stake in the New York–based company (led by Ike Perlmutter and Avi Arid).

Simultaneously, the comic book industry was about to enter a tail spin as the collector craze came to a halt. The 1989 *Batman* film (starring Michael Keaton) and the 1992 *Death of Superman* comic book (six million copies sold) had reinvigorated sales, but that mania fizzled. Marvel was vulnerable despite the successes, particularly since Perelman concentrated on profits over reinvesting in product development. In 1995, Marvel reported its first loss under Perelman, losing $48 million, despite sales of $829 million. Debt swelled to about $600 million, which caused Marvel's investment banks to place the company on watch, essentially cutting off funds for new ventures, like a much-needed Internet division.

Perelman had issued a number of junk bonds to continue the acquisition spree. Fellow corporate raider Carl Icahn (even wealthier than Perelman) viewed Marvel as ripe for a hostile takeover. He purchased about $40 million in bonds. Eventually, when Marvel had trouble paying its debts, Perelman offered to grant $350 million in exchange for more shares, but Icahn, who then owned 25 percent of the company, refused the deal. Suddenly, despite the downturn in the comic book market, two of America's richest men launched a financial war, and Marvel's future hung in the balance. Though Icahn seemed to want to save Marvel, few believed that he wouldn't just buy it and then later sell it off piecemeal.[15]

On December 27, 1996, a day prior to Lee's seventy-fourth birthday, Perelman took his final step, plunging Marvel into bankruptcy in a last-ditch effort to thwart Icahn's takeover. "The news release was short and not so sweet," said former Marvel executive Shirrel Rhoades. "It sent ripples of fear throughout the comics industry."[16] The two sides swapped reorganization plans, neither acceptable. Ironically, the publishing division held Marvel afloat. Trading cards drained the budget, and many advertising and licensing deals evaporated.

In February 1997, the bankruptcy court granted Icahn control. Four months later, he won over the board of directors, enabling him to oust Perelman. Estimates place Perelman's profit under his ownership years at $200 to $400 million. While Icahn named a management team, diminutive Toy Biz—led by Perlmutter and Arad—jumped into the negotiations. They wanted to protect their no-royalty license agreement since more than half their toys were based on Marvel characters.

In December 1997, Marvel's fate fell to trustee John J. Gibbons, appointed by Delaware US District Court Judge Roderick McKelvie. Perlmutter and Arad brought together a group of investors to make a $400 million offer to purchase Marvel outright. Over Icahn's objections, Judge McKelvie approved the counterproposal. The newly merged company owed creditors a portion of the debt and offered equity claims.[17] Arad had convinced many of the debt holders that Marvel's future as a film company warranted the gamble. His impassioned overture would prove prophetic.

★ ★ ★

Lee played good company soldier during the chaos. The bankruptcy didn't affect Stan, really, beyond a few producers getting cold feet due to the financial instability.[18] Lee continued working, focusing on several animated programs so that the writers understood Marvel standards for character development and plot. "I spend most of my time in the office working on movies, television shows, and animation," Lee said.[19]

The bankruptcy battle rocked Marvel but had little personal consequence for Stan. He was too valuable a property to be discarded, no matter who ultimately won control. "I stay out of all that business stuff because my area of concern is the creative ends of things," he explained.[20] And the company saw a payoff for Lee's supervision of the production line: *Spider-Man*, *X-Men*, and *The Incredible Hulk* drew a growing audience as part of the children's television lineup: "Our shows generally do very well. . . . That's the most important thing as far as I'm concerned."[21]

Although frequently overlooked, Stan's efforts to build the animation division greatly expanded Marvel's fan base. But the lifelong film buff still hoped for a movie deal. Slowly, it seemed as if Stan's wish would become a reality. The Spider-Man film got caught up in legal wrangling and ownership disputes, but the *X-Men* and *Hulk* moved closer to production.

Surprisingly, one of Marvel's lesser-known supporting characters—vampire hunter Blade (created by Marv Wolfman and artist Gene Colan)—was its first breakout movie. Released in summer 1998 to mixed critical reviews, fans flocked to see Wesley Snipes in the title role. After opening strong in the US, the movie eventually brought in $70 million domestically and $131 million worldwide. Although Stan's brief cameo ended up on the cutting-room floor, *Blade* proved his long-standing opinion that Marvel characters would do well on-screen.

Although in his seventies (past retirement age for most people), Lee focused on innovations that changed the industry and licensing, including video games, books on CD-ROM, and the burgeoning Internet. For example, Stan answered fan questions on an AOL home page in the late 1990s. He didn't understand how the web worked but realized its vast potential.

As the decade closed, Stan's aspirations for bringing Marvel superheroes to life on film or television had either happened or appeared on the near horizon. Yet Marvel trod on shaky ground. The company's core superheroes were among the most well-known properties in the world, but the various corporate conglomerates that acquired it couldn't seem to formulate a winning strategy. Only Toy Biz's Perlmutter and Arid seemed to grasp how to turn Marvel superheroes into cash, capitalizing first on licensing and later parlaying that stake into buying the company.

Historically, few writers, musicians, artists, or other creative icons remained relevant as they reached Stan's age. Though time seemed against him in the 1990s, he refused to retire, presuming if he stopped, it might sap his will to live. Plus, Stan had a magic elixir—the constant buzz around him at comic conventions, at media opportunities, and with other celebrities. It wasn't that Lee simply didn't want to stop—he genuinely couldn't.

★   ★   ★

Stan Lee Media! The name had a certain gravitas and was recognizable. But who could have imagined that Stan would launch an Internet company?

The January 1999 news caught the world's attention as journalists rushed to cover the story. The marriage of the world's most exciting storytelling channel and the world's most interesting storyteller seemed to promise surefire success. Little did reporters and eager fans know that Stan's new venture was doomed from the start!

Lee was smitten with new business partner (and Hollywood gadfly) Peter F. Paul. The entrepreneur had some big wins—launching a nonprofit with legendary screen star Jimmy Stewart and orchestrating several high-profile fund-raising campaigns. Paul had successfully boosted heartthrob Fabio's career and displayed a knack for making rich and powerful friends, even President Bill Clinton and wife Hillary. But Paul also had a shady past, despite his reinvention as an impresario in LA. Stan Lee Media marketing pieces dubbed Paul a "new media producer," touting his past experience as founder of Digicon Entertainment, which had created a Marilyn Monroe artificially intelligent/virtual reality animation with Sony.[22]

The explosion of interest in the Internet gave Stan yet another opportunity to show that he could master new media, even at seventy-six years old. "When Peter Paul suggested we start an Internet company, the only thing I really knew about the web was that it was going to be the biggest force for entertainment and communications that the world has ever known. So, naturally, I was excited about getting involved in it," Lee explained.[23] Paul estimated that Stan's name alone accounted for about $30 million in brand value. While the new company could not use the superheroes that Lee created or cocreated—Marvel owned the copyrights—Paul hoped the old master could launch an entirely new superhero universe (that they owned).

The idea of competing with Marvel—and challenging his critics—fueled Stan, who believed he could create a new superhero universe from scratch. At the same time, his long career with Marvel seemed to be ending. He had felt slighted in his most recent contract negotiations, despite ultimately being named "chairman emeritus." Stan chafed at the notion he was little more than a figurehead after a lifetime of service. He also felt hurt and angry that he had to grovel with new Marvel head Ike Perlmutter. Lee found Perlmutter's initial contract insulting: it reduced his previous lifetime contract to a two-year deal at "exactly half what I had been earning." Lee wondered whether the ghost of Martin Goodman might have been guiding the new Marvel leadership team.[24]

Ultimately, Marvel executives realized Lee's value as the spiritual head of comic books and were unwilling to risk a public relations nightmare if Stan went off to DC or another publisher. Attorney Arthur Lieberman negotiated the final deal that gave Lee a raise (to more than $800,000 annually for life) and $125,000 a year for the *Spider-Man* newspaper strip. More importantly, the contract included a $500,000 annual pension for Joanie and a 10 percent stake in future Marvel film and TV profits.[25] Stan also had a clause that permitted him to work on outside projects, regardless of publisher or organization.

With his own shop, Lee could take shots at Marvel, declaring that in contrast, Stan Lee Media would produce online superheroes: "edgy, high-concept, and surprising."[26] He and Paul had visions of partnering with online production firms, creating web pages and virtual comic books, launching interactive games, and offering web-based classes with the comic book legend.

Stan Lee Media was headquartered twenty miles outside LA on Ventura Boulevard in Encino, one in a sea of nondescript office buildings. The flash came in its gaudy marketing campaign, filled with glossy press kits in bright, brassy colors, hyping Lee and his successes. The propaganda was a way to attract investors for a potential IPO (the path to wealth for web companies during the dot-com era). Nothing seemed over the top, with media materials exclaiming Stan "exerted more influence over the comicbook industry than anyone in history" and "more than 2 billion of his comicbooks have been published in 75 countries and in 25 languages."[27] The centerpiece was www .stanlee.net, a hub for new characters and products.

Lee's earnestness and enthusiasm spilled out in interviews and profiles. On NPR, Stan called web-based comics "really miniature movies. We have actors reading the roles. There are no dialog balloons."[28] The idea of creating a new superhero universe intrigued investors and excited fans. If Stan and Peter had one advantage, it was that they moved online quickly. A reporter explained Paul's vision: trading on Lee's past accomplishments to create "a Stan who could be offered up piecemeal to fans and eager licensing partners from the virtual balcony of a new House of Old Ideas built on the fluid foundation of the Internet."[29]

In August 1999, Paul and investment banker Stan Medley concocted a reverse merger with Boulder Capital Opportunities. The new publicly traded entity would be listed as Stan Lee Media (symbol SLEE). As creative lead and chairman, Lee received stock options (more than six million shares), as did Paul and other executives. The options had little initial value but promised to make them extraordinarily wealthy (Lee's annual salary was $272,500). In its first year on the top floor of the Encino building (also HQ for Paul's other shadowy businesses), the company grew to 150 employees.

The flagship franchise was *The 7th Portal*, featuring a superhero team battling villains traveling to Earth through a hidden gateway. Stan took a hands-on approach, according to Buzz Dixon, former VP of creative affairs. Initially, Lee focused on six or seven projects, writing outlines and character sketches. "Everything I saw had Stan's creative imprint on it," Dixon said. While Lee and a new bullpen of writers and artists worked through a multitude of ideas, company officials explained what was really for sale—Stan Lee: "The fact is that Stan is a recognized brand in the global marketplace."[30] No idea seemed too outlandish; Paul and the team also considered starting a Lee clothing line based on his catchphrases and others they might trademark. Interviewers noted that Lee routinely reported to work each morning in his black convertible Mercedes E320 around 9:30 and often stayed until 8 p.m.[31]

On February 29, 2000, *The 7th Portal* debuted at a star-studded gala Paul orchestrated at Raleigh Studios in North Carolina. Television personality Dick Clark hosted the bash, with performances by Jerry Lee Lewis, Ray Charles, and Chaka Khan. Three months later, SLM announced a deal with Paramount Parks to develop a 3-D ride based on the *7th Portal* franchise for its twelve million annual visitors.

The company had brand recognition but not enough content to capitalize on the many deals Paul negotiated. Stan worked earnestly with the creative team, but his cofounder kept the actual wheeling and dealing close to his chest. Paul ultimately prevented Lee from exercising any significant decision-making authority. According to insiders, Stan "would sit in business meetings and occasionally say something. But mainly he'd sit there and doodle, or fall asleep."[32] Paul kept Lee and the startup in the news with the marketing machine operating at full speed. However, fewer and fewer of the deals amounted to any tangible content or products.

With Stan's involvement as a lure, some celebrities jumped on the bandwagon, including high-profile ventures with the Backstreet Boys and Mary J. Blige. Pundits saw SLM as the culmination of Lee's career, even positing that under his supervision, SLM might become the Internet era's Disney. It was one thing for the general public to see the "Stan Lee" name attached to an entity and equate it with Marvel's successes, but it was another for the media, stock analysts, and others to climb aboard. The hysteria surrounding the New Economy bubble far outstripped the media's ability to recognize its farcical elements or anticipate the fated consequences.

In this tech-mad environment, SLM seemed a surefire winner. In early 2000—at the height of the boom—Wall Street valued the company at $31 a share, basically giving SLM the paper wealth ($350 million) to buy Marvel Comics outright. Pop superstar Michael Jackson considered that option, personally asking Lee if he would run Marvel if the deal went through. Of course Lee agreed, but the acquisition never materialized.

Lee excelled at doing what he always did: becoming the face of the organization. More importantly, Stan was the face of a new generation of online comic books and online media. The extraordinary level of hype and willingness to believe in it with little or no validation created the perfect environment for Lee's longing "true believers" to truly believe (and get in on the ground floor of a "Stan the Man" enterprise). When Lee spoke at tech conferences and events, he stood among his people, a generation of self-anointed nerds who grew up on superhero stories and were avid comic book readers.

Although some SLM employees secretly questioned the many partnerships and deals, no one outside Paul and a small group of co-conspirators understood how fast the company burned through its funds. Court documents later revealed that SLM plowed through $26 million from its earliest incorporation to September 2000. In contrast, during that same span, the firm only brought in $1 million in revenue.[33]

Like many other dot-com "bombs," SLM was a house of cards—little more than hype and marketing. While many dot-bombs were the outcome of excessive exuberance, a pervasive stock market bubble, and the notion that size mattered more than profitability, SLM actually engaged in fraud and stock manipulation. The company's 150 workers lost their jobs when the company declared bankruptcy in December 2000, activating SEC and FBI investigations into Paul, Lee, and other executives. While authorities soon cleared Stan, they fixated on Paul's role. Soon, people around the globe would know his name—the criminal who ensnared Stan Lee in one of the world's most egregious Ponzi schemes.[34]

Two weeks before Stan's seventy-eighth birthday, company staffers (despite ominous news stories about Paul's treachery) bought Stan a seven-foot-tall Spider-Man statue imported from Germany. They hoped that in superhero fashion, Lee would somehow save the day. Maybe the webslinger could magically come to life and lead the charge.

No superheroes came to the rescue. At a staff meeting, the remaining SLM executives announced the company was shuttering and the entire staff would be laid off. With tears and stunned faces, the employees could not believe what they were hearing. In less than two years, SLM crashed and burned through tens of millions of dollars—another web venture left to history's dustbin. Stan collapsed after hearing the news. He had to be helped out of the building. The memories of Goodman repeatedly forcing him to fire staffers and freelancers at Marvel still burned in his memory.[35]

If Paul were a supervillain, one can imagine his slick, tuxedo-wearing exterior masking a transformation into a slimy supersnake or energy mass fueled to superhuman power by money, jewels, or other baubles. He conned celebrities and the business press as well. The *Los Angeles Business Journal*, for example, dubbed him "Spider-Man's Business Brain," suggesting he would transform Lee's new characters "into a business empire." Paul himself envisioned SLM as "the Disney of the 21st century."[36]

These over-the-top accolades are chalked up to the dot-com exuberance, but officials unraveled a stock swindle orchestrated by Paul and several henchmen, including executive vice president Stephen M. Gordon (sentenced in 2003 to six and a half years in federal prison for check-kiting).[37] The full scope took investigators years to sort out, but Paul also had more straightforward illegal misdeeds, including reneging on a $250,000 personal loan from Lee. He also forged Stan's signature on multiple contracts (handwriting experts proved that Lee did not sign the documents).[38]

On February 16, 2001, SLM filed bankruptcy petitions in the United States Bankruptcy Court for the Central District of California. In August 2002, the Colorado Secretary of State dissolved the company, and its case was dismissed for failure to pay US trustee fees.[39] While the legal machinations unfurled, Paul fled the country. Hoping to avoid prosecution, he turned up in Brazil. Later, Brazilian agents arrested the fugitive, imprisoning him for two years. US authorities arranged for extradition in September 2003.

Paul attempted to wriggle out of legal troubles, but complaints verified that he bilked various parties out of at least $25 million.[40] In 2005, he pleaded guilty and spent four years under house arrest. In 2009, the criminal began serving a ten-year prison term at a federal institution in Anthony, Texas (paroled in late 2014).

Generations of accumulated goodwill helped Lee dodge the fallout. Stan physically looked the part of an eccentric grandpa, not a high-tech criminal. Investigators realized that he indeed had been duped, but many revelations were unkind, including articles in the business press revealing Stan had slept through meetings or not paid attention. Clearly, authorities understood Lee did not control the finances or orchestrate the illegalities, but he did rather recklessly keep his head in the sand, which allowed a company bearing his name to swindle investors and other stakeholders.

Perhaps the saving grace for Stan fixed on Paul's remarkable level of corruption. He duped many people much more powerful than Lee, including the Clintons and Muhammad Ali. Labeled a "sometimes-mysterious figure with searing eyes and grand gestures," Paul became one of the more fantastical, infamous figures of the dot-com age. As if the story weren't screwy enough, Paul even began claiming ties to secret government agencies. The charges, in his mind, were an effort to silence him.[41]

The SLM debacle virtually erased three years of Lee's life and changed his basic outlook. "No platitude will ever repair the harm that's been done, to me and countless others," Lee explained. "But one thing's for sure—I'll never be so stupidly trusting again."[42] Most observers deduced Lee's career would slowly fade to black—the superhero industry's greatest showman finally calling it quits after decades in the public spotlight. Few believed that even the ever-resilient Lee could sidestep the scandal.

From a broader perspective, though, the collapse of the dot-com boom crushed the reputations of many organizations and executives with much more experience than Stan in business affairs. The resulting hit to the global economy made the SLM boondoggle seem like just another dot-com nightmare. Plus, as Peter Paul's criminal past, outlandish lengths to deceive Wall Street, and zany claims about working for secret military operations became public, it seemed that the conman intentionally targeted Stan, using their friendship to trigger the devious plot.

Almost immediately, Stan fought back in the press, not willing to let the debacle dictate his legacy. He turned to his strength—comic books—inking a deal with *Batman* film producer Michael Uslan to reimagine DC's famous characters. They called the series *Just Imagine Stan Lee*, which allowed him to reconceptualize the major characters in the DC pantheon, including Superman, Batman, and Wonder Woman. The DC deal—after a lifetime of battling the company for industry supremacy—was a coup for Stan. The series led to private negotiations with DC (and parent company Time Warner) to expand its relationship with Lee. The possible creation of a boutique publishing operation, according to one insider, would "remove that yoke of worry from Stan's shoulders." Within months of the SLM bankruptcy, Lee and his advisors moved to deflect the negative publicity from the fiasco.[43]

Despite turning seventy-nine years old at the end of 2001, Lee vowed to continue producing superheroes and launching new projects. As usual, Stan tapped into his seemingly endless supply of creativity to fashion a new image—pop culture's elder statesman and the godfather of comic books.

• *14* •

King of the Cameo

$\mathscr{B}$efore *X-Men* hit the big screen in July 2000, Stan met with director Bryan Singer to discuss bringing the characters to life. "There was no template for it," Singer explained. "Comic book movies had died[;] there was no concept of one as anything but camp." Lee's advice took film in a new direction. He encouraged Singer to research the characters himself and scrap earlier scripts.[1]

The strategy worked! After an extensive marketing campaign, *X-Men* set a then-record for comic book films, earning $54.5 million opening weekend. Lee appeared in the movie playing a hot dog vendor. The cameo allowed fans to see "Smilin' Stan," but the box office success ($296 million worldwide) proved superhero films were viable.

Stan's appearance gave him a shot in the arm popularity-wise for a new generation. "It became tradition to see Stan the Man wandering through Marvel productions," he explained.[2] The cameos would continue for more than a generation (even after his 2018 death). During that time, the Marvel cinematic universe came to dominate contemporary cinema, making Lee one of the most recognized figures in the world.

Yet Stan's astonishing popularity came with some controversy. The success of Marvel films dwarfed his failures, but as he aged, Lee got caught up in a string of mediocre productions and lofty announcements of new projects that led nowhere. Fans still viewed Lee as the face of Marvel, but his work outside the cameos was uneven at best. Stan continued to push new ideas, but the concepts simply didn't click. Despite setbacks, Lee responded by playing his most enduring (and endearing) role—himself. Stan amped up his public persona, focusing on nostalgia for the good old days of early comics.

The shifting winds of pop culture helped Lee recalibrate. Just as he and his colleagues had caught the cultural zeitgeist in the early 1960s, Lee did it again in the early 2000s. Something peculiar took place in the fusion of the Internet, cable television, and expanding film—geek culture took over, with superheroes at its epicenter.

Marvel films made superheroes even more hip in the new century than in Lee and Kirby's heyday. Fans lined up for hours just to see Stan or get his signature on their plastic-sealed, cardboard-packaged comics. Time eventually paid Lee back in dividends. People who grew up reading comics (and idolizing Stan) came into power. They paid tribute to their hero.

★   ★   ★

In November 2001, Lee joined with attorney Arthur Lieberman and producer Gill Champion to form POW! Entertainment (official title: chief creative officer). "I just wanted to show that I can succeed," Lee explained. He emphasized what had been missing at SLM: "working with people who are honorable and competent." The work, however, remained similar to SLM—Stan's ideas for new characters.[3]

Lee's embellishment continued too. An early press release announced a three-film deal with the Sci-Fi Channel, touting Lee as "creator and inventor of the modern superhero," who "revolutionized the comic book industry" via characters that had superpowers but were "none the less plagued by the same doubts and difficulties experienced by ordinary people."[4] The document accentuated Stan's role in creating Marvel's most popular heroes, calling them "his most enduring characters" and then naming Spider-Man, the Hulk, and the X-Men. These public announcements were written to rehabilitate Stan's reputation and underline his place in comic book history.

POW! negotiated a string of new projects designed to take advantage of Lee's status as pop culture's elder statesman. However, the constant hyperbole and lack of completed products left observers shaking their heads. Inevitably, critics questioned the company's viability since its potential success solely centered on Stan's creativity.

There were successes, though, particularly when the boss utilized the Stan Lee persona. In 2002, mega-popular indie filmmaker Kevin Smith (*Clerks, Dogma*), a lifelong comic book fan (and comic book store owner), released *Stan Lee's Mutants, Monsters and Marvels*, a series of discussions between them, along with additional Lee-centric material, heavy on his glory days and the effects of superheroes on American culture. Smith and Lee had been friends for years, particularly after Stan's extended role in Smith's *Mallrats* (1995). The filmmaker's approval demonstrated how Lee would be placed on a pedestal by his pop culture offspring—a generation of creatives that grew up gazing in wonder at Marvel and "Smilin' Stan."

Lee published his autobiography, *Excelsior! The Amazing Life of Stan Lee* (ghostwritten by George Mair, 2002), depicting himself as heroic, achieving the American Dream through smarts, hard work, and quick wit. For Lee aficionados, it is a priceless examination of his life, providing many details the icon rarely discussed. But Stan could never fully rip himself from the superheroes he helped birth. He crafted a public persona and narrative that stressed his role as the father of the superheroes.

POW! focused on new technology and innovations. In late 2003, Lee served as a consultant for Activision, then a top video game production company. Lee's job—the kind that seemed to suit him best—involved developing superhero video games. When Marvel and Activision agreed to a new licensing deal, which included Spider-Man, Iron Man, the X-Men, and the Fantastic Four, Lee provided input on game design, story ideas, and character development. These types of consulting jobs played into Lee's strength as a creator and idea man, while others worked the details and executed the vision he outlined.

Many other agreements, projects, and partnerships were in the works, but the same challenges that had dogged him since the 1970s still existed: the slow pace of creation and producing an end product. Sometimes POW! overreached, while other partnerships simply dissolved. These bombs were a black eye for Stan. News headlines blared, but only a small number of projects were ever completed. As a result, some of the deals and business leaders signing them seemed shady, fueling the notion that Stan was selling his name and past successes for a quick buck. Visions of another SLM hung in the air.

Critics lambasted projects that seemed sordid. In 2003, for example, Lee launched *Stripperella*, an animated series with *Playboy* pinup, *Baywatch* actor, and paparazzi provocateur Pamela Anderson. Jumping in bed with Anderson—literally—and other kinds of campy, adult content seemed tacky and mercenary, like Stan was simply selling his name to D-level projects.

Yet there seemed to be no basement in America's desire for garish entertainment. Anderson found him "kooky" and "very eccentric" but loved the idea of an animated series of a stripper turned crime fighter.[5] Part of Spike TV's ("first network for men") animated block of programming, Lee did not write *Stripperella*, but served as coproducer, art director, and story editor. He didn't shy away from the cartoon's racy aspects: "It's not what I would call a dirty show. It's kind of funny-sexy, bad taste, as treated tastefully." Stan even compared it to a "late-night version of *The Simpsons*."[6] Although the adult cartoon only lasted one season (thirteen episodes), it was picked up globally, often running uncensored (Spike blurred out topless scenes), including in Australia, the United Kingdom, Germany, Brazil, and Italy.

The success led to a series of deals with MTV and its sister networks. Stan also served as executive producer of MTV's animated *Spider-Man* show. The network needed content that appealed to a young demographic, and Lee had that pedigree.

In late 2004, Lee began working with *Playboy* founder Hugh Hefner on *Hef's Superbunnies*. Similar to *Charlie's Angels* (the hit ABC show that launched Farrah Fawcett's career), Hefner would send out Playmates to save the world. In his distinctive overblown style, Lee praised Hefner: "As a fan who bought and cherished the very first copy of *Playboy* in 1953, it is an enormous thrill for me to be partnering with a man who has done so much to shape the culture of the times we live in."[7]

Stan always seemed to have a soft spot for Hefner. The two had much in common, both born in major American cities in the same decade (Hefner in Chicago on April 9, 1926). Hefner took a more traditional route than Lee: active in high school politics and journalism, he started the school newspaper and created a comic book. Neither saw combat in World War II, and both emerged from the global conflict full of vigor and optimism.

After a brief stint working for *Esquire*, Hefner borrowed heavily from dozens of investors to debut *Playboy* magazine with just $8,000. He even initially wanted to call the magazine *Stag Party* but couldn't because Goodman had copyrighted *Stag*. In December 1953, while Lee was editing and writing romance, Western, and cuddly animal comic books, Hefner published the first issue of *Playboy*, featuring a color pinup of Marilyn Monroe. The magazine was an instant hit, with supporters claiming it as a fresh attack on the repressive postwar era. Hefner focused the magazine on urbane, sophisticated readers, showcasing a playful and aspirational lifestyle. Before the decade ended, *Playboy* surpassed *Esquire*, selling one million copies monthly.

Stan admired Hefner's ability to gain credibility in a part of the publishing industry that many criticized. Over the years, they became friends, but while they each transformed popular culture in their own industries, no combined projects ever appeared. Decades later, Lee's praise for the *Playboy* tycoon went overboard, calling him "one of the great communicators in our society," admitting, "I can't think of anyone I'd rather partner with." The release heaped praise on Lee as well, calling him the "godfather of the modern comic book superhero." Hefner dubbed Stan a "creative genius."[8] Typical for this era in Stan's career, though MTV announced it would run the pilot, the program never aired.

In the wake of SLM and the ongoing desire to show fans, critics, and even Marvel itself that he remained vibrant, Lee latched onto these shady projects. While he hid his true feelings behind his always-smiling, ever-optimistic façade, Stan had something to prove, hoping to finally create franchises that he owned, thereby not having to watch as some new corporate overlord reaped massive profits based on his ideas. He clearly enjoyed signing deals and the resulting media frenzy. What he didn't possess, in contrast to his Marvel years, was a team of creators, artists, and other visionaries that could assist him in transforming ideas into completed projects and products.

★   ★   ★

Stan's attempt to create new characters, products, and heroic plots outside the Marvel universe came about because—like countless other artists and writers— he did not own the copyright for the characters he created or cocreated. Right or wrong, this is how the comic book industry operated in the early days. The difference between Lee and the others (like Superman creators Jerry Siegel and Joe Shuster) was Stan's self-created position as Marvel's public face. Despite being a self-avowed "company man," he resented that Marvel profited off his ideas, particularly after the movie industry finally caught on to what he had been preaching for decades.

In late October 2002, *60 Minutes II* aired a segment about comic books and the tremendous popularity of superhero films. Much of the piece showcased Stan's skirmish with Marvel over contract language and whether he might sue. The popular news show painted Marvel as evil—a greedy corporation reaping huge profits off the work of underpaid writers and artists. Lee's contract seemed straightforward, but when it was inked, no one anticipated how superhero films would explode—*X-Men* (2000) earned $300 million worldwide, while *Spider-Man* (2002) became a global phenomenon, drawing some $821 million. Correspondent Bob Simon, employing a bit of spicy language, asked Lee if he felt "screwed" by Marvel. Lee toned down his customary bombast, expressing remorse: "I try not to think of it."[9] Most Marvel fans sided with Lee.

Just days after the segment aired, Lee filed a lawsuit against Marvel for not honoring his 1998 contract—promising him 10 percent of future profits from film and television productions. Despite a $1 million salary, Stan's attorney argued that the provision prevailed. The grand battle between Marvel and its most famous employee shocked onlookers, sparking headlines around the world. One reporter deduced: "You can't blame the pitchman for standing firm and insisting on his due."[10]

The public nature of the contract and its terms (hefty salary for just fifteen hours of work per week, first-class travel, and large pensions for Joanie and J. C.) led some comic book insiders to once again dredge up the argument regarding how negatively comic book artists and cocreators—most notably Jack Kirby—were treated by Marvel (and by extension Lee).[11] The resulting media buzz and idea that Stan was trying to exploit Marvel turned some against him. Critics deduced: Stan got rich, while Jack (and others) didn't. The injustice had been done, and they weren't going to change their opinions, regardless of Lee's contract.

In early 2005, after the judge ruled in Lee's favor, he again appeared on *60 Minutes*. "It was very emotional," said Lee. "I guess what happened was I was really hurt. We had always had this great relationship, the company and me. I felt I was a part of it."[12] Marvel attempted to bury the settlement agreement in a quarterly earnings press release, but the news quickly spread, suggesting that it cost $10 million. Of course, the idea that Lee had to sue the company that he spent his life working for and crisscrossing the globe promoting gave journalists the attention-grabbing headline they needed. And while the settlement amount seemed grandiose, it was a pittance from the first *Spider-Man* film alone, which netted Marvel some $150 million in merchandising and licensing fees.

The upside for Marvel was that the settlement put in motion plans for it to produce its own movies, a major strategic shift. Since the early 1960s, Marvel had licensed its superheroes. The strategy allowed Marvel to outsource risk but also severely limited profits. The new strategy gave Marvel control not only of the films but the future revenue-generating cable television and video products.

Merrill Lynch extended a $525 million credit line for Marvel to launch the venture (using limited rights to ten Marvel characters as collateral). Paramount signed an eight-year deal to distribute up to ten films, including fronting marketing and advertising costs.[13] Interestingly, the agreement also shed light on the suspect Hollywood accounting practices that film companies use to artificially make it seem as if no single film ever made a profit. For example, the Marvel films collectively raked in $2 billion in revenues between 2000 and 2005 and the cut for licensing equaled about $50 million. Despite his contract, Lee had received no royalties.[14]

Stan realized that in a world driven by pop culture influences and hyperdedicated fans, he could just continue to market himself. He licensed his own image in 2004, founding Stan Lee Collectibles (with personal assistant Max Anderson and entrepreneur Tony Carroll). Fans and collectors could purchase memorabilia signed by Lee and authenticated by the store. For Marvel fans, Lee's image was nearly as recognizable as Spider-Man or Iron Man. Through Stan Lee Collectibles, fans could own a piece of "the Man."

In 2006, in celebration of Lee's sixty-fifth anniversary with Marvel (which would have incorrectly made his start date in 1941 rather than 1939 or 1940), the company released a series of comic books called *Stan Lee Meets . . .* , featuring Lee as a character intermingling with his cocreations. Lee wrote the first adventure with the specific superhero; then other writers, such as Joss

Whedon and Jeph Loeb, penned mini-tributes to him. Comically, most of the heroes and villains Lee meets don't actually like him much or at all.

The episodes Lee wrote were filled with inside jokes and plenty of Lee's corny humor. In the Spider-Man issue, for example, the story opens with Lee in the kitchen baking cookies while wearing a Fantastic Four apron. The web-crawler wants to live a "normal" life, approaching Stan for advice, who jokes: "The next time Spidey has a problem—I wish he'd take it to Ditko." In the issue where he meets the Thing, New York City is filled with billboards that make fun of past Marvel artists, such as Gene Colan and the Buscemas, as well as Lee's 1976 commercial for the Personna razor in which he declared himself "Personna Man."

Stan also took his "King of the Cameos" persona into media outside Marvel. On April 28, 2002, Lee guest-starred as an animated version of himself on *The Simpsons* in "I Am Furious (Yellow)." After a comic book craze erupts in Bart's class, the students rush to create superheroes. Lee waltzes into Comic Book Guy's shop, deftly placing an issue of *X-Men* in front of one of *Superman*. Then he criticizes Danger Dude, a comic book Bart creates, but encourages him to keep trying. Lee jokes, "If you fail, you can always open a comic book store." Then, taking a toy Batmobile from a young patron, he attempts to jam a Thing action figure into the car, smashing it into pieces. While the child cries, Stan counters: "Broke, or made it better?" Later, he is portrayed as insane, ripping off his shirt and attempting to transform into Hulk.

Getting in on the reality television craze, Lee hosted the Sci-Fi Channel's *Who Wants to Be a Superhero?*. Season one, which debuted July 27, 2006, featured twelve contestants who created superhero personas. Similar to reality shows like *Big Brother* or *Survivor*, participants engaged in challenges to prove heroism. Lee evaluated them and eliminated the player who was least heroic. The first season winner was Feedback (aka Matthew Atherton, a thirty-four-year-old computer whiz from New Mexico). His superpower was absorbing limited power from video games and disrupting electronics. Atherton was featured in a Dark Horse Comics issue written by Lee (July 2007). A second season debuted on July 26, 2007, running for eight episodes.

Lee's 1998 contract granted him exclusive rights to his likeness and certain catchphrases, like "Excelsior" and "Stan Lee Presents." POW! used the latter in a series of new animated films released in 2007. *Mosaic* debuted on January 9 and later aired on TV on Cartoon Network. The film starred Anna Paquin (who played Rogue in the X-Men film franchise) as Maggie Nelson, an aspiring actress who gains an array of superhero powers. Returning to the formula he mastered during Marvel's 1960s heyday, Lee created the story lines, but industry veterans completed the scripts. *The Condor*, starring actor Wilmer Valderrama, debuted on Cartoon Network on March 24, 2007, after its direct-to-DVD release several days earlier.

Some fans were disappointed in Lee's POW! work; there seemed to be a fine line between the splashy announcements and marketing hype. To be sure, the company had not produced any memorable characters, much less another blockbuster. Condemning Stan this way might seem disingenuous, though, given the rarity of writers, actors, or artists to continue creating great work at that age. Lee could have retired, living out his remaining years as a cultural icon. Yet he toiled earnestly on new projects, while also fulfilling his Marvel agreements: visiting comic book conventions, appearing in film and television cameos, and various writing projects. Lee's longevity became part of his legend. His tenacity in the early and mid-2000s revealed the depth of his character.

★   ★   ★

As a modern-day celebrity, Stan fell into the trap of being famous for being famous, which the cameos increased geometrically. Fans asked him about Spider-Man, X-Men, and other superheroes but knew precious little about his career or work. At the same time, the Marvel universe became the dominant box office force globally. Moviegoers who knew little about Lee—and would have rarely known what he looked like otherwise—had a face to place with the famous name. Stan's mug was as recognizable in Beijing and Paris as it was in Chicago or New York.

The cameos upped Lee's cool factor among fans and also with celebrities. Much of the *Iron Man* cast appeared at the 2007 San Diego Comic-Con. When director Jon Favreau announced a special guest, star Robert Downey Jr. glanced to his left, then raised his arms in a victory salute. A huge grin spread across his devilish face. The surprise visitor was Stan, greeted by hugs from Downey, actress Gwyneth Paltrow, and others, while applause thundered.

Although fans might never get within a million miles of Downey Jr. or Paltrow, part of Lee's popularity came from accessibility. Fans saw his larger-than-life image on the screen but also could meet him at comic book conventions. Stan's approachability set him apart from iconic artists (like Bob Dylan, Mick Jagger, or Bruce Springsteen) who have fans across generations but are essentially walled from them.

Lee pressed the flesh and constantly met new generations of crazed fans who just wanted a moment, even if they were too overcome with nerves to pose a question or squeak out "thank you." Few iconic figures of Lee's era (or celebs decades younger) could attract similar crowds. How many celebrities live past ninety, let alone gain millions of followers on Twitter and Facebook?

★   ★   ★

Stan was the walking, talking, joking, clowning, self-deprecating heritage of the comic book world in the early decades of the twenty-first century. On November 17, 2008, President George W. Bush honored Lee with the National Medal of Arts and the National Humanities Medal at the White House (the highest award granted by the US government and most prestigious in all the humanities).

Ever the joker, Lee waited behind Academy Award–winning actress Olivia de Havilland. Placing the medal over her head, the president kissed the *Gone With the Wind* actress on the cheek. Lee stepped forward, reaching out his hand, which Bush took in both his. As he smiled, Lee blurted out: "You're not gonna kiss me, are you?" Bush burst into laughter. The next day, media sites around the globe ran photos of Lee and the president sharing a belly laugh.[15]

Most fans did not realize that Stan was not part of Marvel's leadership during the King of the Cameo era. His main work was POW!, slowing down only when his health demanded. Usually, Lee just smiled when continually asked to rehash the Marvel glory days. Sometimes he revealed deeper feelings. In 2009, Lee was asked if Marvel should attempt to acquire Superman when the copyright reverted to the families of Joe Shuster and Jerry Siegel. Lee replied positively but explained, "I'm with Marvel, but I'm not really part of the Marvel decision-making team. . . . I think my title is Chairman Emeritus, but it doesn't really mean much. . . . To prove they haven't forgotten me, I get these cameos in the movies, which is kind of nice."[16]

In 2008, Lee published *Election Daze* under the "Stan Lee Presents" banner, poking fun at political leaders and hearkening back to the 1940s and 1950s when he self-published books of humorous celebrity photos with wiseacre captions. The cover, for example, satirized Bush's mispronunciation of the word "nuclear" and Hillary Clinton's allusion to potential intern challenges. The tongue-in-cheek publication clearly attempted to capitalize on Lee's satire, but the effort lacked much bite in an era when political commentators essentially waged rhetorical warfare twenty-four hours a day on television and the Internet.

In 2009, POW! teamed with Walt Disney Studios Home Entertainment to produce *Time Jumper*, an animated comic book series made explicitly for the web and mobile phones. Stan created the characters, including "Lee Excelsior," the leader of an anticrime operation. He produced the series, allowing a creative team to assemble the scripts and storyboards. The show's lead actress, Natasha Henstridge, joked about Lee flirting with her and talked about what fun they had on set.[17]

Stan's popularity made him a natural for late-night talk shows and popular sitcoms. In March 2010, Lee guest-starred on *The Big Bang Theory*, a show capitalizing on the growing popularity of "geek" culture (later considered one of the most popular TV series of all time). The episode (which attracted sixteen million viewers) has the lead characters attempting to meet the Marvel icon. In a memorable scene, Sheldon visits Lee's house (Stan answers the door wearing a navy Fantastic Four robe). When he barges into Lee's home, Sheldon gets arrested and placed under a restraining order. As the show ends, the offbeat scientist gleefully proclaims that he will hang the order next to the one he received from *Star Trek*'s Leonard Nimoy.

In April 2012, Lee launched a YouTube channel (Stan Lee's World of Heroes) with *Fan Wars*. Dedicated to the "hero lifestyle and enthusiast culture," the channel featured scripted and unscripted shows, as well as comic book convention and news coverage. One of the most popular features was "Stan's Rants," a kind of live-action Soapbox column. In each rant, Lee explored a topic that bothered him with a mix of his distinctive wise-guy style and curmudgeonly charm. One rant had Stan railing against people who claimed they were his "biggest fan." In another he implored people to change "comic book" to his preferred variation: "comicbook." Lee delivered the diatribes in vintage, tongue-in-cheek style, exclaiming about a video game version of himself: "Anybody could be Stan Lee! What if a guy isn't worthy? And I'm pretty particular! Never again will I put myself in a position where you, who may not be deserving, can be me!"[18] After a pretty quick start and initial popularity (garnering about half a million subscribers and 163 million views), the Lee YouTube page eventually died on the vine. Similar to other POW! Entertainment initiatives, the YouTube channel launched with a bang and then withered as Lee's attention moved to other projects.

In 2012, Activision turned the comic book creator into an animated superhero in *The Amazing Spider-Man* video game. As Lee, players could swing high above the streets of New York City, shooting webs and confronting villains, just like Lee's iconic character. Voicing the part, Lee begins his electronic adventure by announcing that he is the "king of cameos" and exclaims: "Take that, Hitchcock!"[19]

In late 2013, Lee again appeared alongside the characters in *Lego Marvel Super Heroes*, a role-playing game. In the Marvel version, players can become any of 180 characters (including Lee) and operate in a Lego rendering of New York City. Lee is part of a mission called "Stan Lee in Peril," which places him in dangerous situations. Three years later, there would be another Lego video game, this time based on the Avengers. Players could play as "Iron Stan" (in Iron Man–like armor), but in a humorous nod, the face mask had a built-in moustache.

In January 2014, Lee returned to Springfield, the fictional home of *The Simpsons*, in the episode "Married to the Blob" (twenty-fifth season). Like the 2002 appearance, Lee was teamed with Comic Book Guy. Early in the episode, he urged the shop owner to ask Kumiko, a Japanese manga writer touring America's most tragic cities, out on a date. At the end, he married the couple in the fabled comic book shop.

While these appearances may have seemed like little more than gimmicks, they introduced Stan to a new generation of young people. Just like a fresh legion of fans turned onto classic rockers Aerosmith based on *Guitar Hero*, young video gamers could learn about Stan. YouTube videos posted of people playing the Spider-Man video game as Lee eclipsed three million views (yes, videos of people playing video games!).

In January 2016, *Stan Lee's Lucky Man* debuted on British television's Sky 1, a drama about a troubled police officer who controlled luck (for decades Lee told interviewers this was the superpower he wanted). Drawing about 1.9 million viewers per episode, the series became Sky 1's most successful original drama. It aired for three seasons, with various streaming networks picking it up later.

In mid-2016, *The Hollywood Reporter* presented *Stan Lee's Cosmic Crusaders*, its first branded show. Fabian Nicieza (cocreator of Deadpool) wrote the animated online series, while the magazine and Genius Brands International coproduced it, along with POW!. Stan conceived the series, edited the script, and voiced his starring role, where he leads a group of seven aliens who crashed on Earth. They lose their superpowers but, under Lee's tutelage, discover how to employ their powers on this planet. The partnership with *THR* coincided with the magazine's "Stan Lee: 75 Years in the Business" special Comic-Con issue. The series provided another opportunity to expand Lee's brand outside Marvel. *THR* also marketed the series across its platforms, including its website, YouTube channel, Facebook, and Twitter, a combined social media audience of about fifteen million monthly.[20]

At the conclusion of *Captain America: Civil War* (2016), a FedEx delivery driver appears at the Stark Enterprises headquarters of the Avengers. Knocking on the glass, he asks, "Are you Tony Stank?"

James "Rhodey" Rhodes, Tony Stark's best friend, points to his buddy and exclaims: "Yes, this is Tony Stank. . . . You're in the right place. Thank you for that!"

The FedEx employee is played by Stan Lee, his twenty-ninth cameo in superhero films. The scene ends the movie on a humorous note and, more importantly, demonstrates Lee's place in the Marvel universe. The package contains a letter from Captain America to Iron Man, turning over leadership of the Avengers to him but also letting Stark know that he will still show up if the Earth faces peril. Lee's cameo may seem a throwaway, but the moment is central to the plot and points to how the Marvel universe unfolds in the future. As Rhodes explains, Lee's character is definitely "in the right place"—at the center of the action.

The cheerful conversation between Stark and Rhodes counterbalances the previous scene in which Rhodes—veteran military hero and War Machine combatant—struggles to walk again after breaking his back in the earlier superhero melee. Despite the dramatic edge, the tone and voice sounds as if Lee wrote the exchange in the early 1960s. Rhodes and Stark trade smirks and jokes, with Rhodes laughing, "Please, table for one for Mr. Stank, preferably by the bathroom." The dialogue is a Lee line, set during a Lee cameo, in Lee's Marvel universe—his personality imprinted on a grand scale. Lee certainly fulfilled Martin Goodman's early directive: go create a bunch of superheroes.

No one realized that the order would transform storytelling and American popular culture.

★   ★   ★

At ninety-three years old and arguably never more popular, Stan embarked on a "final appearance" tour, with several cities proclaiming "Stan Lee Day." His status as eminent statesman fueled the tour. "There is an excitement about these comic conventions that nothing can match," Lee explained. "These people are so in love with the pop culture of comic books."[21] Tens of thousands of fans were willing to do anything—and pay any amount—to see Stan and get his autograph. In the Big Apple, Lee explained to the *New York Daily News*: "It's the most incredible thing in the world, because wherever I go, people want my autograph and people say 'thank you for the enjoyment that you brought me.' . . . I must be one of the luckiest guys in the world. . . . It's just great to know that you're wanted and that people actually appreciate the work that you've done."[22]

The challenge for icons as they age is the questions they face (often unspoken) about living up to their past achievements—a tall order, whether Bob Dylan, Robert De Niro, or the Rolling Stones. Stan's challenge was attempting to create a new universe when young people had countless other ways to slip into the heart of popular culture. Why read about a superhero when you can be one in a video game or watch adventures across streaming services? Today, iconic characters are more likely to be created for television or films rather than comics. Marvel's superheroes are popular in part because they are already established in the public's mind. The origin stories are pervasive and thus adaptable for new generations.

As a result, detractors might have pointed at Stan's post-Marvel work and concluded that he coasted on past successes (or the work of Kirby and Ditko) for far too long. But past ninety years old, how many artists even attempt to remain relevant? Stan's legacy was firmly established—one of the great creative icons in American history.

In late 2016 at the Cincinnati Comic Expo, several hundred people stood in line—waiting. They slowly shuffled step-by-step through roped-off areas, attempting to contain excitement and chatting at length in a communal love fest. When their big moment finally took place—meeting Stan face-to-face—nearly to a person they were too dumbstruck to say anything. Some choked out a whispered "thanks."

On paper, the moment might have seemed anticlimactic, but Stan's presence was enough. After getting their Spider-Man poster or Doctor Strange comic book signed, they turned away sporting huge grins, as if it were Christmas morning. They immediately wanted to relive the moment—searching out family, friends, or complete strangers, anybody who would share their joy. A treasured instant in Stan's light—many likened getting his photo or signature as the culmination of a lifetime of fandom, confessing that this was the best time of their lives.

At Stan's Santa Monica office, one may have mistaken the décor for a Stan Lee museum. The bright space burst with shelves of trinkets, including various action figures of Stan and superheroes. An old-school Captain America sat at the front of the desk, daring visitors to lean closer. A stuffed Hulk guarded the computer monitor. Walls were lined with photos—a group shot with the cast of *The Big Bang Theory* and a drawing of Lee drawn as Clark Kent pulling his shirt open to reveal a red Superman "S" emblazoned across his chest. Another showed Lee and Joanie on the red carpet at a Hollywood premiere, and yet another depicted Lee shaking hands with President Reagan. A large Silver Surfer (awash in deep blue and riding a teal-striped surfboard) adorned the wall behind the desk as if jutting directly out at the visitor.

For someone so steeped in comic book and pop culture history as the creator of a new storytelling sensibility, Lee had a keen sense of his past. However, he claimed to have little use for nostalgia. New waves of journalists, interviewers, and fans yearned for his stories of origins and characters, but Stan's outlook was forward—toward the next idea. He scribbled thoughts on tiny two-by-three-inch notepads, tucked away in his front shirt pocket (a lifelong habit). His left-handed scrawl bordered on indecipherable.

Meeting Stan late in his life, one sensed that his public persona grew out of the furtive teenage desire to act, then later morphed into a kind of celebrity identity that enabled him to play up the brash New Yorker stereotype. The caricature, though, fell by the wayside speaking with him one-on-one. In those moments, Lee was thoughtful and reflective, answering questions as if after the many decades, he still couldn't believe his good fortune. Stan's youthful, appreciative outlook offset the exaggerated public displays of braggadocio.

In his early nineties, he no longer heard well and his eyesight had worsened. A 2012 heart operation led to a pacemaker that regulated his heartbeat, yet he continued to relish his role as the Marvel universe's spiritual leader.

In 2016, when I asked Stan how it felt to inspire generations of fans and artists with his flawed hero narrative, he paused for a moment: "It's an incredibly great feeling, when I think about it. I don't have that much time to think about, but when I do . . ."[23] His voice trailed off. I could see in his eyes that the memories of a lifetime filled his imagination.

The thing about icons is they never really stop creating. Lee's worldview wasn't based on what he did in the 1960s. He believed in the next spark, the new work, always charting a future course.

• 15 •

Saying Good-Bye to a Hero

$\mathcal{I}$n 2018, life turned into a horror film for Stan.

He still grieved Joan's death the previous July 6 at age ninety-five. She had been his bedrock, providing priceless emotional support and keeping a close eye on (and over) his career. Like many creatives, Stan shied away from the intricacies of the business world. Joanie stepped in to oversee those facets and ensured he had the order and creative freedom to continue his hectic schedule of appearances and work. Like many older couples, Joanie's death seemed to accelerate Stan's decline, though no one expected his world to unravel so quickly in his final year.

Over several long months, Lee's support system (including longtime members of his entourage) withered to dust in a flurry of lawsuits, police reports, investigations, accusations, finger pointing, cruelty, and violence. As Stan's closest friends and allies were shut out of his life, they rallied individually and collectively against these forces of evil. In time, as the full picture emerged, a horrific notion took hold: one of the most recognizable names and faces in the world fell victim to elaborate and often violence-filled schemes to rob him of his dignity and fortune. Contemporary society created a new name for this often-misunderstood negligence—elder abuse.

Media reports of the chaos swirling around Lee shocked the comic book world and fans alike. Marvel films were dominating big screens around the world, yet the cocreator of the Marvel universe faced a series of embarrassing and devious plots at the hands of lackeys and hangers-on who wanted a piece of his legacy (and the wealth he would leave behind). After talking with several of Stan's longtime friends and allies who were rushing to his aid, I told *Los Angeles Times* reporter David Ng, "If Stan Lee had a Spidey-sense for con

185

men, the world would be better off and his fortunes would be better off, but he doesn't seem to have that."[1]

One of the primary tenets of elder abuse is that that the wrongdoers scheme to paint a picture to the outside world that counters the internal manipulation actually taking place. Reportedly, 10 percent of the elderly population in America suffers from elder abuse, but the legal system has not caught up, so these crimes are difficult to litigate. For most victims, the crime is hidden behind layers of so-called benefactors who are actually duping the world or counting on no one really paying attention.

Making matters worse, Stan had difficulty advocating for himself. At times it seemed he was exceptionally lucid for a man of ninety-five years old. In other moments, though, he was foggy and unclear. The erratic picture made it difficult to comprehend friend versus foe. Compounding the confusion, the villains largely isolated him. According to *The Hollywood Reporter*, Lee's phone number had been changed and his e-mail commandeered.[2] Stan was basically cut off from his lifetime of friends and supporters. Vultures were circling Lee's Hollywood mansion.

Much of the news that emerged came from police reports and tabloid journalism. One scoundrel after another would claim to be his manager or confidant, accompanying the legend to film premieres or comic conventions, but days or weeks later others would surface, shouting or pointing fingers. There was allegedly a large war chest at the end of the rainbow. No one seemed to know exactly, but some reports pegged Lee's worth at upward of $100 million. With that money on the table, the rats scurried to take their chunk, regardless of the embarrassment, pain, or suffering Stan endured. Attempting to unravel the details, reporter David Hochman explained:

> The very qualities that industrious people of Lee's generation pride themselves on—working hard, trusting people, showing respect for authority, raising children to be better off—were traits that did not serve him well as he grew more vulnerable with age. On top of that, Lee didn't like banks and was thought to be stockpiling cash at home, an irresistible temptation for unscrupulous employees.[3]

Sadly, according to Hochman and other investigators, Stan and Joanie's daughter, J. C., was caught up in the misconduct. She probably didn't know it, but she was a conduit, getting involved with unscrupulous people who had targeted her to get closer to her father. But she also had demons. Portrayed by many observers as quick-tempered, prone to violent rages, and supremely entitled by her charmed (and wealthy) life, at times she seemed unhinged, ranting about what she was due and later unleashing a barrage of lawsuits.[4] An influential media outlet called her Stan's "long-troubled dilettante daughter . . . a prodigious shopper with an ill-tempered personality."[5]

One handler connected first to J. C. eventually wormed his way to Stan, illegally purchasing $1 million of real estate in Lee's name by forging his signature and stealing $4.6 million from a bank account. If the money alone weren't enough, the situation turned sick and depraved when reports surfaced that he even took vials of Stan's blood to mix with ink and later sell in comic books. Another sycophant—Keya Morgan—was in the eye of the storm of alleged Lee abuse. His misdeeds led to his arrest in 2019 on felony charges related to Stan's final months, including false imprisonment and theft. Some media report that Morgan embezzled about $5 million worth of assets from Lee in the final months of his life.[6]

The intensity of the chaos left fans and allies in disbelief (even devolving to groping charges against Lee by a live-in nurse that seemed to be an effort at extortion). Clifford Meth, a longtime friend and writer who had worked with the icon, led an effort by insiders to get the elder abuse case launched, going to the authorities and bringing the abuse to light. "Stan was being picked apart by vultures," Meth explained. "It was disgusting and broke our hearts. Those who knew him were appalled."[7] Others checked in on Stan personally in an attempt to ascertain his well-being, including Spawn creator and artist Todd McFarlane and Stan's longtime friend and colleague Roy Thomas. McFarlane told the press that in their last meeting about a month before he died, Stan told his friend that he looked forward to seeing Joanie soon.

★   ★   ★

On November 12, 2018, Stan Lee passed away.

Paramedics received an emergency call from Lee's Hollywood Hills home at 8:34 a.m. and took the ailing icon to Cedars-Sinai Medical Center. According to his brother, Larry, Stan had been in ill health over the previous several months, including heart issues and pneumonia. He had breathing problems that were complicated by age and his failing health.

People around the world used to seeing Stan's cameos were shocked. Certainly, most did not know he had been in ill health, despite the tabloid reports about his final months. For contemporary audiences, it seemed there were more lessons Lee still had to teach. For example, fans who only knew Stan from the Marvel films and convention appearances later learned of his deep commitment to social justice and human rights in the United States and globally. What we collectively recognized is that the ideas Stan embodied and promoted in Marvel comic books and discussed as a public figure reflected the deeply held beliefs that fueled him as a person. Stan Lee believed that human beings should care for one another and treat each other with respect and dignity.

The staggering news triggered a global reaction and outpouring of love and affection.

In China, where they respectfully referred to Stan as "Grandpa," a hashtag honoring him was viewed some 1.21 billion times within twenty-four hours after the news hit. A Chinese site dedicated to sci-fi posted: "Maybe to some people this is just another famous person who passed away, but to us the god of creation has fallen from the sky, a disaster so great that neither the reversal of time nor the assemblance of heroes can correct."[8] This is a tribute that Stan himself might have deemed worthy. Fans could not imagine their hero being gone or what the MCU would look like without a Stan cameo.

On *PBS NewHour*, I spoke with host Judy Woodruff about Stan's unique impact on popular culture, explaining: "Stan's real power was capturing this kind of everyday superhero mentality that people were really attracted to. It wasn't the godlike speaking of a Superman or the stilted language of Batman. It was a language that people could really relate to and understand on a deeply personal level."[9] Tributes from stars of the MCU flooded Twitter and other social media outlets. While billions of fans across the world mourned, a wide range of celebrities joined them, from Paul McCartney and Patrick Stewart to Robert Downey Jr. and Tom Holland. Dozens of other stars from the MCU also chimed in, thanking Stan for his role in creating modern storytelling.

In the years since Lee passed away, November 12 has become a kind of Stan Lee Day around the world. Each year, countless fans flock to social media to rejoice in his life and work. In 2021, Stan's name began trending when fans posted photos posing with him at comic book conventions, while others followed with gifs of his MCU appearances. Given the state of technology, it's no wonder that Stan also made additional posthumous cameos in several Marvel video games for *Spider-Man*, *Miles Morales*, and *Guardians of the Galaxy*. The success of Marvel film and television properties and the billions of dollars bet on its continued popularity ensure that Marvel—and Stan—will remain at the heart of global popular culture.

★   ★   ★

Is it possible to assess someone like Stan Lee?

Was he simply the superhero invention of Stanley Lieber, the desperately poor Depression-era kid from New York City? Was this new character—like a mask—what the youngster had to create to overcome the odds stacked against him?

If we accept this vantage point, Stan embodies a version of the fabled American Dream—a mainly twentieth-century story of accomplishment following on the back of hard work and tenacity. Others might claim that Lee's success was a combination of talent and lucky timing as the wave of baby boomers came of age and had an overriding influence on American culture.

In some ways, though, we reduce him and the comprehensive range of his experiences if we simply categorize or label him. After all, underneath the celebrity and global fame there was a person—one filled with the complexities of human life. Stan had dreams and aspirations. Although he achieved heights that even his mind probably couldn't have imagined as a young man looking to the future, along the way he also confronted a myriad of personal and professional challenges. As Frank Sinatra sang, "That's life." Every up comes with a down, but character is shaped when a person gets on their feet and "back in the race." Stan's life is about nothing if it isn't about resiliency, created from childhood trauma, willpower, and hard work.

Shifting to pre–Fantastic Four times, Lee carried wounds from the public shaming he felt about working in comics, which included the 1950s national uproar against their alleged "immorality." The humiliation had consequences. After the Marvel explosion that he and others birthed and American culture shifted in their favor, Stan worked the room like a person who had been the lifelong ugly duckling. As a swan, Lee spread his wings, but the self-doubt still festered. So how does a person feel less than and extraordinary simultaneously? The human mind is a complex organ.

When someone like Lee becomes an "overnight sensation" after toiling in a field for decades, the resulting fame has consequences. For every observer who believes that Stan saved comic books and expanded their popularity in the 1960s by becoming the face of the industry, there are others who view him as media-hungry and money-grubbing. Lee wasn't perfect and didn't have an unflawed life, but what he retained was an aura of authenticity, despite an otherworldly level of celebrity that only increased well past the time it falls off for most stars. He was authentic in his passion for life, which resulted in creating characters that people wanted to know better: first talking to children, then teenagers, and eventually adults.

Perhaps even more important, his authenticity rang true with fans. They clamored to meet him and kept him popular for nearly sixty years. His interest in fan engagement could be viewed callously as a way to make money, but autographs and memorabilia have been part of popular culture for decades, if not centuries. Like many people who grew up in the Depression, Stan never trusted that his last paycheck would be followed by another. If he had stopped working at traditional retirement age, it would have been about a decade before the first Marvel film hit theaters. Stan kept working because he saw no other way. The childhood scars never healed.

There is also "inside baseball"–level detail about Lee's role at Marvel during the 1960s heyday that much of the general public knows little about. At the core of this hullabaloo is the fight over who gets the credit (or lion's share of the credit) for creating the Marvel superheroes. There are countless Stan supporters and innumerable others who believe he is some kind of devil based on how one divvies up provenance. For many, this debate represents a line in the sand that cannot be crossed and is at the heart of countless social media arguments.[10]

In many interviews, Stan unequivocally credited Jack Kirby for his role in creating the Marvel universe: "He was a genius. He was terribly important to Marvel. It's very unfortunate that some people think he did half the work and I took all the credit. That just isn't so. Every time I was interviewed, I would always say how great Jack was. Very often, the interviewers just left that part out. I had no control over what was written about us."[11]

If you've read this book carefully, you will appreciate a middle ground between Stan and Jack on many fundamental issues—including perspectives they shared about their work and the comic book industry as a whole. Some critics utilize analogies in an attempt to describe their working relationship— from songwriters like John Lennon and Paul McCartney to likening them to filmmakers. None of these comparisons seem to fully capture the connection better than the most frequently used term: cocreators. What emerged from their creative collision is some of the greatest work in American art history. *Their* work.

According to comic book historian and writer Clifford Meth, it's the consequences of Stan's work that matters the most. "At the end of the day," he explained, "it doesn't matter who spins the history of the comics, nor how they spin it. One fact is indisputable: Stan Lee changed comics, which changed most of *us*." There will surely be people who read that statement and chalk it up as expressed by yet another "Stan lover" intent on shortchanging the artists. As a writer who is benefited by a team of editors, copyeditors, design-ers, and other professionals, I know that there is no comprehensive way to demarcate or parse the idea of cocreation. Again, Meth provided insight on the complexities of the thinking: "It would be impossible to reconstruct where and when one man's thoughts began and the other's ended without records of these transactions, which no one kept."[12]

One of the most frequently overlooked aspects of Lee's career is how he managed and ran the comic book division from the time he was a teenager through the early 1970s, an era spanning parts of five decades. In this sense, he truly was the man behind Marvel as the editorial director and talent manager.

He brought in the writers, artists, inkers, and others who made the company great long past his own tenure as editor-in-chief. He also approved all the merchandise that was licensed, so the man constantly worked—and his work ethic was off the charts.

Stan had a gift for spotting talent and then creating an environment where the creatives were able to do their best work. Jack Kirby never achieved the broad public acclaim that Stan did, but he is the greatest comic book artist of all time. When he and Stan put their efforts together in the early 1960s, they needed each other and that drove their combined success. Together they revolutionized comics.

If you take a deep dive into Stan's official archive, housed at the American Heritage Center at the University of Wyoming, you will find file after file filled with office memoranda, advertising and circulation studies, countless fan letters, human resources paperwork, and other corporate effluvium that might make most researchers' heads spin.[13] From a different perspective, though, what seems like miscellany actually reveals the depth of Lee's work across the entire Marvel enterprise. His responsibilities not only covered writing, editing, and approving artwork but extended to general managerial and editorial work that most people do not contemplate when they think of Lee as a writer or the elderly person in the cameos.

Of course, like any good leader, when Marvel's popularity exploded, he hired people to help keep pace. Yet the archive uncovers a leader fully in charge, despite his carefree persona. Lee created and cocreated countless superheroes, villains, and plots, all while simultaneously running the comic book business as it grew from a virtual one-man operation in the mid- to late 1950s to an empire across the 1960s and into the 1970s.

Turning to Stan's promotion of Marvel—and himself—as brands, one finds a shrewd promoter who instinctively understood what audiences wanted. On the college speaking circuit, for example, Lee frequently moved away from the typical lecture, instead turning his appearances into audience-led question-and-answer sessions. He knew this is what the fans wanted: a combination of "insider" information and the chance to interact with the cocreator of their superheroes. When Stan realized how his own celebrity could work to increase his prestige, he fully embodied the notion. He may have seen this as a way to get back at Martin Goodman, who never really appreciated his cousin-in-law the way the younger man hoped. With distance from the publisher's meddling, bad decisions, and egregious orders, Stan created his own power after dutifully playing company man for decades.

Any discussion of Marvel's success should include analysis of the context of the 1960s and the comic book industry. A key challenge is that, with many of the superheroes, Jack and Stan had no idea that the characters would become iconic or that their stories would be used to drive billions of dollars in the global economy. At the time, they were a means to an end—work that paid the bills, not anything approaching a legacy or fame. From 1939 to 1961, few people (aside from the most dedicated fans) could have named a single comic book creator. *The Fantastic Four* turned this notion on its ear. Marvel's unheralded success created egos, altered memories, and fueled animosities. The simple fact of the matter is that Stan and Jack both took liberties with the facts over the decades. The full truth about the superhero creation process died with them and Steve Ditko. Everyone else is just spouting opinion.[14]

One might ask (semi-rhetorically) if there is an American author more widely read than Lee or a voice heard more often across the culture. Similar to Henry Ford, who did not invent but rather perfected the assembly line, Stan sharpened and defined the antihero character and sold them by the millions to generations of consumers. Unlike Ford's Model T, however, Lee's superheroes adapted as culture changed. That's why today's Fords have little in common with earlier models, but we have had multiple Spider-Mans on the big screen alone. Ford's achievement is the stuff of legend, but Lee's creations have become mythology. Stan's legacy is that Marvel superheroes are the foundation of modern storytelling.

Although Stan was not a baby boomer, he had an undeniable impact on that incredibly large and powerful generation. That generation that would become witty, full of angst, and a myriad of dichotomies also showed the country what it was to be human. Heroes *and* human—like a teen with unbelievable superpowers or a self-loathing pilot who becomes a hulking, living, breathing pile of rocks. Lee gave teens and college-aged readers a voice by creating superheroes readers could relate to. Like so much of the boomer era, the influences get messy as locked-down Cold War culture shapeshifted into something different, then transformed again as the 1960s kids became the 1980s Gordon Gekko corporate raiders.

The Fantastic Four transformed the kinds of stories comic books could tell. *Spider-Man*, however, brought the idea home to a global audience. Lee told an interviewer that he had two incredibly instinctive objectives: introduce a "terribly realistic" superhero and one "with whom the reader could relate."[15] While the nerd-to-hero storyline seems like it must have sprung from the earth fully formed, Lee gave audiences a new way of looking at what it meant to be a hero and spun the notion of who might be heroic in a way that spoke to the rapidly expanding number of comic book buyers. Spider-Man's popularity revealed the attraction to the idea of a tainted hero, but the character hit the newsstands at the perfect time; ranging from the growing baby boomer generation to the optimism of John F. Kennedy's Camelot, this confluence of events resulted in a second golden age for comic books.

Just like novelists and filmmakers had always done, it is as if Lee put his hands up into the air and pulled down fistfuls of the national zeitgeist. In this sense, he understood his audience in the same way as Walt Disney or John Updike, who at about the same time was crafting Harry "Rabbit" Angstrom, the American everyman (a character one could certainly imagine reading comic books). Lee as writer did what all iconic creative people do: he improved on or perfected his craft, thus creating an entirely new style that would have broad impact across the rest of the industry and later the world.

Stan shares the same stage that once held Ella Fitzgerald and F. Scott Fitzgerald, as well as Babe Ruth, Sinatra, and Andy Warhol. He sits there proudly with Bob Dylan, Toni Morrison, Tom Hanks, Hank Aaron, and Elvis ('cause he just might still be out there somewhere). His legacy is undeniable: Lee transformed storytelling by introducing generations of readers to flawed heroes who also dealt with life's challenges, in addition to the threats that could destroy humankind.

Generations of artists, writers, actors, and other creative types have been inspired, moved, or encouraged by the universe he gave voice to and birthed. Lee did not invent the imperfect hero—one could argue that such heroes had been around since Homer's time and even before—but Lee did deliver it—Johnny Appleseed style, a dime or so a pop—to a generation of readers hungry for something new.

The vision of what the future might hold separated Stan from other comics professionals. Unlike comic book experts and insiders who focused on monthly sales figures and audience demographics, Lee understood that Marvel's horde of superheroes could form the basis of a multimedia empire. He spoke about turning Marvel into the next Disney decades before Walt's company gobbled up the superhero shop. Back then, Lee's idea drew derision and people openly scoffed at such a notion.

We must always remember that Stan did not do it alone. It is impossible to quantify the number of people it has taken to keep Marvel operating and producing since 1939. Artistic collaboration has always been the bedrock of the comic book industry, just like so many other forms of commercial entertainment. Where is the director without the cinematographer or the actor? Where is the writer without the editor and publisher? Heck, those examples are compounded and extended by the hundreds of people it takes to get a creative product into the world. Authors, for example, need the bookseller to physically place thousands of items on a shelf to reach the public.

Looking back at Lee's work can give today's readers new ways of thinking about race and racism, identity issues, culture, and gender. In this way, comic books—then and now—promote two incredibly important skills: critical thinking and contextual analysis. These abilities allow readers to understand themselves and their societies more fully, while simultaneously broadening comprehension of the wider world and its interlocking historical impulses.

Through Lee, Spider-Man famously stated: "With great power there must also come great responsibility." From his writing and editing, as well as the life he led, we learn that great responsibility can include a fundamental commitment to humanity, compassion, and self-respect.

Stan's role as voice of the superheroes cannot be underestimated. He created a narrative foundation that has fueled pop culture for nearly six decades. By establishing the voice of the Marvel universe and shepherding the comic books to life as the head of Marvel, Lee cemented his place in American history.

Acknowledgments

$\mathscr{I}$s it possible to calculate all that goes into writing a book? *Stan Lee: A Life* is the culmination of a lifetime of reading, research, and enjoying comic books within the long through line of studying popular culture. I taught myself to read so that I could unlock the joys of *Spider-Man* and the *Avengers*. Later I grew obsessed with the reality-bending *What If* series. I do not remember a time without Stan Lee. The "Stan Lee Presents" banner is ever-present in my mind's eye.

I was lucky enough to spend some time with Stan in late 2016. When I asked him how it felt to inspire generations of fans and artists with his flawed hero narrative, he paused for a moment. Looking wistfully off into the distance, he explained: "It's an incredibly great feeling, when I think about it. I don't have that much time to think about, but when I do . . ." Then his voice trailed off. With a brief grin and eyes almost sparkling behind his semidark glasses, my wife, Suzette, and I could see his pride and hear it in his voice. Thinking back on that time now, my hands still tremble a bit. How often does one get to stand in the shadow of greatness?

As you have read in the preceding pages, Lee's career and impact on popular culture has not been without controversy. Given the billions of dollars at stake in the Marvel universe across films, comics, merchandise, and everything else related to the company across the globe, the hullabaloo will likely never end. As you've also now learned, I think *both* Stan Lee and Jack Kirby deserve equal credit for their creations, as does Steve Ditko for his cocreation of Spider-Man. Equal. My advice to those so quick to argue for or against these creators is to dig in and come to your own conclusions.

My attempt to tell Stan's story centered on multi-archival research and using that material, plus interviews, newspaper articles, essays, blogs, and all other information I could get my hands on to create my own interpretation. That's all history is, in the end. History is not what *actually* happened, rather a snippet and an elucidation. As such, the ideas and analysis are mine, as are any errors of judgment. I would like to extend my deepest appreciation to the amazing team at the American Heritage Center (AHC) at the University of Wyoming. How Lee's papers got to Laramie, Wyoming, is itself a great story. The archivists and librarians I worked with were so professional and provided access to material that few had previously seen.

I would also like to thank the team at the Billy Ireland Cartoon Library and Museum at Ohio State University. Additional resources, including rare books and Marvel materials, were hunted down at the Cincinnati and Hamilton County Public Library, Stow-Munroe Falls Public Library, and Lane Public Library in Oxford, Ohio. Newspapers.com is an invaluable source, as are the many digital databases that help the historian find and utilize materials. I read deeply in the Marvel back catalog via the Marvel Unlimited subscription service.

Thanks to the many editors and staffers I have had the great pleasure to work with at Rowman & Littlefield! Christen Karniski has been a wonderful editor and guide as we took another headlong dive into Stan's epic life. Her steady and thoughtful work made this a much better book. I would also like to thank everyone who had a hand in this book at R&L over the years, including the design team, copyeditors, marketing team, and the production staff—first-rate one and all. A huge thanks to illustrator, comic artist, and storyteller Jason Piperberg for his Marvel comic book–inspired cover design. His work on this book and the young adult version brings Stan alive for a new generation of readers.

I would like to thank several friends and scholars who helped me along the way, including Arthur Asa Berger, who is simply one of the nation's great creative minds. His friendship with Stan gave me another point of reference, and I greatly appreciate his advice and support. Thanks too go to Carl Rollyson—in my mind the dean of American biography—who always says, "The answer to one biography is another biography." His work is inspirational, and I used his thinking as a guide as I wrote this book! Thanks as well to my mentor and friend Phillip Sipiora and to the memory of the great historian Lawrence S. Kaplan. I am constantly inspired to be a stronger writer and thinker by Jerome Charyn. He has had a profound impact on me. Thank you, too, to Jerome's wife, Lenore Riegel, for continued friendship and support.

A big shout-out to several friends who have offered unwavering support on the journey, including Brian Jay Jones, one of America's best biographers, and Kyle Sarofeen, the publisher of Hamilcar Publications and a guy I'm happy to call friend! I would also like to thank Jim Thompson, Alex Grand,

and the Comic Book Historians group they run on Facebook. I have learned so much as a member. I have also learned so much at Comics' Silver Age, run by the eminent Clifford Meth.

Josh Schwartz is a trusted friend, advisor, and confidante. Thanks, buddy, for all you've done for me and Stan's story! My thinking about history, life, and friendship has been shaped and formed by Thomas Heinrich. He is more than a friend—a brother for life.

Imagine my surprise when Tom DeLonge agreed to write the foreword! Thanks to everyone on Tom's team for making this happen, particularly Kari DeLonge. From music superstar to To the Stars★ to major motion pictures, Tom has shaped contemporary culture in a way few can claim. Thanks, Tom, for lending your insight—Excelsior!

This book is dedicated to the memory of my mother-in-law, Josette Hérupé Percival Valois. I would also like to extend my thanks to Michel Valois, Carole and Laurent van Huffel, Matthew van Huffel and Trang, Benjamin van Huffel, and Nicholas van Huffel.

Finally, nothing is possible without the love and support a writer receives from their family. Thank you to Kassie and Sophia for all the love in the world and being the wonderful young women you are! My wife, Suzette, is also my research partner, cowriter, best friend, and north star. Thank you, my love, for everything.

Notes

CHAPTER 1

1. Quoted in Nancy Tartaglione, "Marvel's Victoria Alonso," *Deadline*, June 14, 2021.

2. Sophie Vallas, ed., *Conversations with Jerome Charyn* (Jackson: University of Mississippi Press, 2014), 157, 60.

3. Spencer Harrison, Arne Carlsen, and Miha Škerlavaj, "Marvel's Blockbuster Machine," *Harvard Business Review*, July–August 2019, https://hbr.org/2019/07/marvels -blockbuster-machine.

4. Ibid. The Harrison et al. article is brilliant! Please go find it online and read it.

5. Tartaglione, "Marvel's Victoria Alonso."

6. Brad Meltzer, "Stan Lee," *Entertainment Weekly*, December 14/21, 2018, 90–91.

7. Frank Pallotta, "Marvel Heroes," CNN, November 12, 2018.

8. Roy Thomas, "Roy Thomas, Former Marvel Editor, Pushes Back on New Stan Lee Biography," *The Hollywood Reporter*, February 23, 2021, https://www.holly woodreporter.com/movies/movie-news/roy-thomas-former-marvel-editor-pushes -back-on-new-stan-lee-biography-guest-column-4136571/.

9. Danny Fingeroth, *A Marvelous Life: The Amazing Story of Stan Lee* (New York: St. Martin's Press, 2019), Kindle edition.

CHAPTER 2

1. The sum equates to about $3,500 (Samuel H. Williamson, "Seven Ways to Compute the Relative Value of a U.S. Dollar Amount, 1790 to present," Measuring-Worth.com, 2021).

2. Dana Mihailescu, "Images of Romania and America in Early Twentieth-Century Romanian-Jewish Immigrant Life Stories in the United States," *East European Jewish Affairs* 42, no. 1 (2012): 28.

3. Gur Alroey, *Bread to Eat and Clothes to Wear: Letters from Jewish Migrants in the Early Twentieth Century* (Detroit, MI: Wayne State University Press, 2011), 32.

4. Alroey, *Bread to Eat*, 12.

5. Lee said relatively little about several significant topics: his parents, relatives, ethnicity, or religion. See Stan Lee and George Mair, *Excelsior!: The Amazing Life of Stan Lee* (New York: Simon and Schuster, 2002), 5; Stan Lee, Peter David, and Colleen Doran, *Amazing Fantastic Incredible: A Marvelous Memoir* (New York: Touchstone, 2015), n.p.

6. Many basic facts about Lee's extended family are unknown. In the archives, his father's name changed from Hyman in 1910 to Jacob in 1920, while his birthdate is listed alternatively as 1886 or 1888. If the latter is correct, then he was only seventeen years old during the transatlantic journey. Later, Lee mentioned Jacob's sisters (Becky and Bertha), but they do not show up in any further documentation, nor does he mention them in his memoirs. Joanna Lieber to Stan Lee, e-mail message, April 26, 1998, Correspondence, 1998, Box 196, Stan Lee Papers, American Heritage Center, University of Wyoming.

7. Stan Lee, interview by Mark Lacter, "Stan Lee Marvel Comics Always Searching for a New Story," *Inc.*, November 2009, 96.

8. Stan Lee, "Excelsior!" (Autobiography) Outline, July 30, 1978, Box 96, Stan Lee Papers, American Heritage Center, University of Wyoming.

9. Lee and Mair, *Excelsior!*, 7.

10. Lee, "Excelsior!"

11. Lee and Mair, *Excelsior!*, 11.

12. Jordan Raphael and Tom Spurgeon, *Stan Lee and the Rise and Fall of the American Comic Book* (Chicago: Chicago Review Press, 2003), 4.

13. Lee and Mair, *Excelsior!*, 12.

14. Ibid., 9.

15. Lee, "Excelsior!"

16. Lee and Mair, *Excelsior!*, 10.

17. Stan Lee, "Comic Relief: Comic Books Aren't Just for Entertainment," *Edutopia*, August 11, 2005, http://www.edutopia.org/comic-relief.

18. Lee and Mair, *Excelsior!*, 13.

19. Lee, "Excelsior!"

20. Quoted in Stan Lee, interview by Mike Bourne, "Stan Lee, The Marvel Bard," in *Alter Ego*, 3, no. 74 (2007): 26.

21. Quoted in *With Great Power: The Stan Lee Story*, directed by Terry Douglas, Nikki Frakes, and William Lawrence Hess (Los Angeles: MPI Home Video, 2012).

22. Stan Lee, "History of Marvel (Chapters 1, 2, 3)," Unpublished, 2. Marvel Comics—History (Draft of "History of Marvel Comics"), 1990, Box 5, Folder 7, Stan Lee Papers.

23. Quoted in Raphael and Spurgeon, *Stan Lee*, 8.

24. Lee and Mair, *Excelsior!*, 15.

25. Raphael and Spurgeon, *Stan Lee*, 7.

26. United States, Bureau of the Census (8 April 1940). 1940 U.S. Census: Jacob Lieber Family. Sheet 6-B. Barb Sigler. New York, Bronx County, New York; enumeration district 3-1487, household 61. *HeritageQuest Online.*

27. Robert A. Margo, "Employment and Unemployment in the 1930s," *Journal of Economic Perspectives* 7, no. 2 (1993): 43–44.

28. Lee and Mair, *Excelsior!*, 6.

29. Stan Lee, interview by David Hochman, "Playboy Interview: Stan Lee," *Playboy*, April 11, 2014.

30. Lee and Mair, *Excelsior!*, 7.

31. Mark Alexander, "Lee & Kirby: The Wonder Years," *Jack Kirby Collector* 18, no. 58 (Winter 2011): 5.

CHAPTER 3

1. Blake Bell and Michael J. Vassallo, *The Secret History of Marvel Comics: Jack Kirby and the Moonlighting Artists at Martin Goodman's Empire* (Seattle: Fantagraphics, 2013), 98.

2. Stan Lee interview, "Interview with Stan Lee (Part 1 of 5)," *IGN*, June 26, 2000, https://www.ign.com/articles/2000/06/26/interview-with-stan-lee-part-1 -of-5.

3. Lieber's exact hiring date is still a mystery. In an unpublished draft of the history of Marvel, Lee wrote "early 1940," but in other publications and places, he says or infers 1939. Lee, "History of Marvel (Chapters 1, 2, 3)," Marvel Comics— History (Draft of "History of Marvel Comics"), 1990, Box 5, Folder 7, Stan Lee Papers, American Heritage Center, University of Wyoming, 1.

4. Gerard Jones, *Men of Tomorrow: Geeks, Gangsters, and the Birth of the Comic Book* (New York: Basic, 2004), 97.

5. Ibid., 108.

6. Ibid., 158.

7. Ibid., 159.

8. Sean Howe, *Marvel Comics: The Untold Story* (New York: Harper, 2012), 14.

9. Ibid.

10. Quoted in Mark Evanier, *Kirby: King of Comics* (New York: Abrams, 2008), 45.

11. Joe Simon, *Joe Simon: My Life in Comics* (London: Titan, 2011), 92.

12. Howe, *Marvel Comics*, 20.

13. "The Marvelous Life of Stan Lee," *CBS News*, January 17, 2016, https://www .cbsnews.com/news/the-marvelous-life-of-stan-lee/.

14. Stan Lee and George Mair, *Excelsior! The Amazing Life of Stan Lee* (New York: Simon and Schuster, 2002), 26.

15. Stan Lee, "1975 San Diego Comic-Con Convention," YouTube, https:// youtu.be/MhJuBqDTM9Q.

16. *Captain America Comics #3*, May 1, 1941, 37.

17. Simon, *My Life in Comics*, 114.

18. Quoted in ibid., 113.

19. Ibid.

20. Ibid., 114.

21. Quoted in Stan Lee, Peter David, and Colleen Doran, *Amazing Fantastic Incredible: A Marvelous Memoir* (New York: Touchstone, 2015), n.p.

22. Lee and Mair, *Excelsior!*, 30.

23. Lee, "History of Marvel (Chapters 1, 2, 3)," 9.

24. Quoted in Shirrel Rhoades, *A Complete History of American Comic Books* (New York: Peter Lang, 2008), 36.

25. Stan Goldberg, interview by Jim Amash, "The Goldberg Variations," *Alter Ego* 3, no. 18 (October 2002): 6.

26. Arie Kaplan, *Masters of the Comic Book Universe Revealed!* (Chicago: Chicago Review Press, 2006), 49.

27. Quoted in Rhoades, *A Complete History*, 36.

28. Lee and Mair, *Excelsior!*, 30.

CHAPTER 4

1. Rebecca Robbins Raines, *Getting the Message Through: A Branch History of the U.S. Army Signal Corps* (Washington, DC: Center of Military History, US Army, 1996), 256.

2. Mike Benton, *The Comic Book in America: An Illustrated History* (Dallas, TX: Taylor, 1989), 35–41.

3. Sean Howe, *Marvel Comics: The Untold Story* (New York: Harper, 2012), 24. In 2020 terms, Fago's salary based on "relative income value" was $51,400, while "relative output value" was $126,000 (Samuel H. Williamson, "Seven Ways to Compute the Relative Value of a U.S. Dollar Amount, 1790 to present," MeasuringWorth.com, 2021).

4. Catherine Sanders et al., eds., *Marvel Year by Year: A Visual Chronicle* (New York: DK, 2013), 20.

5. Quoted in Howe, *Marvel Comics*, 25.

6. During the time Lee was stationed at Fort Monmouth, Julius Rosenberg carried out a clandestine mission spying for Russia. He also recruited scientists and engineers from the base into the spy ring he led in New Jersey and funneled thousands of pages of top-secret documents to his Russian handlers. In 1953, Rosenberg and his wife, Ethel, were arrested, convicted, and executed.

7. Stan Lee, interview by Steven Mackenzie, "Stan Lee Interview: 'The World Always Needs Heroes,'" *The Big Issue*, January 18, 2016, http://www.bigissue.com/features/interviews/6153/stan-lee-interview-the-world-always-needs-heroes.

8. Stan Lee, "Excelsior!" (Autobiography) Outline, July 30, 1978, Box 96, Stan Lee Papers.

9. Quoted in Stan Lee and George Mair, *Excelsior! The Amazing Life of Stan Lee* (New York: Simon and Schuster, 2002), 37.

10. Ibid., 40; quoted in Clifford Meth, *ComicBook Babylon* (Rockaway, NJ: Aardwolf Publishing, 2014), Kindle edition.

11. Stan Lee, "Comic Relief: Comic Books Aren't Just for Entertainment," *Edutopia*, August 11, 2005, http://www.edutopia.org/comic-relief.

12. Quoted in Meth, *ComicBook Babylon*.

13. Lee and Mair, *Excelsior!*, 44.

14. "Venereal Disease and Treatment during WW2," WW2 US Medical Research Centre, n.d., https://www.med-dept.com/articles/venereal-disease-and-treatment-during-ww2/.

15. Ibid., 45.

16. George Raynor Thompson and Dixie R. Harris, *The Signal Corps: The Outcome (Mid-1943 through 1945)* (Washington, DC: Center of Military History, United States Army, 1991), 555.

17. Blake Bell and Michael J. Vassallo, *The Secret History of Marvel Comics: Jack Kirby and the Moonlighting Artists at Martin Goodman's Empire* (Seattle: Fantagraphics, 2013), 158.

18. Stan Lee, "Only the Blind Can See," *Joker* 1, no. 4 (1943–1944): 39; reprinted in Bell and Vassallo, *Secret History*, 159.

19. Lee and Mair, *Excelsior!*, 43–44.

CHAPTER 5

1. Equivalent to more than $3,000 in today's wealth; see Samuel H. Williamson, "Seven Ways to Compute the Relative Value of a U.S. Dollar Amount, 1790 to present," MeasuringWorth.com, 2021.

2. Stan Lee, "Excelsior!" (Autobiography) Outline, July 30, 1978, Box 96, Stan Lee Papers, American Heritage Center, University of Wyoming.

3. Stan Lee and George Mair, *Excelsior! The Amazing Life of Stan Lee* (New York: Simon and Schuster, 2002), 56.

4. Timely script editor Al Sulman claims he created the character after Lee asked him to come up with a Wonder Woman–like heroine.

5. Joe Simon, *My Life in Comics* (London: Titan Books, 2011), 166–67.

6. Comic books were not uniformly numbered, titled, retitled, or renumbered, which had to do with printing and distribution processes as well as postal regulations. Traditional methods were developed from pulps, which led to similar tactics in the comic books. For more, see John Jackson Miller, "Where Did Comics Numbering Come From?" *Comichron*, July 10, 2011, http://blog.comichron.com/2011/07/where-did-comics-numbering-come-from.html.

7. Lee and Mair, *Excelsior!*, 64.

8. Stan Lee, *Secrets Behind the Comics* (New York: Famous Enterprises, 1947), 6, 22.

9. Ibid., 64, 66.

10. Blake Bell and Michael J. Vassallo, *The Secret History of Marvel Comics: Jack Kirby and the Moonlighting Artists at Martin Goodman's Empire* (Seattle: Fantagraphics, 2013), 72.

11. Stan Lee, interview by David Anthony Kraft, "The FOOM Interview: Stan Lee," 1977, in *Stan Lee Conversations*, ed. Jeff McLaughlin (Jackson: University Press of Mississippi, 2007), 68.

12. Stan Lee, "Excelsior!" (Autobiography) Outline.

13. Ibid.

14. Stan Lee, "Where I Span a Hero's Yarn," *Sunday Times*, May 12, 2002, F3.

15. Lee, "Hero's Yarn."

16. Jordan Raphael and Tom Spurgeon, *Stan Lee and the Rise and Fall of the American Comic Book* (Chicago: Chicago Review Press, 2003), 38.

17. Lee, "Excelsior!" (Autobiography) Outline.

18. "Urges Comic Book Ban," *New York Times*, September 4, 1948, 16.

19. Quoted in Thomas F. O'Connor, "The National Organization for Decent Literature: A Phase in American Catholic Censorship," *Library Quarterly: Information, Community, Policy* 65, no. 4 (1995): 390.

20. Ron Goulart, *Great American Comic Books* (Lincolnwood, IL: Publications International, 2001), 210–12.

21. Lee's glib discussion of the debates is in Lee and Mair, *Excelsior!*, 92–94.

22. Ibid., 91.

23. Ibid., 92, 93.

24. Quoted in David Hajdu, *The Ten-Cent Plague: The Great Comic-Book Scare and How It Changed America* (New York: Farrar, Straus and Giroux, 2008), 264.

25. Ibid., 269ff, 270–73.

26. Goulart, *Great American*, 217.

27. Lee and Mair, *Excelsior!*, 93.

28. Ibid., 94.

29. Stan Goldberg, interview by Jim Amash, "The Goldberg Variations," *Alter Ego 3*, no. 18 (October 2002): 9.

30. Alexandra Gill, "Captain Comics," *Globe and Mail*, September 29, 2003, R1.

31. Richard Harrington, "Stan Lee: Caught in Spidey's Web," *Washington Post*, February 4, 1992, D1.

32. Lee and Mair, *Excelsior!*, 99.

33. Quoted in Sean Howe, *Marvel Comics: The Untold Story* (New York: Harper, 2012), 32.

34. Lee and Mair, *Excelsior!*, 87, 88.

35. Quoted in Howe, *Marvel Comics*, 35.

CHAPTER 6

1. John Romita, "Face Front, True Believers! The Comics Industry Sounds Off on Stan Lee," *Comics Journal* 181 (October 1995): 83.

2. Roy Thomas, "All-Schwartz Comics: A Conversation with Editorial Legend Julius Schwartz," *Alter Ego* 3, no. 7 (2001), http://www.twomorrows.com/alterego/articles/07schwartz.html.

3. Shirrel Rhoades, *A Complete History of American Comic Books* (New York: Peter Lang, 2008), 70–71.

4. Ibid., 72–73.

5. Blake Bell and Michael J. Vassallo, *The Secret History of Marvel Comics: Jack Kirby and the Moonlighting Artists at Martin Goodman's Empire* (Seattle: Fantagraphics, 2013), 75.

6. Quoted in ibid., 45.

7. Stan Lee and George Mair, *Excelsior! The Amazing Life of Stan Lee* (New York: Simon and Schuster, 2002), 112.

8. Stan Lee, *Origins of Marvel Comics*, revised edition (New York: Marvel, 1997), 10.

9. Craig Tomashoff, "Move Over Batman . . ." *Los Angeles Reader*, January 26, 1990.

10. *Stan Lee's Mutants, Monsters, and Marvels*, directed by Scott Zakarin (Burbank, CA: Sony Pictures, 2002), DVD.

11. Roy Thomas, "A Fantastic First," in *The Stan Lee Universe*, ed. Danny Fingeroth and Roy Thomas (Raleigh, NC: TwoMorrows, 2011), 17.

12. Stan Lee and Jack Kirby, *Marvel Masterworks: Fantastic Four, Nos. 1–10* (New York: Marvel, 2003), n.p.

13. *Stan Lee's Mutants.*

14. Stan Lee, Peter David, and Colleen Doran, *Amazing Fantastic Incredible: A Marvelous Memoir* (New York: Touchstone, 2015), n.p.

15. Quoted in Les Daniels, *Marvel: Five Fabulous Decades of the World's Greatest Comics* (New York: Harry N. Abrams, 1995), 87.

16. The popularity of *The Fantastic Four* enabled Goodman to raise the price of all comics from the traditional ten cents to twelve cents per issue. The increase took place with the third issue dated March 1962.

17. "Fantastic Four #1 Synopsis," reprinted in Thomas, "A Fantastic First," 16.

18. Ted White, "Stan Lee Meets [Castle of] Frankenstein: An Early Marvel Age interview with Stan," in *The Stan Lee Universe*, ed. Danny Fingeroth and Roy Thomas (Raleigh, NC: TwoMorrows, 2011), 11.

19. Lee and Mair, *Excelsior!*, 124.

20. Stan Lee and Jack Kirby, *Marvel Masterworks: Fantastic Four, Nos. 11–20* (New York: Marvel, 2003), n.p.

21. Quoted in Daniels, *Marvel: Five Fabulous Decades*, 85, 87.

22. Stan Lee, *Bring on the Bad Guys*, revised edition (New York: Marvel, 1998), n.p.

23. Ibid.

24. Lee and Kirby, *Marvel Masterworks, Nos. 11–20*, n.p.

CHAPTER 7

1. Mark Lacter, "Stan Lee, Marvel Comics Always Searching for a New Story," *Inc.*, November 2009, 96.

2. Don Thrasher, "Stan Lee's Secret to Success: A Marvel-ous Imagination," *Dayton Daily News*, January 21, 2006, sec. E.

3. Lacter, "Stan Lee, Marvel Comics Always Searching," 96.

4 Quoted in John Morrow, *Kirby and Lee: Stuf' Said!*, expanded 2nd ed. (Raleigh, NC: TwoMorrows, 2019), 15.

5. Quoted in Lacter, "Stan Lee, Marvel Comics Always Searching."

6. Stan Lee and George Mair, *Excelsior! The Amazing Life of Stan Lee* (New York: Simon and Schuster, 2002), 126–27.

7. Ibid., 126.

8. Roy Thomas, "Stan the Man and Roy the Boy: A Conversation between Stan Lee and Roy Thomas," in *Stan Lee Conversations*, ed. Jeff McLaughlin (Jackson: University Press of Mississippi, 2007), 141.

9. Ibid.

10. Lee and Mair, *Excelsior!*, 127.

11. Thomas, "Stan the Man," 141.

12. Lee and Mair, *Excelsior!*, 127.

13. Ibid., 128.

14. Ibid., 128.

15. Leonard Pitts Jr., "An Interview with Stan Lee," in *Stan Lee Conversations*, ed. Jeff McLaughlin (Jackson: University Press of Mississippi, 2007), 96.

16. Quoted in Lee and Mair, *Excelsior!*, 128.

17. Stan Lee, Peter David, and Colleen Doran, *Amazing Fantastic Incredible: A Marvelous Memoir* (New York: Touchstone, 2015), n.p.

18. Lee and Mair, *Excelsior!*, 135–36.

19 Quoted in Morrow, *Kirby and Lee*, 167.

20. Stan Lee, "That's My Spidey," *New York Times*, May 3, 2002, https://www.nytimes.com/2002/05/03/opinion/that-s-my-spidey.html.

CHAPTER 8

1. Stan Lee and George Mair, *Excelsior! The Amazing Life of Stan Lee* (New York: Simon and Schuster, 2002), 120.

2. Quoted in Roger Sabin, *Comics, Comix and Graphic Novels: A History of Comic Art* (New York: Phaidon, 1996).

3. Stan Lee, *Son of Origins of Marvel Comics*, revised edition (New York: Marvel, 1997), 69.

4. Pierre Comtois, *Marvel Comics in the 1960s: An Issue by Issue Field Guide to a Pop Culture Phenomenon* (Raleigh, NC: TwoMorrows, 2009), 20.

5. Stan Lee, *Origins of Marvel Comics*, revised edition (New York: Marvel, 1997), 165.

6. Larry Lieber, interviewed by Danny Fingeroth, *WriteNow!* 18 (Summer 2008): 5.

7. Quoted in Will Murray, "Stan Lee Looks Back: The Comics Legend Recalls Life with Jack Kirby, Steve Ditko, and Heroes," in *Stan Lee Conversations*, ed. Jeff McLaughlin (Jackson: University Press of Mississippi, 2007), 182.

8. Lee and Mair, *Excelsior!*, 160.

9. Quoted in Les Daniels, *Marvel: Five Fabulous Decades of the World's Greatest Comics* (New York: Harry N. Abrams, 1995), 99.

10. Lee, *Origins of Marvel Comics*, 215.

11. Lee, *Son of Origins*, 110.

12. Quoted in John Morrow, *Kirby and Lee: Stuf' Said!*, expanded second edition (Raleigh, NC: TwoMorrows, 2019), 35.

13. Ibid., 10.

14. Jack Kirby disputed Lee's origin story decades later, writing: "In the early 1960s, everyone was wondering what radioactivity would do to us. My imagination took over and that's how I came up with The X-Men! The X-Men are people who have suffered radiation and they all change in a variety of ways." Quoted in Morrow, *Kirby and Lee*, 162.

15. Quoted in Dick Cavett, "The Dick Cavett Show: An Interview with Stan Lee," in *Stan Lee Conversations*, ed. Jeff McLaughlin (Jackson: University Press of Mississippi, 2007), 15.

16. Quoted in Dewey Cassell, ed., *The Art of George Tuska* (Raleigh, NC: Two-Morrows, 2005), 57. In 1972, Tuska was the first artist to illustrate Luke Cage for the Black superhero's series. Two years later, he worked on the revamped Luke Cage, Power Man.

17. Ibid., 58.

18. Gene Colan, interviewed in Tom Field, "The Colan Mystique," *Comic Book Artist* 13 (May 2001), http://twomorrows.com/comicbookartist/articles/13colan.html.

19. Dennis O'Neil, interviewed in Danny Fingeroth, *The Stan Lee Universe*, ed. Danny Fingeroth and Roy Thomas (Raleigh, NC: TwoMorrows, 2011), 53.

20. Ibid.

21 The new style of creating comic books grew out of Lee's determination to keep freelance artists working. If they had to wait around while he finished writing a script, they were essentially losing money.

22. *Stan Lee's Mutants, Monsters, and Marvels*, directed by Scott Zakarin (Burbank, CA: Sony Pictures, 2002), DVD.

23. Ibid.

24. Quoted in Chris Gavaler, "Kirby vs. Steranko! Silver Age Layout Wars," *The Hooded Utilitarian*, July 12, 2016, http://www.hoodedutilitarian.com/2016/07/kirby-vs-steranko-silver-age-layout-wars/.

25. Ibid.

26. Lee, *Origins of Marvel Comics*, 164.

CHAPTER 9

1. *Stan Lee's Mutants, Monsters, and Marvels*, directed by Scott Zakarin (Burbank, CA: Sony Pictures, 2002), DVD.

2. Quoted in Paul Lopes, *Demanding Respect: The Evolution of the American Comic Book* (Philadelphia: Temple University Press, 2009), 65.

3. Craig Tomashoff, "Move Over Batman . . ." *Los Angeles Reader*, January 26, 1990.

4. David Kasakove, "Finding Marvel's Voice: An Appreciation of Stan Lee's Bullpen Bulletins and Soapboxes," *Write Now* 18 (Summer 2008): 57.

5. Mark Alexander, "Lee & Kirby: The Wonder Years," in *Jack Kirby Collector* 18, no. 58 (Winter 2011): 8.

6. Ibid.

7. Quoted in Danny Fingeroth, *The Stan Lee Universe*, ed. Danny Fingeroth and Roy Thomas (Raleigh, NC: TwoMorrows, 2011), 52.

8. Ibid.

9. Stan Lee interview in Dan Hagan, "Stan Lee," *Comics Interview*, July 1983, 55.

10 Quoted in John Morrow, *Kirby and Lee: Stuf' Said!*, expanded second edition (Raleigh, NC: TwoMorrows, 2019), 167.

11. Leonard Sloane, "Advertising: Comics Go Up, Up and Away," *New York Times*, July 20, 1967.

12. Ibid.

13. Quoted in ibid.

14. Lopes, *Demanding Respect*, 66.

15. Mike Benton, *The Comic Book in America: An Illustrated History* (Dallas, TX: Taylor, 1989), 71.

16. Stan Lee, "Excelsior!" (Autobiography) Outline, July 30, 1978, Box 96, Stan Lee Papers, American Heritage Center, University of Wyoming.

17. Stan Lee and George Mair, *Excelsior! The Amazing Life of Stan Lee* (New York: Simon and Schuster, 2002), 142.

18. Quoted in Dick Cavett, "The Dick Cavett Show: An Interview with Stan Lee," in *Stan Lee Conversations*, ed. Jeff McLaughlin (Jackson: University Press of Mississippi, 2007), 16.

19. Ibid.

20. M. Thomas Inge, "From the Publisher's Perspective: Comments by Stan Lee and Jenette Kahn," in *Stan Lee Conversations*, ed. Jeff McLaughlin (Jackson: University Press of Mississippi, 2007), 105.

21. Stan Lee, Peter David, and Colleen Doran, *Amazing Fantastic Incredible: A Marvelous Memoir* (New York: Touchstone, 2015).

22. Lee and Mair, *Excelsior!*, 179.

23. Quoted in Sean Howe, *Marvel Comics: The Untold Story* (New York: Harper, 2012), 92.

24. Ibid., 100ff.

25. Quoted in ibid., 104.

26. Quoted in Cavett, "The Dick Cavett Show," 18.

CHAPTER 10

1. Norman Mark, "The New Super-Hero (Is a Pretty Kinky Guy)," *Alter Ego* 3, no. 74 (2007): 20.

2. Michael Goldman, "Stan Lee: Comic Guru," *Animation World Magazine*, July 1997, 8.

3. Quoted in Mark, "The New Super-Hero," 20.

4. Ibid.

5. Quoted in ibid., 21.

6. Quoted in Brian Cunningham, ed., *Stan's Soapbox: The Collection* (New York: Marvel, 2009), 16.

7. Quoted in Stan Lee, interview by Mike Bourne, "Stan Lee, The Marvel Bard," *Alter Ego* 3, no. 74 (2007): 30.

8. Quoted in Cunningham, *Stan's Soapbox*, 31.

9. Mark Evanier, *Kirby: King of Comics* (New York: Abrams, 2008), 157.

10. Joe Simon, *Joe Simon: My Life in Comics* (London: Titan, 2011), n.p.

11. Ibid.

12. Lawrence Van Gelder, "A Comics Magazine Defies Code Ban on Drug Stories," *New York Times*, February 4, 1971, 37.

13. Quoted in ibid., 38.

14. Ibid.

15. Ibid.

16. "Stan Lee," Billy Ireland Cartoon Library and Museum Biographical Files, Ohio State University Billy Ireland Cartoon Library and Museum.

17. "Comics Come to Carnegie," *New York Post*, January 6, 1972, 44.

18. Quoted in Van Gelder, "A Comics Magazine," 28.

19. Ibid., 33.

20. Roy Thomas, interview by Jon B. Cooke, "Son of Stan: Roy's Years of Horrors," *Comic Book Artist* 13 (May 2001), http://twomorrows.com/comicbookartist/articles/13thomas.html.

21. Ibid.

22. *Stan Lee's Mutants, Monsters, and Marvels*, directed by Scott Zakarin (Burbank, CA: Sony Pictures, 2002), DVD.

23. Quoted in Thomas J. McLean, "Unique Collaborations Set Marvel Apart," *Variety*, July 19–25, 2004, B12.

24. Thomas, "Son of Stan."

25. Ibid.

26. Stan Lee, *The Best of Spider-Man* (New York: Ballantine, 1986), 10.

CHAPTER 11

1. Memo, "Marvel Comics, Classification and Frequency of Titles," January 16, 1973, Memoranda 1969–1976, Box 7, Folder 1, Stan Lee Papers, American Heritage Center, University of Wyoming.

2. Ibid.

3. Stan Lee, Memo, "Approval of Covers, Etc.," n.d., Memoranda 1969–1976, Box 7, Folder 1, Stan Lee Papers, American Heritage Center, University of Wyoming.

4. Stan Lee, interview by David Anthony Kraft, in *Stan Lee Conversations*, ed. Jeff McLaughlin (Jackson: University Press of Mississippi, 2007), 65.

5. Mike Benton, *The Comic Book in America: An Illustrated History* (Dallas, TX: Taylor, 1989), 74.

6. "ABC Audit Report-Magazine: Marvel Comic Group," Memoranda 1969–1976, Box 7, Folder 1, Stan Lee Papers, American Heritage Center, University of Wyoming.

7. Jonathan Hoyle, "Comic Sales (Monthly Average in Millions) for Marvel and DC, 1950 to 1987," The Fantastic Four 1961–1989 Was the Great American Novel, http://zak-site.com/Great-American-Novel/comic_sales.html.

8. Quoted in Brian Cunningham, ed., *Stan's Soapbox: The Collection* (New York: Marvel, 2009), 59.

9. Quoted in Les Daniels, *Marvel: Five Fabulous Decades of the World's Greatest Comics* (New York: Harry N. Abrams, 1995), 156.

10. Memo, "We Must Be Doing Something Right!" Memoranda 1969–1976, Box 7, Folder 1, Stan Lee Papers, American Heritage Center, University of Wyoming.

11. Peter Gorner, "Stan Lee's Superheroes," *Chicago Tribune*, July 17, 1975, B1.

12. Stan Lee and George Mair, *Excelsior!: The Amazing Life of Stan Lee* (New York: Simon and Schuster, 2002), 183.

13. Sherry Romeo, "Inter-Office Memo," December 17, 1974, Memoranda 1969–1976, Box 7, Folder 1, Stan Lee Papers, American Heritage Center, University of Wyoming.

14. Stan Lee, "Introduction," in *George Lucas, Star Wars* (New York: Del Rey, 1977), 1.

15. Daniels, *Marvel*, 177.

16. Ibid.

17. Stan Lee, "Streaking," *Crazy*, July 1973, 16. San Francisco Academy of Comic Art Collection, Ohio State University Billy Ireland Cartoon Library and Museum.

18. Quoted in David Hench, "Maine Artist Recalls Spider-Man Work," *Portland Press Herald* (Maine), May 5, 2007, A1.

19. Stan Lee and Frank Springer, *The Virtue of Vera Valiant* (New York: Signet, 1976), 9, 10.

20. Stan Lee, interview by Dan Hagan, "Stan Lee," *Comics Interview*, July 1983, 57.

21. Stan Lee, *Best of Spider-Man* (New York: Ballantine, 1986), 6.

22. Dewey Cassell, ed., *The Art of George Tuska* (Raleigh, NC: TwoMorrows, 2005), 105.

23. Lee, *Best*, 8.

24. Lee, interview by Hagan, "Stan Lee," 57.

25. Memo, "S&S Sales," Marvel Comics Group—Facts and Figures 1976–1978, Box 6, Folder 4, Stan Lee Papers, American Heritage Center, University of Wyoming.

26. Lee, interview by Kraft, 67.

27. Stan Lee, *The Superhero Women* (New York: Simon and Schuster, 1977), 8.

28. "Fireside Paperbacks Marketing Flyer," Articles—1977, Box 32, Folder 2, Stan Lee Papers, American Heritage Center, University of Wyoming.

29. Lee, interview by Kraft, 67.

30. Stan Lee, *The Best of the Worst* (New York: Harper & Row, 1979), 10.

31. Stan Lee, interview by Mike Gold, in *Stan Lee Conversations*, ed. Jeff McLaughlin (Jackson: University Press of Mississippi, 2007), 43.

32. Mark Evanier, *Kirby: King of Comics* (New York: Abrams, 2008), 189.

33. George Kashdan, interview by Jim Amash, "Sales Don't Tell You Everything," *Alter Ego* 3, no. 94 (June 2010): 49.

34. Evanier, *Kirby*, 191.

35. "'Spider-Man' to be Featured in Action Film," *New Castle (PA) News*, April 16, 1975, 8.

36. Lee Stewart, "Spinner Takes All," *The Sunday Times* (London), May 12, 2002, Newspaper Source, EBSCOhost (accessed February 21, 2015).

37. N. R. Kleinfield, "Superheroes' Creators Wrangle," *New York Times*, October 13, 1979, 25.

38. Ibid.

39. Quoted in ibid., 26.

40. Paul Lopes, *Demanding Respect: The Evolution of the American Comic Book* (Philadelphia, PA: Temple University Press, 2009), 71.

41. Quoted in Sean Howe, *Marvel Comics: The Untold Story* (New York: Harper, 2012), 215.

CHAPTER 12

1. Stan Lee and George Mair, *Excelsior!: The Amazing Life of Stan Lee* (New York: Simon and Schuster, 2002), 202.

2. "Marvels of the Mind: The Comics Go Hollywood," *Time*, February 5, 1979.

3. Quoted in Paul Weingarten, "The Hulk," *Chronicle-Telegram* (Elyria, OH), October 30, 1978, B-9.

4. Ibid.

5. Craig Tomashoff, "Move Over Batman . . ." *Los Angeles Reader*, January 26, 1990.

6. Stan Lee, interview by Pat Jankiewicz, in *Stan Lee Conversations*, ed. Jeff McLaughlin (Jackson: University Press of Mississippi, 2007), 108.

7. Tomashoff, "Move Over Batman."

8. Stan Lee, interview by Jim Salicrup and David Anthony Kraft, "Stan Lee," *Comics Interview*, July 1983, 48.

9. Tomashoff, "Move Over Batman."

10. Letter, Stan Lee to Alain Resnais, May 23, 1979, Correspondence 1977–1980 (Folder 1 of 2), Box 14, Folder 1, Stan Lee Papers, American Heritage Center, University of Wyoming.

11. Stan Lee, Peter David, and Colleen Doran, *Amazing Fantastic Incredible: A Marvelous Memoir* (New York: Touchstone, 2015), n.p.

12. Letter, Stan Lee to Alain Resnais, Stan Lee Papers.

13. Letter, Michael Herz to Sam Arkoff, July 5, 1979, Correspondence 1977–1980 (Folder 1 of 2), Box 14, Folder 1, Stan Lee Papers, American Heritage Center, University of Wyoming.

14. "Marvel Entertainment Group Forms Marvel Productions Ltd.," Marvel Update, Summer 1980, 6. Scrapbook Feb. 1980–Nov. 12 1984, Box 129, Stan Lee Papers, American Heritage Center, University of Wyoming.

15. Ibid., 1.

16. Quoted in ibid., 2.

17. "Marvels of the Mind."

18. Lee, interview by Salicrup and Kraft, "Stan Lee," 47.

19. Ibid., 48.

20. Ibid.

21. "Comic Characters Put a Zing in Product Promotion," *The Sales Executive*, April 1, 1980, 4.

22. Quoted in Judy Klemesrud, "Savage She-Hulk New Comic Heroine," *New York Times News Service*, January 20, 1980.

23. Terry Young, "Spider-Man's About to Get Real, Says His Creator," *Toronto Star* (Canada), July 6, 1986.

24. Stan Lee to Francelia Butler, November 21, 1980, Correspondence, Box 14, File 4, Stan Lee Papers, American Heritage Center, University of Wyoming. The fee would be between $10,000 and $20,000 in 2020 (Samuel H. Williamson, "Seven Ways to Compute the Relative Value of a U.S. Dollar Amount, 1790 to present," MeasuringWorth.com, 2021).

25. Stan Lee, interview by Margaret Jones and John R. Gambling, "Good Afternoon New York," WOR/Radio, June 22, 1984. Interviews with Stan Lee 1970–1989, Box 3, Folder 10–11, Stan Lee Papers, American Heritage Center, University of Wyoming.

26. Stan Lee, *Best of Spider-Man* (New York: Ballantine, 1986), 9.

27. Ibid., 10, 12.

28. Ibid., 12–16.

29. Quoted in Sean Howe, *Marvel Comics: The Untold Story* (New York: Harper, 2012), 294.

30. Lee and Mair, *Excelsior!*, 209–10.

31. Quoted in Howe, *Marvel Comics*, 295.

32. Ibid., 309.

33. Quoted in ibid., 311–12.

CHAPTER 13

1. Mike Wallace, "Ronald Reagan Remembered," *60 Minutes*, June 6, 2004, http://www.cbsnews.com/news/ronald-reagan-remembered.

2. Quoted in Dan Raviv, *Comic Wars: How Two Tycoons Battled over the Marvel Comics Empire—And Both Lost* (New York: Broadway, 2002), 12.

3. Ibid.

4. Quoted in Les Daniels, *Marvel: Five Fabulous Decades of the World's Greatest Comics* (New York: Harry N. Abrams, 1995), 225.

5. Michael E. Hill, "Where Does The Hulk Buy Clothes?: Anywhere He Wants, Of Course," *Washington Post*, February 18, 1990, O8.

6. Stan Lee, ed., *The Ultimate Spider-Man* (New York: Berkeley, 1994), 10.

7. Ibid., 11, 13.

8. John Updike, "Cut the Unfunny Comics, Not 'Spiderman,'" *Boston Globe*, October 27, 1994. July 1994 to November 1994, Coll 8302, Box 137, Stan Lee Papers, American Heritage Center, University of Wyoming.

9. Lee, *Ultimate*, 22.

10. Ibid., 110.

11. Ibid., 342.

12. Ibid., 7.

13. Adam Bryant, "Pow! The Punches that Left Marvel Reeling," *New York Times*, May 24, 1998, http://www.nytimes.com/1998/05/24/business/pow-the-punches -that-left-marvel-reeling.html.

14. Ibid.

15. Shirrel Rhoades, *A Complete History of American Comic Books* (New York: Peter Lang, 2008), 153–54.

16. Ibid., 155.

17. Ibid., 160–61.

18. Raviv, *Comic Wars*, 230.

19. Michael Goldman, "Stan Lee: Comic Guru," *Animation World Magazine*, July 1997, 8.

20. Ibid.

21. Ibid.

22. Stan Lee Media Press Kit, 1999, Stan Lee Media Publicity Folder 1999, Box 127, Stan Lee Papers, American Heritage Center, University of Wyoming.

23. Quoted in Gary Dretzka, "At 77, 'X-Men' Creator Stan Lee Is as Busy as Ever," Knight Ridder/Tribune News Service, July 22, 2000.

24. Stan Lee and George Mair, *Excelsior! The Amazing Life of Stan Lee* (New York: Simon and Schuster, 2002), 223.

25. Figures noted in Sean Howe, *Marvel Comics: The Untold Story* (New York: Harper, 2012), 398.

26. Quoted in Dretzka, "At 77."

27. Stan Lee Media Press Kit, 1999, Stan Lee Media Publicity Folder 1999, Box 127, Stan Lee Papers, American Heritage Center, University of Wyoming.

28. Quoted in Madeleine Brand, "Growing Trend of Online Comics," *Morning Edition*, NPR, January 20, 2000.

29. Michael Dean, "If This Be My Destiny," *Comics Journal* 232 (April 2001): 8.

30. Quoted in ibid., 8, 10.

31. Jordan Raphael, "The Invincible Stan Lee?" *Los Angeles Times Magazine*, July 16, 2000, 20.

32. Quoted in Howe, *Marvel Comics*, 408.

33. Anthony D'Allessandro, "Lee Bounces Back into Business with POW!" *Variety*, July 19–25, 2004, B14.

34. "Co-Founder of Comic Company Pleads Guilty," *Los Angeles Times*, March 10, 2005, http://articles.latimes.com/2005/mar/10/business/fi-rup10.4.

35. Howe, *Marvel Comics*, 408–9.

36. Shelly Garcia, "Spider-Man's Business Brain," *Los Angeles Business Journal*, August 21, 2000, 29.

37. "Ex-Exec of Stan Lee Media Sentenced," *Los Angeles Times*, August 5, 2003, http://articles.latimes.com/2003/aug/05/business/fi-stanlee5.

38. Jon Swartz, "Stan Lee Rises from Dot-Com Rubble," *USA Today*, May 12, 2004.

39. *Stan Lee, Plaintiff, -against- Marvel Enterprises, Inc. and Marvel Characters, Inc., Defendants*. 02 Civ. 8945 United States District Court for the Southern District of New York 765 F. Supp. 2d 440; 2011 U.S. Dist. LEXIS 11297 February 4, 2011, Decided. February 4, 2011, Filed.

40. *United States of America, Appellee, -v.- Peter Paul, Defendant-Appellant, Stephen M. Gordon, Jeffrey Pittsburg, Charles Kusche, Jonathan Gordon, Defendants*. Docket Nos. 09-3191-cr (L), 09-4147-cr (con) United States Court of Appeals for the Second Circuit, 634 F.3d 668; 2011 U.S. App. LEXIS 4473, February 17, 2011, Argued. March 7, 2011, Decided.

41. Swartz, "Stan Lee Rises."

42. Lee and Mair, *Excelsior!*, 233.

43. Larry Schultz, e-mail message to Stan Lee, January 12, 2001, Correspondence, 1995–2010, Box 106, (2016-09-22 142037), Stan Lee Papers, American Heritage Center, University of Wyoming.

CHAPTER 14

1. Bryan Singer, interview by Adam Chitwood, "The Epic Bryan Singer Interview: 'X-Men Apocalypse,' the Superhero Genre, Timelines, and More," *Collider*, April 21, 2016.

2. Stan Lee, Peter David, and Colleen Doran, *Amazing Fantastic Incredible: A Marvelous Memoir* (New York: Touchstone, 2015), n.p.

3. Anthony D'Alessandro, "Lee Bounces Back into Business with POW!" *Variety*, July 19–25, 2004.

4. "POW! Entertainment Partners in the Production of Three Live Action Flicks," *PR Newswire*, October 6, 2004.

5. Quoted in Virginia Rohan, "Stan Lee's Project with Pam Anderson Looks Like a Bust," *The Record* (Bergen County, NJ), June 26, 2003.

6. Ibid.

7. "Alta Loma Entertainment & POW! Entertainment to Develop Animated Series Hef's Superbunnies," *PR Newswire*, July 18, 2003.

8. Ibid.

9. Quoted in Michael Dean, "Stan Lee's Hour of Glory," *Comics Journal* 267 (April/May 2005): 23.

10. Brent Staples, "Marveling at Marvel: You Say Spider-Man, but I Say the Thing," *New York Times*, March 25, 2005.

11. "Who Deserves the Credit (and Cash) for Dreaming Up Those Superheroes?" *New York Times*, January 31, 2005.

12. Quoted in David Kohn, "Superhero Creator Fights Back," *60 Minutes*, October 30, 2002.

13. "Marvel Settles Suit with Lee," *Los Angeles Times*, April 29, 2005.

14. Ibid.

15. Joel Garreau, "Stan Lee and Olivia de Havilland Among National Medal of Arts Winners," *Washington Post*, November 18, 2008; Lee, David, and Doran, *Amazing Fantastic Incredible*, n.p.

16. Stan Lee, "Stan Lee Talks about Time Jumper at San Diego Comic-Con 2009," bigfanboy, July 30, 2009, YouTube video, https://www.youtube.com/watch?v=hixwR_c_R_4.

17. Ibid.

18. Stan Lee, "Stan Lee is Spider-Man," Stan Lee's World of Heroes, June 21, 2012, YouTube video, https://youtu.be/I-lL8LD8SJQ?list=PL027ADE83FF495FA3.

19. Matt Clark, "Amazing Spider-Man Game Features Playable Stan Lee," MTV .com, May 9, 2012.

20. "Stan Lee's POW! Entertainment Teams with Hollywood Reporter on New Series 'Cosmic Crusaders,'" *The Hollywood Reporter*, June 21, 2016.

21. Stan Lee, interview by Ethan Sacks, "Stan Lee Muses on His Final New York Comic Con," *New York Daily News*, October 10, 2016.

22. Ibid.

23. Stan Lee in discussion with the author, Cincinnati Comic Expo, September 24, 2016.

CHAPTER 15

1. David Ng, "As Marvel Movies Soar," *Los Angeles Times*, June 29, 2018.

2. Gary Baum, "Stan Lee Needs a Hero," *The Hollywood Reporter*, April 10, 2018, https://www.hollywoodreporter.com/movies/movie-features/stan-lee-needs-a-hero -elder-abuse-claims-a-battle-aging-marvel-creator-1101229/.

3. David Hochman, "The Last Days of Stan Lee," *AARP Magazine*, October/November 2020.

4. See Eriq Gardner, "Stan Lee's Daughter Sanctioned," *The Hollywood Reporter*, June 26, 2020, as well as the many other stories about her frivolous lawsuits since Stan's death.

5. Baum, "Stan Lee Needs."

6. Bernie Zilio, "Marvel Legend Stan Lee Was a Victim in His Final Days, Reveals REELZ Documentary," *Radar*, June 25, 2021, https://radaronline.com/p/marvel-stan-lee-victim-final-days-death-autopsy-reelz-documentary/.

7. Peter Sblendorio and Nancy Dillon, "Stan Lee," *New York Daily News*, November 12, 2018.

8. Jake Newby, "China Reacts," *Radii*, November 13, 2018.

9. "How Stan Lee Helped 'Revolutionize' Comic Books," *PBS NewsHour*, November 12, 2018.

10. Abraham Reiser in *True Believer: The Rise and Fall of Stan Lee* (New York: Crown, 2021) portrays Lee negatively at just about every turn. Roy Thomas called it good "95 percent of the time" but said the remaining 5 percent make it "a very bad biography," explaining: "The author often insists, visibly and intrusively, on putting his verbal thumb on the scales, in a dispute he seems ill-equipped to judge." Roy Thomas, "Roy Thomas, Former Marvel Editor, Pushes Back on New Stan Lee Biography," *The Hollywood Reporter*, February 23, 2021, https://www.hollywoodreporter.com/movies/movie-news/roy-thomas-former-marvel-editor-pushes-back-on-new-stan-lee-biography-guest-column-4136571/.

11. Quoted in John Morrow, *Kirby and Lee: Stuf' Said!*, expanded second edition (Raleigh, NC: TwoMorrows, 2019), 166.

12. Clifford Meth, *ComicBook Babylon* (Rockaway, NJ: Aardwolf Publishing, 2014).

13. Visit http://www.uwyo.edu/ahc/index.html for more information.

14. For an interesting blow-by-blow account, see John Morrow's valuable *Kirby and Lee*.

15. *Stan Lee Conversations*, ed. Jeff McLaughlin (Jackson: University Press of Mississippi, 2007), 77.

Index

About the Author

Bob Batchelor is an award-winning cultural historian and biographer who has published books on Bob Dylan, *The Great Gatsby*, *Mad Men*, and John Updike, among other topics. *Rookwood: The Rediscovery and Revival of an American Icon, An Illustrated History* won the 2021 Independent Publishers Book Award for fine art. *The Bourbon King: The Life and Crimes of George Remus, Prohibition's Evil Genius* won the 2020 Independent Publishers Book Award for historical biography. *Stan Lee: The Man behind Marvel* was a finalist for the 2018 Ohioana Book Award for nonfiction.

Bob's books have been translated into a dozen languages, and his work has appeared or been featured in the *New York Times*, *Cincinnati Enquirer*, *Los Angeles Times*, and *Time* magazine. Bob is also the creator and host of the podcast *John Updike: American Writer, American Life*. He has appeared as an on-air commentator for the National Geographic Channel, PBS NewsHour, PBS, and NPR. Bob hosted "TriState True Crime" on WCPO's *Cincy Lifestyle* television show.

Bob earned his doctorate in American literature from the University of South Florida. He has taught at universities in Florida, Ohio, and Pennsylvania, as well as Vienna, Austria. Bob and his wife, Suzette, live in North Carolina and have two teenage daughters.

Other books by Bob Batchelor are:

Aging Heroes: Growing Old in Popular Culture (editor)
Bob Dylan: A Concise Biography
The Bourbon King: The Life and Crimes of George Remus, Prohibition's Evil Genius
Gatsby: The Cultural History of the Great American Novel
Heroines of Comic Books and Literature: Portrayals in Popular Culture (editor)

Heroines of Film and Television: Portrayals in Popular Culture (editor)
John Updike: A Critical Biography
Mad Men: A Cultural History
Michael Chabon's America: Magical Words, Secret Worlds, and Sacred Spaces (editor)
Rookwood: The Rediscovery and Revival of an American Icon, An Illustrated History
Stan Lee: The Man behind Marvel
Stan Lee: The Man behind Marvel, Young Adult Edition